PUBLIC NO MORE

PUBLIC NO MORE

*A New Path to Excellence for
America's Public Universities*

Gary C. Fethke and
Andrew J. Policano

Stanford Business Books
An Imprint of Stanford University Press
Stanford, California

Stanford University Press
Stanford, California

Special discounts for bulk quantities of Stanford Business Books are available to corporations, professional associations, and other organizations. For details and discount information, contact the special sales department of Stanford University Press. Tel: (650) 736-1782, Fax: (650) 736-1784.

Printed in the United States of America on acid-free, archival-quality paper.

Library of Congress Cataloging-in-Publication Data

Fethke, Gary C. (Gary Craig), 1942- author.
    Public no more : a new path to excellence for America's public universities / Gary C. Fethke and Andrew J. Policano.
        pages cm
    Includes bibliographical references and index.
    ISBN 978-0-8047-8050-6 (cloth : alk. paper)
    1. Public universities and colleges—United States.   I. Policano, Andrew J., 1949-author.   II. Title.
    LB2328.62.U6F48 2012
    378.050973—dc23
                                                                    2011052266

Typeset by Newgen in 10/14 Minion

Contents

Preface

It is not enough that we do our best; sometimes we have to do what's required.

—*Winston Churchill*

With combined experience of almost fifty years as academic leaders in four different public university systems, we have participated in periods of state budget shortfalls, university cost-cutting exercises, and debate over the social and private returns from higher education and who should pay. This collective experience includes positions as interim president, dean of social and behavioral sciences, and long-time deanships of schools of business. While both of us are trained as economists, that orientation has been tempered by our observations of complex human behavior within organizations.

One impetus for writing this book comes from our knowledge of how business schools have evolved over the past two decades in response to a dramatically shifting environment. We have witnessed many changes in instruction and research and, especially, in sustaining financial models. Business schools have been magnets for students willing to pay for their education, and that has led to declines, if not reversals, in their public support. Alumni are interested in giving back, and corporate donors are generous with their time and money. Business schools and several other programs have become externally focused, increasingly entrepreneurial, and financially self-sustaining. Success is both shaped by and limited by competition, by the continued review and assessment of professional organizations, and by media rankings against aggressive groups of peers.

Fethke's experience as interim president at the University of Iowa (UI) provided a strategic view of university's enterprises, including athletics and hospitals, which are independent financial entities that weigh prominently in the strategies of major public universities. In their incentive and operating structures, these enterprises overlap with well-run private companies. It became apparent to both of us that the features of competition, consumer focus, and accountability to donors and alumni that now define business schools and some enterprises provide insights that can be applied more broadly in public universities. Not all things apply, but many do.

The academic core of major public universities, which includes liberal arts, the humanities, and the basic sciences, has suffered with a decline in public support and the associated need to accommodate more students, who are often not well prepared. The cuts deriving from the Great Recession, which began in 2008, continue to wreak havoc on the budgets of subsidized academic programs. These cuts are not temporary; rather, they portend the extinction of the low-tuition–high-subsidy financing model that has been the backbone of public higher education for over a century. While tuition revenue has increased to partially close the gap left by reduced public support, it cannot increase by enough to offset the reduction; as a result, universities can no longer sustain the array of cross-subsidies that prop up the high-cost–low-revenue programs.

Things have to change. "Wasteful" spending can be reduced, there is room for further tuition increases, and some programs can be eliminated. Responses such as these are routinely seen in private business and, indeed, in some areas of public universities. Change in response to environmental factors does not come readily in higher education, which is a culture based on preservation of agendas and equitable treatment for all; it is not a culture that embraces enhanced efficiency.

We decided to assess the issues and make suggestions for responding to permanent lower public support predicated on our interests and experiences in administration, applied economics, and business strategy. In this book, we examine how public universities, which have been protected by exclusive franchises, low tuitions, and subsidized access, can survive, if not thrive, in an environment where these protective mechanisms are eroding. Accepting the new reality is a necessary first step, and we encourage greater acceptance of the changes that are occurring.

However, what we suggest requires not marginal but, rather, transformational realignment of practices and processes. The necessary adjustments involve changes in the way value is measured, incentives are structured, budgets are allocated, and universities are organized and governed. Attention will have to be refocused away from the preferences of internal constituencies, including faculty and administrators, and toward those of external constituencies, especially students, taxpayers, and donors. Greater emphasis needs to be placed on financial viability and innovative, market-responsive solutions. Recognizing that rising enrollments and higher quality will cost more and that those objectives will compete with one another requires strategic attention. Policies for determining both tuition and academic and research quality need to be based on the willingness of students and taxpayers to pay and on the university's cost structure. Unfunded research and programs will continue to exist, with some acquiring and retaining distinction, but only if subsidized programs are complemented by revenue-generating programs and they are aligned with the positioning strategy of the university.

Our intended audience includes university administrators and faculty, legislators, members of university governing and advisory boards, researchers and students of higher education, and interested business executives. We attempt to develop a context-rich discussion of issues using the prospective of economics and modern strategic and competitive analysis. We illustrate issues as much as possible using numerical examples and supporting data. The analytical models underlying our analysis are developed in chapter appendices, endnotes, and references.

Organization of the Book

We first provide a historical overview of the erosion of state support and the mostly tactical adjustments that have been made by public universities. We then characterize the future environment and develop a roadmap for a successful move to greater self-sufficiency, especially as universities adopt a strategy of higher tuition, lower subsidy, and higher financial aid. We examine academic culture and impediments to change, and argue that an initial step in the process is accepting that the subsidy is permanently reduced. We develop a series of recommendations for university leadership based on how universities add value and can protect quality, how tuition and quality might be determined, and how resources can be better allocated across large complex entities.

Within public universities there are programs that already adhere to market forces and seek greater efficiency and financial viability. Most of these are "enterprises" that are not part of the academic core, but there are also academic programs that have attained financial viability without sacrificing quality and research productivity. These "public-no-more" programs provide one plausible forward-looking template, and we offer the public business school as an illustration. We predict that schools that move toward self-reliance, with strategies that identify and implement a financially viable plan, will become the top public universities; those that do not will fall into competitive decline.

We divide the book into four parts. In Part I, Environmental Issues, Chapters 1 and 2 provide a review of the primary issues facing public higher education. In Part II, Practices, Procedures, and Strategies, Chapters 3 through 6 consider strategy in the context of public higher education, with discussions focusing on common tuition-setting practices; on university finances and academic and enterprise programs; and on two common budget practices: central-administrative and responsibility-centered management. In Part III, Policy and Analysis, Chapters 7 through 9 provide arguments for and against a public subsidy and investigate the setting of optimal tuition and quality. Finally, in Part IV, Culture and Governance, Chapters 10 through 12 examine both impediments and positive adjustments to change. Here we present examples of successful program implementation and examine what "public-no-more" universities may be like and whether they will benefit society.

Acknowledgments

This book has benefited from the advice and support of many people. We were both recruited into academic leadership almost thirty-five years ago by George Daly, then dean of the College of Business at the University of Iowa. George championed the new reality of business school education and research with an emphasis on developed strategy, external focus, and prominent advisory boards. We also learned much over many years from the late Marvin Pomerantz, an unfailing champion of excellence in higher education. Henry B. Tippie urged us to use (and teach) common sense and to always try to "keep it simple." Chuck Martin, CEO of Mont Pelerin Capital, devoted considerable time to a careful reading of the manuscript, provided many provocative comments, and challenged our arguments, always with great encouragement and enthusiasm.

We benefited from the advice and many detailed suggestions of Provost Joe Alutto of Ohio State and Dean John Kraft of the University of Florida.

We would like to acknowledge Iowa provost, Barry Butler, and University of California, Irvine, provost, Mike Gottfredson, for comments and suggestions pertaining to Chapters 5, 6, and 10. We are grateful to Paul Merage, former CEO of Chef America, Don Beall, former chairman and CEO of Rockwell International, Kent Oliven, finance director, Village of Calumet Park, Illinois, Professor Ron Ehrenberg of Cornell University, Dr. Michael Shasby, Senior Associate Dean Charles Whiteman, and Associate Dean Jay Sa-Aadu of the University of Iowa for ongoing discussions.

Many people were helpful with the development of key chapters: Ed Fuller, president of Marriott International Lodging, for his counsel on strategy; Jerre Stead, CEO of IHS, Inc., for his long participation in graduate strategy courses and his personification of value-based leadership. Professor Randy Bezanson, Don Szeszycki, Rhonda Simpson, Marilyn Brown, and Patricia Millard all at the University of Iowa, Dean Labh Hira at Iowa State University, and Dean Alison Davis-Blake at the University of Michigan all assisted us in the development of Chapter 6. We also benefited from the suggestions of Iowa regents Jack Evans and Michael Gartner, Professor Rick Cosier of Purdue University, and Valerie Jenness, dean of social ecology at UC Irvine, for their perspectives on faculty culture and shared governance in Chapter 10.

Diane Sagey and Maureen Bresse, UC Irvine, provided excellent technical assistance, Lari Fanlund at the University of Wisconsin-Madison offered helpful comments on the Wisconsin Plan in Chapter 10, and Emily Ambrosy and Linda Knowling at the University of Iowa disentangled one of us from the mysteries of word processing. Margo Beth Fleming at Stanford University Press, our editor, has been both responsive and delightful to work with.

Andrew Policano would like to thank the California Institute for Management Leadership for providing financial support, and Gary Fethke appreciates the funded professorship support provided by Leonard Hadley, retired CEO of Maytag. Pam Policano read parts of the manuscript and helped enhance the perspective and delivery. The person who lived with this project from the beginning was Carol Fethke, who reread every chapter with a critical eye, made numerous suggestions for improving the focus and expression of our ideas, contributed many of her own ideas, and encouraged us to make timely and quality-improving changes. Carol's imprint is everywhere on this project.

PUBLIC NO MORE

I ENVIRONMENTAL ISSUES

1 Introduction

Challenges, Solutions, and Themes

> Faced with the choice between changing one's mind and proving that there is no need to do so, almost everyone gets busy on the proof.
>
> —John Kenneth Galbraith

Challenges

The belief that higher education should be funded by society dates back at least to the fourth century BCE, when Plato's Academy offered free admission to selected students—a philosophy that prevailed throughout most of history. Today we face a different and challenging environment, with collapsing government budgets and rising tuition revenues. The emphasis of *Public No More: A New Path to Excellence for America's Public Universities* is that the long-standing dependence on state subsidies that facilitated low tuition and easy student access to public higher education is unsustainable. We view the recent cuts in public university funding as permanent and their consequences, both for higher education and for society, as profound. Public universities can either recognize and confront major strategic challenges or face prolonged financial stress, deteriorating quality, and eventual competitive decline.

To retain both access and quality, many public university systems are dramatically increasing tuition and fees to high-income students while providing an internal subsidy to low-income students. In effect, external market forces and internal reallocations are replacing state financial support. The inevitable outcome of these forces is that the traditional high-subsidy–low-tuition model, which helped to create the premier system of higher education in the world, is on a steady path toward extinction. Its emerging replacement will feature high tuition for some, high aid for others, and substantially reduced public support. The consequences will be less discretion in subsidizing inefficient programs, regardless of their appeal to basic notions of academic taste and fairness.

While public financial support, along with the award of an exclusive franchise, has led to a level of academic research, open inquiry, and scientific investigation that is the envy of the world, it has also acted to isolate public universities from competition and has engendered a sense of privilege and entitlement. Greater reliance on tuition revenue, better-informed and more selective students, rapidly emerging national and international competition, and stunning new technologies present a different reality. The question is not whether public universities will adjust to reflect this new reality—because they must; rather, it is whether they can react quickly, successfully, and sensibly enough to sustain their competitive position as premier providers of instruction and research.

One of the major impacts of increased market competition is to drive the prices of products of given quality toward average cost, thereby reducing operating margins and forcing a relentless quest for operational efficiency. Competition is a healthy force; countries with open markets, well-developed institutions for the protection of private property, and transparent legal processes have the most innovative and dynamic organizations. Vibrant economies provide the highest levels of sustainable economic growth and productivity. However, there are also the apparent downsides to enhanced competition. In particular, individuals and organizations that are threatened and displaced by existing or new rivals will not welcome competitive pressure; they will typically resist the implications of competition both politically and economically. For these reasons, the critical choice confronting public universities is whether to compete aggressively in the new environment or to retrench and do everything possible to resist competition and to avoid making needed changes to practices and processes.

Some public university leaders deny the implications of this new funding reality and continue aggressive lobbying of their state legislatures to return to the high-subsidy model. Often, they feel empowered in this by a conservative faculty and staff governance process that promotes strong resistance to change. Although some level of advocacy is important and can be effective, demands on state and federal funds and the lack of appetite for additional taxation offer little hope that future needs can be funded through traditional public sources. Excessive lobbying, accompanied by denial of a permanent problem, has the potential of distracting university leaders from refocusing on needed strategic adjustments. More important, attempts to block impending competitive forces by resistance and delaying actions are self-defeating.

As increases in tuition revenue replace state subsidies as the main funding source for public universities, the vitality of the research enterprise is threatened. In the traditional funding model, a significant fraction of research activity was supported by block grants from state governments, which financed both reductions in faculty teaching loads and a significant portion of the required research infrastructure. These grants were also used to sustain an extensive and nontransparent system of internal cross-subsidies. With this support structure, the subsidy helped to develop the defining features of distinctive public universities, which are based on the concept that teaching and research are complementary and that research-intense universities provide a challenging, high-quality learning environment. To continue to fund their research mission, public universities have implemented less expensive ways to deliver the curriculum, including increased use of adjunct and part-time faculty, compressed pay, and increased class sizes. However, these cost-saving instructional initiatives threaten to erode educational quality and value and thereby to precipitate a negative reaction from students who become less willing to pay if they perceive a reduction in value. If dissatisfied students choose to go elsewhere, efforts to spread resources and sustain cross-subsidies by reducing quality can be self-defeating.

Solutions

Significant challenges arise as universities attempt to sustain the long-standing goal of excellence in instruction and research in the face of declining public subsidies. What is necessary are new and effective positioning strategies that focus more narrowly on academic programs that can distinguish a university relative to existing and emerging rivals. Each public university must identify a unique strategy and invest in programs that align with it, and at the same time decrease resource allocations to programs that do not align. The obvious but rarely acknowledged implication is that the scope of academic programs will have to be reduced. Confronting this issue reveals the tension between the benefits associated with greater differentiation of each institution and the desire to offer broad products that are attractive to a large student base.

Ultimately, public universities cannot be all things to all people. Programs that offer neither distinctive features nor a coherent financial model and those not aligned with the intent or viability of the university face being downsized or eliminated. The essence of an effective strategy is that it provides a logically consistent framework for making challenging decisions in an uncertain environment. To protect and enhance the university's unique (distinctive) market position, top leadership must define a vision and then find the courage to enact these difficult choices.

Moving from subsidy to self-reliance presents significant challenges for public research universities. As increased revenue comes from tuition-paying students rather than from public support, students will seek out academic and professional programs that help them succeed in both life and the workplace, providing the return they expect on their investment in education. Some will not be satisfied with the assertion that what they need is a politically adjudicated liberal education that prepares them for life's intellectual challenges. Nor will they be especially supportive of the notion that their tuition should be diverted to support research and exclusive high-cost programs at the expense of their own instruction.

The traditional approach of setting a base tuition for resident undergraduates that applies generally to all programs and majors leads to various distortions, particularly because it ignores substantial differences in program costs as well as differences in student willingness to pay. A policy of increased tuition-setting discretion can recognize cost and student demand differences, hopefully in the context of a tuition structure that leads to minimal departures from efficiency standards. Education quality rises as student preparedness improves and as the resources devoted to educational quality increase. Like tuition, entry standards and the funds spent on programs are key decisions that must be made in the context of environmental opportunities and the university's aligned positioning strategy.

As shown in the Table 1.1, the new reality facing public universities requires many changes in the practices and processes used in the traditional structure. It is not clear that the required transformation is feasible for many of the institutions that constitute the current broad spectrum of public higher education. Moreover, a basic question is whether the transformation, even if possible, will be beneficial for society. The changes we envision will require a major shift in culture on the part of faculty and administration. While the main drivers of change are the permanent decline in the level of real public

TABLE 1.1 Traditional structure versus new reality

Traditional structure	New reality
Regulated tuitions	Increased tuition discretion
Low tuition–high subsidy	High tuition–low subsidy–high financial aid
Fixed entry requirements	Flexible entry requirements
Unrestricted subsidy use	Restricted subsidy use
Spending of revenues received	Increased operational efficiencies
Limited external accountability	Increased external accountability
"Hourglass" governance structure	Top-down governance emphasis
"All things to all people"	More focused strategic vision
Opaque financial reporting	Financial transparency
Innumerable internal cross-subsidies	Fewer internal cross-subsidies

support per student and the unprecedented emergence of new competitors, the principle inhibitors of change are entrenched ideologies, resistant internal cultures, and budgeting and resource-allocation processes that are predicated on the once, but no longer, predictable receipt of public support.

The transformation from subsidization to greater self-sufficiency necessitates different strategic and operational models from those that have dominated at public universities throughout their history. The repositioning and re-evaluating of academic program scope recognize that greater importance must be given to societal needs and student demands. In the process, programs and services that have low demand, generate little revenues, or are too costly must be identified for the possibility of downsizing or elimination. The new model encourages productivity enhancement, entrepreneurship, and greater attention to relentless competitive forces.

Themes

We summarize a number of key themes that underlie the major tenets of this book:

1. Replacing state support with tuition revenue will require more emphasis on the efficient allocation of resources to achieve as much as possible with limited funds. The traditional appeal of fairness, where

low-tuition access is subsidized, is challenged by an economic efficiency argument.

2. The choice between greater efficiency and enhanced fairness (equity)
   seems to be the critical issue, but in fact there is only one option. Unless public universities become more efficient, they will not survive in
   their current form.

3. With a decline in direct state support, internal cross-subsidies that
   support high-cost, limited-access programs at the expense of low-
   cost, broader-access programs are going to be difficult to maintain.
   More specialization across public universities provides one answer,
   and public universities will have to make choices that limit program
   scope.

4. Increased market competition both reduces overall demand and increases demand elasticity. This will put pressure on the traditional
   positioning of public research universities. Increases in tuition elasticity will limit the ability to raise tuition, and reductions in demand
   will increase unit fixed cost.

5. Impediments to change are embedded in culture and traditional ways
   of doing things. The shared-governance structure of public universities is inherently conservative, internally focused, and discipline
   based. Needed changes cannot be implemented easily by a central
   administration that is directed by governing boards to achieve greater
   access and constrained to recognize faculty rights.

6. There are numerous examples in public universities of independent
   programs that must adhere to market forces and seek efficiency and
   financial viability. Most of these units are "enterprises" that stand
   apart from the academic core, but there are also independent academic programs, like those in public business schools and other
   entrepreneurial units, that have attained financial viability without
   sacrificing quality and research productivity. These "public-no-more"
   programs provide one plausible forward-looking template.

2 Challenges Facing Public Research Universities

The difficulty lies, not so much in developing new ideas, but in escaping from old ones . . .

> —J. M. Keynes, *The General Theory of Employment, Interest and Money*

The Blame Game

A familiar pattern takes shape when state appropriations for public higher education are reduced. Universities raise tuition and admit additional students. Given strong enrollment demand, it is possible at public research universities to increase tuition by enough to replace lost public support, but it is not politically easy to do so as students and their parents (voters), long accustomed to subsidies, exert political pressure to restrain tuition increases. One politically sensitive argument is that qualified low- and struggling middle-income applicants are being shut out of higher education as tuition goes up. Student protests over higher tuition are supported by the same legislators who reduced the appropriations in the first place.[1] Disliking rising tuitions, legislators sometimes turn on universities and assert that the main problem is not state budget decisions but wasteful spending of scarce taxpayer funds. At the same time, university leaders make appeals for a return to the golden years of high-subsidy–low-tuition programs of public funding—presumably the 1970s (see, for example, Miles and Evans [2011]).

Adopting financially self-reliant strategies, reducing expenses, or eliminating nonviable programs are not the embraced alternatives. On the contrary, the reward for university leaders who do make such difficult decisions is usually a shortened tenure and reduced options for subsequent employment. Instead of laying out a vision and taking bold strategic steps, administrators often take the safer route of defending the core principles and social benefits of higher education. In appealing for additional subsidy support, they make extraordinary claims to persuade legislators of the high rate of return to the state's higher education "investment."

Unfortunately, the benefits are difficult to quantify and the arguments lack credibility. Few administrators can defend higher education by showing that it provides a greater return than health care, K–12 education, or job training. Meanwhile, legislators call for elimination of waste and a renewed focus on teaching. The result of this "volley the blame" game is a continuation of the status quo, endless appeals to restore state funding, reluctant adjustments in academic programs to keep costs from exceeding revenues, increased use of tuition to accommodate some of the loss of state funding, and gradual erosion of the vitality and quality of public research universities.[2]

In this chapter we describe the evolving external educational environment and the tactical responses to it made by public universities. This information lays the foundation for later chapters on strategy and the actions necessary to sustain the quality and financial health of these universities.

Changing Environmental Factors

Public institutions are of fundamental importance to the quality of U.S. higher education. Guided by a broad and bold mission to create and disseminate knowledge, and ranging from two-year community colleges to comprehensive undergraduate and graduate research universities, they enroll over seventy-five percent of college students.[3] Our primary concern is with the economic environment of universities that the Carnegie Foundation defines as "very high research universities" (referred to as "RU/VH").[4] These have been largely responsible for the global acclaim for public higher education in the United States. They also provide a range of benefits to their host communities, including medical services, technology transfer, and extension activities. Most are ranked in the top 100 nationally by *U.S. News & World Report,* although that particular ranking is dominated by the selective private universities also ranked by Carnegie as RU/VH. While our focus is on this category of schools, much of the analysis is also pertinent to many large, comprehensive (four-year) public universities.

A range of substitute educational providers, both public and private, featuring lower tuition and various advantages such as location and convenience, have exerted competitive pressure on the teaching and research mission of public RU/VHs. These alternative providers typically do not have research-based missions, and they are not constrained by the need to employ an expensive faculty and infrastructure to produce research products. Similar competitive pressures affect academic health centers, which face declining reimbursement rates and increasing clinical and inpatient-based competition from providers who are not burdened with subsidizing teaching and research missions.

Today this system faces unprecedented challenges. Competition is squeezing the major public research universities from above and below on the quality spectrum. At the high end, selective private universities offer restricted access and the perception of higher-quality education and research. At the other end, the instructional market share of major public universities is slipping and is being captured by community and for-profit colleges that offer low-tuition options and open admission. Competition for talented students is extending globally as countries like Australia, Canada, China, Germany, and Singapore expand government support for education even as public spending in the United States and the United Kingdom declines. While all of these issues are significant, there are some central financial questions that affect quality and survival: Who is expected to pay for higher education—taxpayers or students? And how will universities decide to respond to changing patterns of customer demand, competition, and financial support?

We focus on choices in tuition, access, quality, and organizational structure, in an environment of declining public support and increasing competitiveness, to show how these choices impact both instructional and research missions. The differentiator for major research universities is the complementarity between teaching and research. When research and instruction are complements, enhancement of research increases the incremental return to instruction. The problem is that research activities, even those funded by external sources, are partially subsidized and reduced support places stress on both research and instruction. The future of very-high-research public universities depends on getting the financial model right.[5]

A Permanent Decline of State Support

For generations public universities were supported by state funding, but this historical financing model, which we refer to as "high subsidy–low tuition,"

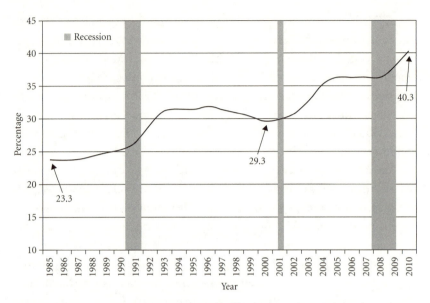

FIGURE 2.1 Net tuition as percentage of public higher education total educational revenue (U.S. fiscal years 1985–2010)

SOURCE: SHEEO (2010b).

NOTE: Net tuition revenue used for capital debt service is included in net tuition revenue but excluded from total educational revenue in the calculations.

has been eroding for decades.[6] The decline in public support reflects growing skepticism regarding the importance of positive externalities of public higher education, combined with increasing demands for state funds (e.g., Medicaid, prisons, pensions) and a general reluctance to pay higher taxes. As shown in Figure 2.1, the dynamics of state funding has settled into a predictable pattern. Whenever a recession hits the U.S. economy, stressed state legislatures are forced to make significant cuts. Because a sizeable portion of state spending is nondiscretionary, legislators have few alternatives and so cuts are made to the discretionary areas, including public higher education. Moreover, as the economy recovers, the cuts are rarely fully restored.

In fact, with each decline in the state subsidy, there has been a shift of financial burden from the state to students and their parents. Following each recession starting in the early 1980s, the percentage of educational expense paid by net tuition increased: in 1985 net tuition amounted to 23.3 percent; in 2000 it increased to 29.3 percent; and by 2010 it accounted for 40.3 percent (SHEEO, 2010b). In 2010 the percentage of total revenue covered by state appropriations in Iowa, for example, was 46 percent, with subsequent declines predicted. While public universities have become accustomed to, and have accommodated, gradual declines in state support, few predicted the sea change that occurred as a result of the "Great Recession" beginning in 2008. Many state legislatures have now acquiesced to large tuition increases, essentially abandoning the philosophy that higher education is primarily a social responsibility.

Recent actions suggest that many universities see the most realistic option for generating increased revenue as higher tuition charged to the large cohort of undergraduate students. In 2009 fewer than five state systems held tuition increases at under 5 percent. At the same time, at least thirty-three public universities increased tuition by more than 10 percent; at least a dozen, by more than 20 percent; and at least four, by more than 30 percent. Florida intends to raise public university tuition by 15 percent per year until the national average tuition is achieved, and academic leaders in Georgia argue that tuition will need to be increased by 77 percent to offset proposed cuts in state spending. Most likely, the list of universities increasing net tuition will expand in coming years.[7]

Perceptions of and Reactions to Rising Tuitions

The traditional low-tuition–high-subsidy model in public higher education focused on student access and equality of opportunity. Now declining public support is being offset, one to one, by increased tuition revenue so that students and their parents are paying more and taxpayers are paying less for educational products whose costs have not changed greatly. There are both misperceptions and misunderstandings concerning this situation. Perceptions of rising cost, rather than declining subsidies, have precipitated widespread calls for universities to cut expenditures and increase productivity. Ironically, the same legislators who are cutting state appropriations deny their role in increasing listed tuitions.[8] The frequent claims made in the press asserting that increased tuition implies high costs, inefficient operations, and low productivity in public higher education are just not supported by the facts.[9]

It is true that published tuitions ("sticker prices") have increased significantly, exceeding the rate of CPI inflation by 60 percent.[10] These increases have led parents, students, and the media to express concerns about the affordability of public universities. But although published tuitions are rising, the costs incurred to provide the education they pay for are not. Much of the confusion centers on the relationships between tuition, subsidy, and cost. The *list price* is the published tuition before grants, aid, and other discounts, and it is increasing but not everyone pays it. *Net tuition*, which reflects financial aid and other support, is the price students actually pay. *Subsidy* is what taxpayers and donors contribute. Finally, *costs* are what the university pays to various providers (salaries, utilities, supplies, etc.) to deliver its products. For a public university to break even, net tuition revenue plus public subsidy must equal total cost. In recent years, a determined effort has been made by public universities to hold costs to a level that can be supported by the combination of tuition revenue and public subsidy. With expenditures held constant, a decrease in the level of public support has been mostly offset with a combination of increases in tuition and increased enrollment. What has changed is who pays the bill.

Many assert that restraining spending on instruction as enrollment rises adversely affects the quality of higher education because the higher enrollments needed to increase tuition revenue are being accommodated within fixed expenditure levels. Equally concerning to some is that access for lower-income students may be reduced as public universities increasingly cater to students who can afford higher tuition. To these critics it appears that public universities are dealing with higher enrollments of less prepared applicants by discounting tuition and offsetting the reduced subsidy by lowering the quality of their academic offerings.[11]

The data in Table 2.1 highlight some key points of the revenue/cost reality. They present an image of an awkward business model. Too much media emphasis is placed on published prices, which few pay. Indeed, students pay a fraction of the cost of higher education; the average two-year community college student, for example, is provided with a grant that can be used to offset expenditures. The trends in these averages, which are not presented, are also interesting. Instructional spending per full-time equivalent (FTE) and net tuition have been remarkably constant over the last decade, with average net tuition *declining* in public four-year institutions. Market shares are relatively stable as well, although an increasing share (not reported) goes to for-profit institutions. Private universities are increasing their real spending per FTE at nearly twice the rate of public universities, which is one consequence of lower public support per FTE at public institutions. Enrollment trends

TABLE 2.1 Net tuition, instructional expenditure, market share, and graduation rate for U.S. colleges and universities in 2010

	Average net tuition ($)[a]	Instructional expenditure per FTE ($)	Market share of FTE (%)	Six-year graduation rates (%)[b]
Public two-year	−670	10,400	25	17.6
Public four-year	1,540	15,600[c]	46	57
Private	11,320	34,340[d]	20	>90

SOURCE: Data for net tuition, instructional expenditure, and market share from College Board Advocacy and Policy Center (2010a). Instructional expenditure per FTE does not include spending on research. The tables presented in the College Board report provide considerable longitudinal information as well.

[a] Net tuition is the published tuition (sticker price) minus grants, tax credits, and related deductions.

[b] Bound and Turner (2010, 7–10). Average completion rate for 2009 is reported as 53.2%. Reported percentages in the table, which estimates for all public and private colleges and universities, were adjusted by Bound and Turner for student achievement measures.

[c] Only public institutions awarding doctorates.

[d] Only private institutions awarding doctorates.

show little evidence that aspiring students are prevented from attending colleges and universities; rather, enrollment is at an historic high. The problem appears to be that lower percentages are completing a four-year degree, even after six years.

U.S. public higher education offers a wide range of choices in terms of price and quality. In 2010, tuition at very-high-research universities ranged from $4,526 at the University of Mississippi to $19,154 at the University of Pittsburgh.[12] Where a student begins her college career does indeed matter, and what matters most appears to be what institutions choose to spend on instruction. After accounting for student ability, patterns of spending per student vary considerably across types of institution, and these patterns affect six-year graduation rates. After adjusting for student achievement, Bound and Turner (2010) predict that the penalty for attending a low-cost public two-year college is a reduction of about 32 percentage points in the likelihood of graduating from a college or university in six years.

Even sophisticated commentators in the financial press may be missing portions of the bigger financial picture as presented in Table 2.1. They often question, correctly, the actions of universities in the face of increasing tuition. These include sustaining low teaching loads, supporting areas that are far removed from increased enrollment demands, and failing to provide adequate stewardship and accountability for, albeit reduced, state support. But, their too-focused emphasis is on wasteful practices and not on declining revenue; this creates confusion. Critical positions are also being taken up by a small group of academics who point to both the high cost and the inadequate delivery systems of higher education (see Hacker and Dreifus [2010]). Some question whether undergraduates are learning anything once they get to college (see Arum and Roksa [2011]). While there is merit in these assertions, they appear to be sideline issues that direct attention away from the major point, which is the permanent shift in the financial model from public to private financing.

As public support has declined, the widening of income and wealth inequality in the United States has placed great financial pressure on lower-income families. This pressure has encouraged legislatures and governing boards to accommodate easier college entry and to subsidize poorer applicants, relying primarily on the tuition revenue of students who have the ability to pay. Federal support of higher education is now more directed to low-income students in the form of Pell grants and forgivable loans. One consequence of these adjustments has been nearly universal adoption of the so-called "high-tuition–high-aid model." As higher-income students are required to pay more to support lower-income applicants, the tuition-discounting practices among public universities are beginning to match the long-standing practice among selective private universities, but for a different reason. In public universities, the purpose of tuition discounting is to maintain access in the face of declining public subsidy. In private universities, tuition revenue is used to increase quality. Access pressures have also led to programs that increase the flow of community college graduates into major public universities. The policies to protect access and keep costs down have even encouraged some universities to consider "streamlining" the basic undergraduate degree from four to three years (see Gordon [2010]).

If the public and the press are confusing differences between published and net tuitions and between net revenue and cost, why is there not a greater effort to present the facts in a way that is transparent and easy to understand? University leadership is not always eager to declare openly that legislatures, which they depend on for support, are responsible for the tuition increases required to offset reduced subsidies. Legislatures, in turn, are frustrated by trying to meet the multiple demands placed on state budgets; they also are the focus of criticism for permitting public institutions to charge outlandish prices. Finally, the substantial efforts made by public universities to hold the line on cost increases has had adverse effects on the quality of their products, and on graduation rates, and it is not prudent to bring attention to these effects.

Even if it is developing by default, the high-tuition–high-aid–low-subsidy formulation has had a number of positive impacts. Universities increasingly recognize the importance of differentiated preferences for programs, differences in student willingness to pay, competition among programs, productivity enhancement, and efficiency.[13] In contrasting this case with the low-tuition–high-subsidy tradition, key societal issues become apparent. They involve a trade-off between equity (fairness) and efficiency, and the associated issues present divergent points of view.[14]

University Responses to Declining State Support

As budget cuts have occurred, central administrations have absorbed some of them but have passed most on to individual academic and administrative units. The academic units, whose largest budget item is the cost of faculty, have responded by implementing less costly methods to deliver the curriculum. Class sizes have increased, and the use of web-based technology has expanded. Most importantly, lower-priced part-time and adjunct faculty have been substituted for more expensive research-oriented faculty. The effect of faculty substitution has been profound: between 1971 and 2003 the number of part-time instructors doubled; by 2003 they accounted for 46 percent of all college faculties.[15] At the same time, administrative units lowered operational costs through initiatives like energy efficiency campaigns, decreases in student and faculty services, and better utilization of space. These tactical actions were designed to maintain the scope of operation and programs. By delaying investments, handing out across-the-board budget cuts, and seeking increased revenue from existing sources and donors, most major public universities have avoided embracing painful reallocation and repositioning strategies. The tactical responses to the state funding problem are to rely increasingly on tuition revenues, endowment income, program fees, and modest cost-cutting measures.

Many public universities also try to increase enrollment of higher-paying nonresidents, a "beggar thy neighbor" policy to recruit "outsiders" to pay for declining subsidy support. However, the scenario of limiting resident tuition and enrolling nonresident students to offset declines in state support leads to a paradox. As out-of-state enrollment increases, the pressure remains to serve residents by offering low-tuition access. When capacity constraints develop, qualified resident students willing to pay even the higher nonresident tuition are prevented from doing so and, in essence, face enrollment rationing.[16] In the supply-constrained states of California and Illinois, this scenario is causing an out-migration of residents who become the nonresident students of neighboring states, respectively Arizona and Iowa.

At the time they were introduced, these tactical reactions in academic and administrative units were both sensible and predictable; indeed, some were innovative. By implementing the adjustments just discussed and others, public universities were able to maintain a relatively flat real per-student cost for over two decades.[17] While there are efficiencies that can yet be gained, the evidence suggests that university costs have not been excessively inflated by wasteful expenditures, which, in our opinion, are not as significant as imagined by some nor as egregious as presented in the media. Rather, we argue that the major inefficiencies are those associated with distortions of relative prices and the continued subsidy to programs and activities that have little market-based demand and no feasible means of continued financial support. In some sense, in trying to control expenditures in the face of declining subsidies, public universities have been doing the "wrong things right."

In general, when an external shock from the environment shrinks resources, appropriate reactions differ depending on whether the change is seen as temporary or permanent. With their tactical responses, universities are behaving as though the reductions in state subsidies are temporary. Thus, rather than face the new financial economic reality, university leaders and their constituents lobby both state and federal governments to increase direct support, student loans, and research funding. They often decry the public finance circumstances that require them to place an ever larger financial burden on students and their parents. In effect, there is an element of collective denial among many university leaders that state funding has *permanently* declined relative to private funding. Appeals to return to the unobtainable, perhaps even laudable, historical norms hamper the ability of public higher education to adapt, and they adversely affect its ability to compete in the new economic environment. Only when reductions in subsidy are perceived as permanent will institutions begin to make appropriate long-term changes.

When drastic budget cuts began in 2008, many public universities, faced with few remaining opportunities to reduce cost, shifted their emphasis to revenue generation. Fundraising efforts increased, although most have been hindered by the poor state of the overall economy. Fundraising activities can indeed provide some measure of relief, and they offer a most useful supplement to budgets, but it is simply unrealistic to assume that endowment income and annual donations can replace a significant amount of the state subsidy. Lobbying has intensified, both to state legislatures to reverse the loss in subsidy and to federal governments to increase research funding. Steps have been taken to increase the scope of entrepreneurial programs, especially instructional and fee-based programs and technology transfer. Most importantly, numerous proposals to increase tuition have been presented to governing boards.

While each of these activities is defensible, we will show that increasing net tuition is the only option that has the potential to replace more than a small portion of declining state subsidies. As governing bodies consider tuition increases, several critical issues need to be considered. How large an increase is necessary to offset lost state funding? To what extent can tuition increases actually generate an increase in net revenue? Are significant increases in tuition politically feasible, or is there a willingness to accept lower quality to maintain access? What levels of nonresident enrollment are acceptable? We address each of these questions in the coming chapters.

The environment just described applies directly to recent university actions and, as an example, is especially applicable to the University of California system. A report from the University of California Commission on the Future (2010) recommends an increase in resident tuition, an increase in nonresident undergraduate enrollment, a change in the mix of faculty to facilitate research, and increased use of online courses. It also calls for spending more internal funds to increase advocacy efforts, eliminating administrative redundancies, and coordinating system-wide planning. What the report fails to consider is changes either in governance structures and budgetary process or in the reward and incentive systems that, as we argue throughout, are critical as universities become more self-reliant.[18] Subsequent to the report, the University of California Office of the President developed a plan to allow each campus in the system to "float on its own bottom." The details of how this new paradigm will evolve are currently being developed.

Pertinent Facts

Here we list some of the salient features of public higher education that will affect and motivate our subsequent discussions:[19]

- Enrollments are increasing, and state appropriations per student are decreasing.
- While list-price tuitions are increasing, net tuitions are decreasing.
- Public support is declining relative to tuition revenue, yet students still pay far less than the full cost of higher education.
- Real revenue and real cost per student have been constant for over a decade, and there is evidence that product quality might be slipping.
- Cross-subsidies are a defining feature of public universities: low-cost programs subsidize high-cost programs; high-income students subsidize low-income students; lower-division students subsidize higher-division students; undergraduates subsidize graduates; teaching-load reductions subsidize research activities; and clinical care subsidizes medical education and medical research. Many of these cross-subsidies are not sustainable.
- The scope and revenue base of noneducational programs ("enterprises") in public universities are growing relative to the scope and revenue of traditional academic programs.

Summary and Conclusions

Given the size of the subsidy relative to tuition revenue, even modest percentage decreases in state funding require a significant increase in tuition to cover lost revenue. Universities in a strong competitive position can increase tuition and revenue because their student demand is relatively insensitive (inelastic) to increases in tuition or decreases in real income. If enrollment demand were both tuition and income elastic, any attempt made to offset declines in state support during economic downturns by increasing tuition would fail, and those public institutions in a poorer competitive position would have less ability to offset the loss of subsidy with tuition increases.

Most public universities are culturally inclined to respond slowly to permanently changing patterns of demand. With the decline in subsidies, demand for public higher education has declined relative to that for private education, and the new pattern is permanent. With more emphasis on tuition, students will be attracted to universities that respond to their needs as well as to societal priorities. While universities have a long-term perspective, they also need to react more aggressively in the short run to areas and programs in demand, generally those favored and supported by expected labor-market conditions. University systems that do not make the necessary structural adjustments are doomed to lose competitive advantage to others that are more market sensitive.

II PRACTICES, PROCEDURES, AND STRATEGIES

3 A Framework for Defining, Creating, and Distributing Value

The essence of strategy is choosing a unique positioning and a distinctive value chain to deliver on it.
—Michael Porter and Mark Kramer

The Planning Process

Every major public university engages in some form of planning, often with considerable fanfare and typically on a five-year basis. The outcome is usually a massive document that is seldom read, widely ignored, and sometimes ridiculed, even by those responsible for implementing decisions. Any senior administrator who tries to engage the faculty in a discussion about strategic planning can easily relate to our characterization of the strategic planning process. Many faculty view the process as a pro forma exercise that wastes valuable time and resources. The reason for this attitude, besides the usual resistance to change, is that the "plan" is usually not strategic. In particular, it fails to delineate the boundaries of the organization; it does not specify the difficult program trade-offs required; it fails to create a defensible competitive position relative to rivals; it typically offers no financial program to accomplish its goals; and it sets few time-bound metrics for measuring subsequent results. The paradox is that, given the conservative culture of higher education, an effective strategic plan can likely lead to the demise of public university leadership. Many faculty members do not want leadership to change the status quo. The goal of this chapter is to provide a template for planning and then to use it to address some of the most relevant issues facing public higher education.

Value Creation in Higher Education

The ultimate purpose of any public university is to create value for society and itself through contributions to research and education. Thus, understanding how the value created by the institution is defined, measured, and distributed to various constituents is critical. Interestingly, while educational leaders often decry reductions in the public subsidy based on the loss of education value to society, rarely do they try to precisely define or measure this loss. Moreover, there is often a failure to recognize that determining the value of education involves comparing consumer benefits against taxpayer costs. Value is not only the measurement of benefits; it is also the consideration of costs.

Value in higher education is often presented in the context of lofty principles because university leaders avoid being precise in defining it. Some perhaps find it easier to use more conceptual, less quantifiable notions— "teaching the ability to think critically" or "the attainment of a liberal education" or the "provision of the skills to analyze critically today's changing societal problems"—than to offer a measurable, implementable definition. Many in higher education still heartily agree with the nineteenth-century position of John Stuart Mill, who asserted that "the object of universities is not to make skillful lawyers, physicians or engineers" but "to make capable and cultivated human beings." Along this line, a letter sent to the *Guardian* (Lawson, 2010), signed by over 100 members of higher education and public life, stated,

> We start from the belief that education cannot just be a debt trap on a learn-to-earn treadmill that we never get off as the retirement age is extended. Education in our good society is a universal public good which all explore to reach their fullest potential. It is about the protection and extension of a precious public realm where we know each other not as consumers and competitors but as citizens and co-operators. What is happening [extension of tuition fees and the decline in public support of instruction] is wrong and we must say so in every legal and peaceful way we can—in Parliament, in the media, and in the sites of education and on the streets.

We argue that value is not usefully defined only as reflecting a set of intrinsic and ethereal features of higher education. A major weakness in the strategic planning process of public universities is their inability to readily quantify, or even seek to quantify, the value created by their activities. How can an organization develop a meaningful strategic plan and set realistic goals without understanding how to measure and track the plan's outcomes? Unfortunately, it is rare for universities to set goals systematically based on a precise definition and measure of value and then carefully monitor performance. In the following, we offer a definition of value and discuss how universities can make strategic decisions based on the value propositions they construct.

We prefer to measure the value of higher education in real dollars by the difference between what consumers and users, both public and private, are willing to pay for an educational product and the opportunity cost of all resources devoted to providing that education. Thus,

Value = willingness to pay − opportunity cost of resources

A rise in educational value occurs when willingness to pay increases relative to the cost of the associated resources used to provide the education. It is important to note that willingness to pay for public higher education originates from several diverse sources. Students and their parents express willingness to pay. State and federal governments, and the taxpayers they represent, are willing to pay for both teaching and research through subsidies and grants, with private donors becoming an increasingly important part of the equation.[1] Students and parents are providing more tuition revenue, and taxpayers are providing less. Changes in the overall contributions of taxpayers, donors, and students reflect differences in their preferences and in their capacities to pay for public higher education.

Willingness to pay is observable. Each student will enroll in higher education if his personal willingness to pay exceeds tuition. Students display different degrees of willingness of pay; as tuition rises, fewer choose to enroll. For the last student who enrolls, willingness to pay exactly equals tuition; if tuition rises further, this student will choose not to enroll. Thus, the current level of tuition provides an observation of willingness to pay for the last student who enrolls. For all other enrolled students, willingness to pay is greater than tuition. Similarly, an enrollment subsidy rate reflects the state's willingness to pay for the marginal enrollment. If the subsidy per enrollment declines, there is a reduced public willingness to pay. All private consumers with a willingness to pay in excess of tuition receive a benefit that is called *net consumer surplus*. This is an intuitive concept, with some flaws, but it can be measured using the demand curve. If no one is willing to pay tuition, then this definition implies that there is no private value. This simple proposition has profound consequences. Many products offered in public higher education do not attract sufficient tuition revenues to cover their costs, including areas in the sciences, technology, engineering, and mathematics (referred to as "STEM"), and in medicine. To survive and attract needed enrollments, these areas require a public subsidy. If taxpayers and their representatives are willing to subsidize them, then public willingness to pay reflects their attached value. This notion of value therefore includes potential benefits that accrue to society (public benefits paid for by subsidies) as well as those that accrue to individuals (private benefits paid for by tuition and donations).[2] The challenge for university leadership is to examine the areas of the university under this definition and then to identify programs that provide a social return and deserve a subsidy. The critical decision of what not to produce because there is limited willingness to pay is as important as the decision of what to produce, with both guided by a measurement of value.

Assessing the value of education is complex because it is affected by underlying variables that change over time. Willingness to pay can be influenced by university choices such as quality of instructional improvements, investment in research faculty, or higher graduation and placement rates. Thus, economic value can be created when a university develops or invests in new products, devises new methods of program delivery, or develops more accessible academic programs. The introduction of cost-reduction methods of continuous improvement creates value by reducing costs and improving process flow. Using a value proposition that weighs benefits against cost, one can avoid common misconceptions. For example, value can increase even as tuition increases as long as the increases in perceived return from education exceed its underlying cost.

Willingness to pay can reflect many budgetary and preference factors, including family income dynamics, social demographics, and perceived changes in the return of education (benefit) to both individuals and society.[3] The private benefits of education vary widely depending on a student's major. In a report on the economic value of 171 majors, Carnevale, Strohl and Melton, at the Georgetown University Center on Education and the Workforce, report that undergraduates' average lifetime earnings range from $1,090,000 for engineering majors to $241,000 for education majors. Importantly, a four-year bachelor's degree earns a premium of 84 percent over a high school diploma. Majors also affect the probability of unemployment (Carnevale et al., 2011).

Factors external to the university can also affect willingness to pay. Innovation and product development that increase the need for a more highly educated workforce will increase the value of education to individuals and society. The difficulty in obtaining certain skills can limit their acquisition and thereby increase the return to the few who have the ability or the perseverance to succeed. Monitoring changes in the underlying determinants of willingness to pay is a critical element in establishing an effective strategy.[4] Some contributors to willingness to pay and cost can be influenced by purposeful decision making, and some will remain outside direct control.[5]

Many assert that the key to increasing educational value lies in pursuing efficiency improvements and cost reductions. Certainly, the value proposition previously given implies that becoming more efficient and more productive does increase value. This point of view is popular with supporters of higher education from the business community, government, and many external governing boards, who propose applying the same cost discipline to public higher education that is routinely applied to private businesses that face a dynamic, intense, and increasingly competitive economic environment. This argument usually asserts that competition is a healthy force and that protecting public universities from competition leads to waste and inefficiency. While there is merit in this view, few public university leaders embrace restructuring and cost reduction as the primary imperative for increasing value. Nevertheless, increasing competitive pressure on universities will begin to force the issue regardless of any expressed reluctance to change.

The economic cost of higher education includes faculty and staff compensation, facilities and libraries, information technology, and other services. The unit cost of instruction in public higher education, adjusted for inflation, has remained relatively constant over the last decade. In 1999, the real instructional cost per full-time equivalent (FTE) was $11,242 and by 2009 had become $11,036 (SHEEO [2010b]). While cost inefficiencies do exist, the relevant discussion cannot focus exclusively on the "increasing" cost of higher education, which is a small part of the problem, but must also focus on the burden carried by those who pay for it. It appears that the determination of who pays is more contentious than the issue of whether the total value of higher education is increasing or decreasing.[6]

Educational value can be viewed as flowing to two groups: society (composed of students who receive the education and others in the public who benefit) and the providing university. We can explore how this value is distributed and consider the changing distributional burden between the price paid by students and the subsidy paid by taxpayers. The distribution of value can be represented by an extension of the basic expression

Value = (net benefit to society) + (net benefit to the university)

The *net benefit to society* measures the collective willingness to pay of both students and taxpayers minus tuition revenue and the public appropriation. If students and society perceive higher returns from education, they will express a higher willingness to pay. The *net benefit to the university* is the sum of tuition revenue and the public subsidy minus the opportunity cost of education.[7] The value of education is thus distributed to those who benefit from education and to those who provide it. Finally, because public universities are not-for-profit enterprises, a common condition imposed on university net revenue is that the university can only break even. This means that the net benefit to the university after covering its opportunity cost is zero, and all net benefits accrue to society (students and the public).[8]

Because tuition revenue plus the subsidy are subtracted and then added back into each part of the value expression, the distribution of who pays has no effect on *total* value, but it does affect the *relative* well-being of students and taxpayers (the public). So, while there is a clear trend to redistribute the share of funding responsibility from the public to the private sector, it is not clear how total value is changing. Indeed, the total value of education and, certainly, the value per student can be either increasing or decreasing even as the distribution of who pays changes.

The value expression provides a basis for guiding the objectives of the university and society with respect to higher education. Using this concept, many conceptual questions can be addressed:

- How can major public research universities increase total value?
- Can each university develop a unique value proposition that distinguishes it from rivals and provides incremental value?
- Can desirable features be added to the product to increase willingness to pay?
- Should ways be sought to reduce cost, possibly by reducing the quality of education?
- What investments will increase willingness to pay or reduce costs?

- Should the costs of higher education be covered by the public subsidy or by private tuition?
- What is the ideal distribution of this burden?

The rest of this chapter focuses on these questions in the context of strategic planning and provides useful tools for analysis.

Competitive Forces and the Creation and Distribution of Value

Quite possibly the most widely adopted framework for analyzing the creation and distribution of value is the continuingly popular Five Forces Framework, developed by Michael Porter (1980). This approach recognizes that value can be diminished by the creation of substitute products, by the entry of rivals, by internal rivalry, and by the appropriative actions of sellers and buyers. This framework provides a useful way to identify and assess the forces that affect the creation and distribution of value, and it allows a more systematic strategic analysis than the usual lists of environmental conditions. Dynamic responses to the forces of competition affect nearly all industries and apply as well to higher education. If competitive pressures from new products, new entrants, existing rivals, sellers, and buyers become more intense, the ability of public universities to create and capture economic value will diminish. Specifically, if society's willingness to pay (the sum of tuition revenue, research funding, and public subsidy support) is driven toward opportunity costs by unfavorable competitive pressures, some universities will suffer financially and some may fail.

An extension of the Porter Five Forces Framework, which deals with the creation and especially the distribution of value, is provided by the Value Net (illustrated in Figure 3.1), which is a modified construct introduced by Brandenburger and Nalebuff (1996, p.23) in their well-received book *Co-Opetition*. The "players," who both create and receive value in this construct are customers, substitutors, suppliers, complementors, and the university. A key question is "What is the value that I bring to this game?" A player cannot extract more value from the game than he brings to it, but he certainly can extract less.

A key implication of the combined frameworks of Porter and Brandenburg and Nalebuff is that environmental factors work through both the

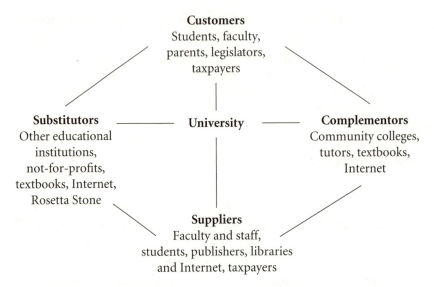

Customers
Students, faculty,
parents, legislators,
taxpayers

Substitutors
Other educational
institutions,
not-for-profits,
textbooks, Internet,
Rosetta Stone

University

Complementors
Community colleges,
tutors, textbooks,
Internet

Suppliers
Faculty and staff,
students, publishers, libraries
and Internet, taxpayers

FIGURE 3.1 Public university value net

competitive forces and the actions of the game participants to change the total value of public higher education and its distribution. One such environmental factor, the permanent reduction in demand for higher education by taxpayers and state legislatures, is having the predictable impact of reducing value. The entry of for-profit providers, the global expansion of supply, the development of potentially disruptive substitute products in the form of web-based instruction, and the increasingly aggressive tuition practices of existing and emergent rivals all adversely affect the ability of public research universities to capture value. Other factors contributing to value erosion include the continued entry of unevenly prepared high-school graduates and the replacement of tenure-track faculty by part-time and adjunct instructors. The confluence of these factors, and others, implies that the ability of universities to create and capture value is changing, which creates new threats and new opportunities.

The Value Net can be used to address the fundamental questions posed by the Carnegie Foundation for the Advancement of Education (1973): *Who Pays? Who Benefits? Who Should Pay?* The answers have changed. In 1973, the Foundation recommended that governments assume a larger role in financing public higher education, but the opposite has occurred. State governments in particular are assigning less value to public higher education and so are less willing to pay. The public subsidy is declining because there are an increasing number of compelling alternatives for public expenditure such as pensions and prisons, and these are "crowding out" higher education spending. There is also a growing reluctance to pay higher taxes and, perhaps, some disenchantment with the claim that higher education is primarily a social, rather than a private, good. Regardless of the contributing factors, tuition revenue is rising to fill the void left by declining public support.

A Framework for Strategic Planning

The considerable jargon in discussions of strategy can detract from the usefulness of key concepts in organizing thinking. Still, a hierarchy of statements can be a helpful frame of reference, as shown in Figure 3.2. There the concepts move from a general statement of purpose and basic existence to ways that an organization can align itself to achieve that purpose, then to specific measures of success and finally to the challenges of implementation. We reluctantly use the term "values" in this hierarchy, but we acknowledge that it is often used to identify the governing principles and standards that guide decisions and actions. In contrast, our definition of values relates to the material or monetary worth that we previously emphasized.

Public universities generally do a good job in articulating their mission and guiding principles. They state why they exist and usually express the standards and values under which they operate. According to the mission statement of the University of Wisconsin-Madison,

---

Mission: Why we exist

Vision: What we want to be

Values: What we believe and how we behave

Strategy: Positioning: our competitive game plan; objectives/goals; program scope; competitive advantage

---

FIGURE 3.2 Hierarchy of statements

The primary purpose of the University of Wisconsin-Madison is to provide a learning environment in which faculty, staff and students can discover, examine critically, preserve and transmit the knowledge, wisdom and values that will help ensure the survival of this and future generations and improve the quality of life for all. The University seeks to help students to develop an understanding and appreciation for the complex cultural and physical worlds in which they live and to realize their highest potential of intellectual, physical and human development.[9]

The mission statement for the University of Iowa is perhaps a bit more specific:

The University seeks to advance scholarly and creative endeavor through leading-edge research and artistic production; to use this research and creativity to enhance undergraduate, graduate, and professional education, health care, and other services provided to the people of Iowa, the nation, and the world; and to educate students for success and personal fulfillment in an increasingly diverse and global environment.[10]

In contrast, most universities do a poor job of developing the steps: vision, strategy, and implementation. Often a mission statement is followed by a predictable list of commonly held *aspirations* presented as the university's vision. Many of these are beautifully written and reflect contributions from a wide range of participants, and nearly all express a desire to provide the highest-quality instruction, distinguished, if not "world-class" research, and comprehensive service to the community. They usually seek to hire and retain the best faculty, to achieve greater diversity, and to become a recognized leader in global education. Emphasis has recently increased on interdisciplinary teaching and research, sustainability of the environment, and extended health care service to a broad local community.

Realistically, statements such as "we will be world class," seem to ignore the fact that there are only ten schools in the "top ten." Aspirations to increase the ranks of under-represented faculty need to address the feasibility constraint imposed by the small pool of candidates. In general, aspirations need to be conditioned by both reality and budget constraints. A wish list is a poor foundation for strategic planning, but most universities offer such lists. Some aspirations are not measurable, have no time-bound commitment for achievement, and are so general that they provide little guidance for action. Examples of aspirations from several major public universities follow:[11]

University of Wisconsin-Madison

1. Provide an exemplary undergraduate education.
2. Reinvigorate the Wisconsin idea.
3. Invest in scholarship in which we have existing or potential strengths.
4. Recruit and retain the best faculty and staff; reward merit.
5. Enhance diversity.
6. Be responsible stewards of resources.

Pennsylvania State University

1. Advance academic and research excellence.
2. Realize Penn State's potential as a global university.
3. Maintain access and affordability, and enhance diversity.
4. Serve the people of the Commonwealth and beyond.
5. Use technology to expand access and opportunities.
6. Control costs and generate additional efficiencies.

University of California, Irvine

1. Pursue research excellence in core disciplines.
2. Increase enrollment at both undergraduate and graduate levels.
3. Reinforce centers of excellence.
4. Develop innovative programs in emerging disciplines.
5. Make UCI the institution of choice for California high-school graduates.
6. Increase diversity.
7. Expand housing opportunities for students and faculty.
8. Improve the transfer of innovation.
9. Expand UCI's role in the community.
10. Launch a major fundraising campaign.

All of the statements listed express laudable aspirations, but they delineate preferences with almost no recognition of budget realities or the effects of immediate rivals on the ability of a particular institution to achieve its goals. All seek to hire the best young faculty to replace an aging baby-boomer cohort with little recognition that everyone else is doing exactly the same thing. Indeed, many areas face a declining supply of emerging Ph.D.s even as world demand for them increases. To generate revenue, most public universities have prioritized increasing enrollment of nonresidents without analyzing the competitive environment or noting that the home states of these students also want greater undergraduate enrollments to enhance their own revenues. All major public universities seek greater federal funding for research without examining the overall trends of that funding. Everyone aspires to more diversity, mostly ignoring the fact that Ph.D. programs in the STEM areas, for example, are producing few women and minorities. Much emphasis is placed on the potential for private fund-raising, often ignoring the feasibility of acquiring the enormous endowment that is required to replace a significant amount of public support.

The first step in moving away from aspirational goals is to assess the university's competitive environment and the financial reality. What determines the willingness to pay of the identified student base? Who are the competitors for potential students? These competitors are the ones whose actions will affect financial viability. Most universities consider their competitors to be their "peer" group—those they use for comparison of key factors like faculty compensation, program quality, budgets, and tuition. While peer research institutions are often national and increasingly international, rivalry for students is mostly regional. Universities tend to ignore the economic reality of their environment. Trends in state or federal support, shifting technology, or the presence of a disruptive technology can have permanent effects that will profoundly impact the value proposition. When times are difficult, too many plans assume the status quo and hope for a return to better times.

Analyses of both external environments and the strategies of competitors provide critical input to the creation of value and vision. A vision statement expresses what the institution wants to become. Most of us understand the irony of saying, "We want to be like everyone else" or "We want to be the top"; yet that is exactly what many aspirational plans state. Public universities do a rather poor job of developing unique visions of how they want to distinguish themselves from their peers. Every major public research university seeks to develop academic excellence in teaching and research, but the pressing issue is *exactly how* this can be accomplished in ways that differentiate one university from all others. To be "different" suggests that there are peers or rivals similar to you and that you can take actions to improve your position relative to theirs in ways that provide clear value. But if rivals are not acknowledged, relative positioning strategies will not be articulated. Can anyone imagine the retail giant Target ignoring Wal-Mart in planning what it wants to be in the next three to five years? Is Apple's vision "to be just like Hewlett-Packard?" Can Boeing ignore what Airbus might be planning? Ignoring rivals' actions is the rule in public higher education, where each institution seems to act and plan as if it were operating in a vacuum. This behavior is manifest in the lack of "competitive game plans."

What Is Strategy?

An orderly planning framework begins with a fundamental question: What is the *unique* value proposition offered to students and society by our institution? The goal is to match what is offered to the desires and abilities of students. What is uniquely right about the University of Iowa that might convince a student to enroll there rather than at the University of Illinois, Iowa State University, or the University of Northern Iowa? How do we create value that distinguishes our institution so that, with proper implementation of decisions, we can sustain and measure performance in learning, service, and research outcomes? The analysis of these questions is the distinguishing feature of true strategic planning versus a generic overall mission statement followed by lofty governing principles or tactical responses to current crises.

Answering such questions involves selecting activities and programs that can distinguish a public research university from others, and then demonstrating the courage to focus on and invest in these choices rather than in programs that do not support distinctiveness. Effective strategy involves developing a prescriptive model and then implementing and communicating decisions that are consistent with it. Failure can result when university leadership is unable to identify a need for change, to articulate an improved model, to make trade-off decisions, to provide the necessary financing, or to execute effectively.

Programs, degrees, and research outcomes are the competitive products offered by public universities to students and society. Their configuration represents a value proposition to students, who compare competing programs. When facing a competitive environment, it becomes harder for universities to capture a portion of the value being created, even as total value increases. It also becomes harder to sustain waste, inefficiencies, cross-subsidies, and poor cost control measures as market competition intensifies. That competition, while threatening their ability to capture value, forces public universities to seek ways to enhance their productivity, to develop new products that attract customers, and to achieve better processes for product delivery. These characteristics of markets both attract and frighten many in public higher education. Failure to act quickly and responsibly will lead to declining market share, a loss of resources, and, in some cases, the inability to compete with more responsive rivals. Some nonsubsidized public universities will fail, just as private firms that face declines in their subsidies often fail.

Four key choices in strategic planning can identify a university's positioning strategy and distinguish it from its competitors. These choices involve level of tuition, amount of subsidy, program scope, and quality of instruction, and all take into account the desired mix of student types (resident/nonresident, graduate/undergraduate, etc.). Taken together, tuition, subsidy, scope, and quality define the university's distinctive position. For example, community colleges set low tuition, receive a low subsidy, have open access, make no pretense of carrying out extensive research, and rely primarily on a high mix of faculty with applied experience. Elite private universities discount tuition, offer relatively large subsidies, and seek to attract the highest-quality students.

A broad range of investment decisions are required to create a hard-to-imitate set of specific activities and capabilities. The selected activities align (strategically fit) with the identified position. Defending a unique position among rivals requires making hard choices not to copy others but rather to distinguish oneself. Reading the annual reports of companies like IBM and GE is illuminating in this regard because they focus on issues of relative positioning. The laptop business, which IBM invented, did not fit with its current strategic image as an IT service company, so that business unit was sold. GE sold its long-standing plastics business for the same reason. These examples demonstrate that neither the overall environment nor the intensity of competitive threats is by nature static. Public universities also need to take a hard look at whether many long-offered programs, even those that were once distinguished and defining, still fit with their current vision in an increasingly competitive environment. Some programs and activities, however excellent or long-standing, simply do not fit with the chosen market position.

How does one make this important positioning decision? At the most basic level, an organization can compete by being distinctive (high quality) in the delivery of its products and services or by being the low-cost provider. Another possibility is that offered by so-called brand differentiators that operate at lower cost but provide considerable product differentiation. A comparison of Wal-Mart and Nordstrom offers an excellent example of low cost versus distinctive differentiation. Wal-Mart competes effectively as a low-cost provider to consumers who value low prices more than distinctive service. Nordstrom offers a distinctive niche set of products and associated services to high-income consumers who express variegated preferences. These quite different, but defensible positions require a unique, complementary set of highly differentiated value-added activities to enable effective execution. Nordstrom may emphasize the hiring of a highly skilled sales force that provides individualized attention to choosy customers. Wal-Mart works to develop the most sophisticated distribution capabilities in retailing, if not in all business. In higher education, Williams College offers a high-price, distinctly differentiated product whereas Kirkwood Community College offers a low-price option.

Major public research universities are examples of medium-price differentiators. Their positioning strategies are what attract particular patterns of student demand and provide protection from competitor encroachment. It seems reasonable to assert that the instructional programs of these medium-price differentiators are so-called "search" goods—that is, consumers can access the dimensions of the product's quality prior to purchase.[12] The potential for differentiation in this case involves enhancement of observable program features. The challenge is that, if students can evaluate product characteristics so can competitors, and so there is the potential for innovative academic programs, enhancements, and product extensions to be copied or imitated. The differentiated public university has to work to keep its costs as low as possible because the competitive success of search goods depends on the university's ability to maintain a beneficial cost advantage. A superior cost advantage can be based on such drivers as economies of scale and scope, learning economies, and the relentless pursuit of operating efficiency. In particular, large public universities might enjoy the advantage of scale economies over smaller rivals. Even here, the growing importance of Internet delivery of education products is seen as both a threat and an opportunity.

The feature that distinguishes major public universities from low-cost alternatives is their expensive and visible research-related activities. This research structure provides little opportunity for economies of scale, and it requires employing highly specialized resources whose expenditures, once made, are best defined as sunk costs. Sunk costs are fixed costs that have no other use apart from their intended purpose. For example a nuclear physics lab has little use for faculty outside the narrow nuclear physics subspecialty.

Alternatively, the discrete activities required for excelling at low-cost delivery of instructional services such as by a community college may imply little product differentiation and the use of routine replicable activities. Attempts to succeed by straddling these polar positioning strategies usually fail because the culture, processes, and structure required for success with one platform do not generally support those of the other. It is hard to manage distinctive research programs that define niche competencies and, at the same time, compete as a low-cost provider of commodity-like instructional programs, because the activities and capabilities required for success at one do not transfer to the other. There is a big difference in what is required for success by the sales staff at Wal-Mart and that required by the sales staff at Nordstrom.

Many of the very-high-research public universities actually resemble private businesses that face rivalry from both low- and high-end specialist competitors. At the lower-cost end of the competitive spectrum are not-for-profit organizations, community colleges, and some four-year private colleges that direct nearly all of their resources toward undergraduate teaching and community service. At the differentiated end are distinguished private, research-active universities. Today the very-high-research public universities are positioned neither as low cost nor as distinctly differentiated; rather, they appear to "straddle," sometimes quite awkwardly, these two generic positions. This is a problem, especially when the basic funding model is under stress. Underperforming highly specialized programs are increasingly cross-subsidized using the tuition revenues of high-demand programs, and this is a difficult configuration to sustain in a competitive environment.

With some prominent exceptions, it is hard to argue that the lower-division courses offered at many public research universities, taught by teaching assistants, part-time lecturers, adjuncts, or permanent faculty in large lecture formats, provide distinctive value to students.[13] The analogy is that public universities are in too many instances providing a Wal-Mart experience to first- and second-year students and a Nordstrom experience to juniors and seniors. The catch is that the financial cross-subsidy from lower- to upper-division courses is necessary to sustain the latter. Tuition revenue obtained from large lecture classes is the primary support for the small-enrollment specialty classes favored by faculty and upper-division students. Unfortunately, the recently favored option, encouraged by legislators and sometimes regents—of channeling lower-division students through community colleges—has had profound and probably adverse implications for both the quality and the finances of public universities. If this transformation is accomplished on a broad scale, what new sources of income will support the major research universities' distinctive upper-level undergraduate instructional programs?

University Value-Chain Activities

The vision, the value proposition, and the selected positioning strategy provide ways to think of creating and distributing value, and all help to distinguish the institution. If institutions develop the same market position, the only remaining option is to compete through tuition. The value-chain framework presented here is a useful tool for thinking about differentiating programs. One can use it to define, communicate, and illustrate a series of discrete activities and processes that create a unique positioning strategy.

The primary activities of a public university involve recruitment, advising, academic instruction, out-of-classroom enrichment, career placement, and, finally, relationship building and promotion of the university to alumni and donors (both private and public). These primary activities are supported by such secondary activities as the hiring of faculty and staff, purchasing, new-program development (R&D), human resource management, and infrastructure activities such as IT implementation and facilities management. This interrelated set of discrete activities and processes produces the educational outcomes that are valued by students and society.

The value chain, summarized in Figure 3.3, represents an important interrelated system of activities. Many of its primary activities are related as complements, rather than as substitutes, which implies that they need to be mutually coordinated. Complementarity among variables gives rise to system effects, where the value of the integrated system can be greater than the sum of its individual parts. For example, if a better job is done recruiting students, it is easier to teach them; they will be well received in job markets; and subsequent employment success will lead to greater private donations that feed back positively into attracting new students. When things work well, the entire system thrives and reinforces good outcomes. When things go wrong, declines in value can develop that are difficult to reverse.[14] Cooperation among complementary activities is thus the key to effective outcomes. Virtually all major MBA programs in the United States coordinate their recruiting, advising, instruction, and placement functions. This tight coordination is not

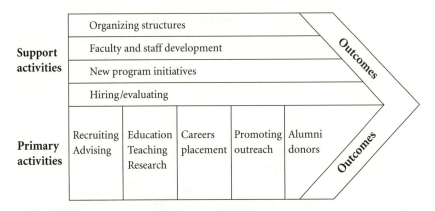

FIGURE 3.3 University value chain

as common in some professional or undergraduate programs, which either loosely assign recruiting and placement to central university units or, worse, pay no attention to them whatsoever. It is revealing to encounter the lack of concern among some university faculty for the placement successes of their graduates. If primary activities are treated as substitutes for one another, the motivation is to encourage internal competition rather than cooperation. It makes no sense, for example, to treat advising and instruction as substitutes because investing in advising will increase the (incremental) return to investing in instruction. Rivalry for resources when activities are complements is ruinous for both morale and outcomes.

Institutions of different types will emphasize different activities in support of their particular competitive advantage. At four-year colleges, the quality of individualized instruction may critically define a competitive advantage; this may be less true at two-year community colleges that offer scores of entry-level courses. The IT capabilities of a for-profit institution like the University of Phoenix might define a core capability that distinguishes it because IT is particularly important in recruiting, advising, and instruction. A specialized recruiting process is an essential competency for some graduate and technical programs and is conducted by individuals who possess insider knowledge of them. The resources spent on recruiting faculty and students at distinguished private universities and the individualized instruction these institutions offer are defining capabilities; they are less emphasized at major public research universities in part because of budget constraints. The point is that different institutions emphasize different parts of the value chain in support of their particular competitive advantage. Wal-Mart focuses on inbound logistics and IT capability; Nike focuses on product development and marketing. Currently, since tuition revenue is growing in importance, a great deal of attention is placed on both "upstream" and "downstream" activities in the public university value chain, particularly recruiting, placement, and donor relations.

Colleges and universities make different choices regarding the configuration of their value chains. The results reflect trade-offs in the expenditure of scarce resources. Public research institutions spend more on research activities than do community colleges. Private institutions spend more per student on academic support, student service, and scholarships than do their public counterparts. These resource allocations reflect the way institutions attempt to position themselves in the higher-education marketplace. The resulting patterns of expenditure choice can be clearly observed in Table 3.1, which contrasts spending by public research universities on instruction, research, and service with that by community colleges.[15]

Supporting the value-chain activities are a series of tangible and intangible resources. Tangible resources include buildings, libraries, IT technologies, and various categories of human resources (faculty, staff, administration, etc.). Intangible resources include reputation, brand image, and, important, hard-to-copy ways of accomplishing key activities and processes. For something to be labeled a "resource," it must be scarce, be in demand, and possess the property that some of its returns are appropriable by the university (see Collis and Montgomery [1995] for an enlightened discussion of resources). Distinct universities reveal a distinct set of resources. The challenge is to recognize that what can legitimately be classified as a resource under one set of environmental conditions will fail under another. Highly specialized faculty members in a discipline that is no longer in demand are not a resource under these criteria.

TABLE 3.1 Spending on instruction, research, and services in 2008

Activity	Public research university ($/FTE student)	Community college ($/FTE student)
Instruction	9,732	5,216
Research	5,567	50
Public service	1,912	367

SOURCE: Wellman, Desrochers, and Lenihan (2008).

The immediate lesson provided by the value chain and associated resources is that coordinated decision making and planning are necessary. A plan that is directed specifically at instruction makes little sense unless it is accompanied by a plan for recruiting and placement. Instruction, recruiting, and placement are all motivated by a statement that describes and defines the characteristics of the students who are being recruited, educated, and placed in the workforce. If the typical student enters a state university after attending a two-year community college, his advising needs will differ substantially from those of a student who begins her education at the state university. If the typical student is a first-generation college student, her chance of completing a degree is reportedly 50 percent of that for a student whose parents both graduated from college. These fundamental distinctions in preparation and family background make a big difference in assessing which parts of the value chain need additional resources. And they make a big difference both in how universities position themselves and in reported outcomes. Ultimately, a successfully created and coordinated system of interrelated activities and processes improves the measured outcomes of student success.

Program Scope

A vision defines the scope of products and services that will be provided. The absurdity of saying the institution will offer a class "in every topic of human knowledge" is clear. Over time, most institutions broaden their program scope to take advantage of faculty, student, and donor interests, as well as funding opportunities. Or they simply copy their peers. Excessively broad scope in academic and research programs and enterprises is a critical issue. The relevant questions for assessing any academic program might be

- Is the program consistent with the university's vision?
- Does the program offer the potential for the chosen quality of instruction and research?
- Can graduates find employment in their chosen field?
- Is there sufficient revenue to cover the financial cost of the program?

If the answer to any of these questions is no, then a decision needs to be made to downsize, eliminate, or expand. Rarely are these key questions used to screen and evaluate programs, and seldom are they asked when a program is being expanded; once established, programs are nearly impossible to dislodge. Decisions regarding scope are especially critical when programs are not self-financed. The decision of what to support when subsidies decline is more difficult. It may be that the only way to retain the distinction of being a very-high-research public university is to shrink program scope. Perhaps a better strategy is to be distinguished in a fewer number of programs than to be mediocre in many. Such questions cannot be answered generally, but one hopes they will be addressed with courage by each institution, because there will be resistance.

What are the strategic limits to regional, national, and, indeed, global expansion? Universities serve an increasing number of customers and provide products and services well beyond those historically purchased by traditional students. This diverse array of products leads to an overlapping of the missions and markets of public universities with those of other institutions. This horizontal broadening scope includes off-campus programs demanded by nontraditional students, ancillary fee-based services, and noncore activities like athletics, clinical health services, and food and housing. The expansion of the horizontal scope of enterprises increases the complexity of governance. Leadership and management challenges are sometimes in the purview of those who are neither experienced nor trained to govern vast, increasingly complex enterprises.

The appropriate scope involves vertical activities in the value chain. Public universities exhibit an excessive vertical scope of activities. With the rapid expansion of effective market specialists, now is a good time to consider outsourcing activities that do not provide competitive advantages. Decisions about what activities to perform internally and what to allocate to market specialists are critical and affect the reputation of institutions. Properly done, the maintenance of quality can be more effective through a mix of internal and external processes. In recent years, IT specialists have begun to replace in-house capabilities; university hospitals have outsourced laundry, cleaning, and food services; dormitories, mail, and food services are managed by outside suppliers; and specialized recruiting and placement for some programs is outsourced. Substantial instruction is outsourced to part-time faculty and adjuncts who work on a piece-rate assignment, although the outsourcing analogy is not promoted. Even so, we suspect that public universities lag well behind private businesses in the effective use of outsourcing. Most probably, outsourcing to specialists will increase in public higher education, and it is just one likely consequence of the changing pattern of financing. The need for and the ability to make scope decisions represent the essence of good strategy, and this is an area where public universities do not excel.

Governing Boards and University Systems

We see the primary role of a governing board, much like that of a corporate board, ideally as establishing a set of principles that can be used by university leaders to guide their decisions and actions. These guiding principles ("goalposts") allow administrators to lead and manage their individual organizations. Each institution then develops a competitive strategy that both suits its vision and is consistent with its governance principles. This ideal underlies successful business practices, and it is helpful to consider how corporations approach these issues to assess whether universities can adopt some of the same perspectives and practices.

In well-known governance structures, a corporation consists of a number of separate businesses, each with its distinct positioning strategy. The businesses are composed of a collection of valuable tangible and intangible resources that are configured to produce value, possibly in different ways across business lines. A guiding overall vision directs the organizing structure. When synergies develop among the separate businesses, a corporate advantage occurs that enhances the value of the overall system.

Using standard corporate strategy as a guiding framework, each separate business seeks to develop a competitive advantage in the markets in which it competes, usually by bringing to bear, and investing in, valuable resources and capabilities around an implementable vision. Similarly, the positioning strategy of each public university defines the way it will compete against rivals. Beyond offering a low-cost option or a distinctly differentiated product, a strategy might be to bring providers of education and students together in a virtual university that features low transaction costs using modern web-based channels.

A *corporate advantage* occurs when there is effective *configuration* and *coordination* of these multiple organizations (Collis and Montgomery, 2005). In public higher education, the separate institutions are the equivalent of individual business units. The board of regents is the governing unit (corporate office) that seeks to configure and coordinate the performance of the individual public universities under its control. Every university is responsible for a unique "business model" that permits it to create value in its respective selected markets. The more effective the individual activities, the more system value can be created. The purpose of the governing board is to leverage the abilities of the collective enterprises and to create a "system advantage," where the value of the system is made greater than it could be by simply adding up the individual parts. The apparent challenge of corporate strategy is to avoid introducing a "conglomerate discount" that destroys some of the value created by the individual units. For example, if the governing board adds monitoring and compliance costs without adding value, system value is destroyed.

In this framework, a system's individual organizations develop a distinctive, viable positioning strategy subject to the general governance principles of behavior and accountability. There is no single positioning strategy that fits everyone, and the available options are many. The function of the governing board is to lay out the guiding principles and to leverage the resources of the system to create additional system value.

Summary and Conclusions

Strategic planning processes can become more rigorous and comprehensive, with emphasis placed on defining value and establishing competitive distinctiveness. Once the university's vision is established, key decisions can be made to determine associated program scope, quality, and tuition. Program scope can be conditioned by always asking: What programs should we offer? What programs should we not offer? For each program, the selected positioning strategy is implemented through a complementary set of value-chain activities (recruitment, advising, instruction, placement, and alumni relations). Time-bound metrics for determining financial viability, quality, and productivity can be developed and widely communicated. Areas of unsatisfactory quality and low productivity can be considered for downsizing or even elimination.

The message for university leadership is that tough decisions are necessary to maintain the discipline required to adopt a unique positioning strategy. Effective strategy involves making trade-offs; for example, higher quality requires higher expenditure. Consensus building, which is widely admired in higher education, does not enhance effective decision making. Perhaps the most difficult choice for leadership is whether to continue to work toward consensus in a declining institution or to take the difficult and precarious path to ensure the university's future excellence. As is often the case in organizational dynamics, the leadership cohort that implements effective change may not survive. One hopes that the new path does not remain, in Robert Frost's words, the "road less traveled."

4 Tuition Setting in Practice

The most unkindest cut of all.
—*William Shakespeare*

Tuition and Enrollment Responses to Declining Subsidies

In Chapter 2 we discussed tactical responses to declining subsidies, including cuts in both instructional and noninstructional costs, postponing capital projects, and raising tuition. We also described recent efforts to raise revenues by increasing enrollment through selective tuition-discounting schemes, lowering admissions standards, and increasing the percentage of nonresidents, who pay higher tuition. All of these tactics relate to a fundamental question: How can public universities continue to deliver high-quality education with reduced state subsidies and, at least in the short term, reduced private donor and other external support? To maintain quality, the leading option is to increase tuition to offset the decline in the subsidy. Whenever tuition increases are proposed, however, there is concern about their necessary magnitude and the impact on enrollment.

The purpose of this chapter is to gain a better understanding of the tuition responses needed to offset subsidy declines. Our intent is to provide a framework that can explain actual tuition-setting decisions, with prescriptive suggestions developed later in Chapter 8. We also discuss the implications of a declining subsidy on access and enrollment, and we examine the efficacy of set-aside programs, which require a portion of tuition to be used for financial aid. When the subsidy declines, say by 10 percent, what is the percentage increase in tuition necessary to offset the university's loss in revenue? Understanding the answer to this question helps to eliminate misconceptions about the relationships between tuition increases, declines in subsidy, and costs.[1]

We begin with an accounting relationship that requires the university to balance its instructional budget annually. This break-even condition is represented as follows: the instructional budget B is constrained to equal the sum of tuition revenue R and the total public subsidy S:

$$B = R + S$$

We exclude other sources of revenue from gifts and entrepreneurial programs, but we will consider their implications later. It is useful to express each of the variables in the accounting relationship in terms of easily understood percentage changes, or growth rates. The growth rate in the budget is a weighted sum of the growth rates in tuition revenue and the subsidy, where the weights k and $(1 - k)$, represent the shares that tuition and the subsidy respectively contribute to the overall budget. For example, $k = 0.4$ means that current tuition revenue accounts for 40 percent of the total instructional budget and the public subsidy accounts for 60 percent:

$$(\% \text{ change in } B) = k \times (\% \text{ change in } R) + (1 - k) \times (\% \text{ change in } S)$$

With the weights held constant, the growth-rate expression is a useful approximation.

A simple way to characterize tuition setting is to assume that the university seeks to maintain its current level of spending. In this case, the percentage change in the budget equals zero, and the university, with S given, sets tuition revenue R to cover its current expenses. For the university to break even in the face of a cut in the public subsidy, tuition revenue must increase. In the accounting relationship, setting the percentage change in the budget equal to zero implies that the percentage increase in tuition revenue necessary to offset a subsidy decrease is determined by the following expression:

$$(\% \text{ change in } R) = -[(1 - k)/k] \times (\% \text{ change in } S)$$

If the subsidy falls, tuition revenue must increase to maintain a constant instructional budget. The percentage increase necessary depends on the contribution to the budget of the subsidy relative to tuition as represented by $(1 - k)/k$.

This basic relation provides insight into how public universities respond to a decline in state support. One key implication is that the necessary percentage increase in tuition revenue can be substantially different from the percentage decrease in subsidy because the two revenue sources represent different initial shares of total revenue. For example, if tuition revenue makes up 40 percent of the instructional budget ($k = 0.4$) and the subsidy declines by 10 percent, then tuition revenue must increase by 15 percent to maintain the current instructional budget. The more significant the subsidy as a percentage of the budget, the larger the percentage change required in tuition to offset a subsidy reduction. Because the subsidy has historically been a large fraction of the total instructional budget, large percentage increases in tuition have been enacted as the subsidy has fallen. Not too surprisingly, much protest has accompanied these increases. With little in the way of alternatives to replace lost subsidy revenue, this kind of response to cuts in state funding is common, and several examples of its application will be provided later.

Because of the required proportional increases in tuition revenue, some argue that the university should offset the decline in state support by increasing entrepreneurial programs and fund-raising. Entrepreneurial programs are those that are financially self-reliant and include off-book instruction, some athletics, and some forms of funded research. There is no problem expanding the formulation to include these other revenue sources. We can gain a sense of needed private giving by looking at the challenges that face the University of Wisconsin (UW). In June 2011 the UW Board of Regents raised tuition 5.5 percent to generate $37.5 million, which offset only about one-third of the budget cut from the state. If, instead, private funds had been raised, the additional endowment necessary would be about $770 million. Any more cuts in ensuing years would require the raising of additional endowments. Apart from the fact that donors are not interested in seeing their gifts replace cutbacks in taxpayer support, this example indicates that replacing declining subsidies with private giving is infeasible.[2]

In the remaining discussion, we will revert to our original formulation, where the effects of increases in gifts or entrepreneurial programs on the university's instructional budget are assumed to be negligible. Offsetting a permanent decline in the subsidy requires a permanent increase in tuition revenue just to maintain the current budget. As was shown in Figure 2.1, tuition revenue rose by over 60 percent in real terms between 1980 and 2009. Given the downward trajectory of the subsidy, this tuition increase was accommodated by tactical cost reductions and, likely, falling educational quality. It is usually not politically feasible to raise tuition to fully cover subsidy losses. Some have tried. At the University of California, a tuition increase of 32 percent was passed in 2009 for 2010, followed by another 17.6 percent increase effective fall 2011; both increases were justified based on cuts in state support (see Bachman [2011]).

The Effects of Tuition Increases on Enrollment

A critical issue concerns the impact on enrollment as base tuition rises to offset a decline in subsidy revenue. The effect on enrollment is not always obvious and depends on demand and supply elasticities, on how much excess demand/supply exists, and on a number of environmental factors. As universities look to increased tuition as a way to solve revenue shortfalls, an assumption is too often made that tuition can be raised without adversely affecting enrollment. In fact, demand curves relating tuition to enrollment display negative slopes, with higher tuition implying lower enrollment. It is useful to think of a willingness-to-pay schedule (an inverse demand curve) that expresses students' preferences, where each student has a unit demand for the education product. Each student either purchases higher education or does not. Ranking students in decreasing order of their individual willingness to pay provides a downward-sloping schedule, where a lower tuition attracts new students who exhibit a lower willingness to pay. If there are a large number of students, the resulting downward-sloping schedule is called the inverse demand curve.

A related concept is the sensitivity, or *elasticity*, of the demand schedule. More formally, tuition elasticity refers to the percentage decrease in enrollment caused by a 1 percent increase in tuition. The available estimates indicate that demand for higher education is inelastic; thus a 1 percent tuition increase leads to a less than 1 percent decrease in enrollment and thereby to an increase in tuition revenue.[3] It should be noted that, because there are substitutes for an individual college or university, their demand is more elastic than is the general demand for higher education. If enrollment declines by a greater percentage than tuition rises (in other words, if the demand schedule is elastic), then tuition revenue does not rise but *falls*, and an increase in tuition becomes self-defeating.

To gain insight into the importance of tuition elasticity, consider a university that enrolls 10,000 students, with tuition equal to $1,000 per student and total tuition revenue equal to $10 million. Suppose that a decline in the subsidy results in a $100,000 decrease in revenue and the university decides to increase tuition to offset this loss. If demand elasticity is zero, a 1 percent increase in tuition will provide sufficient tuition revenue to fully offset the subsidy reduction. More realistically, we assume that tuition elasticity equals −0.50, which implies that every 1 percent increase in tuition results in a 0.50 percent decrease in enrollment. Now, a 1 percent increase in tuition will decrease enrollment by 50 students, which represents a loss in tuition revenue at the new level of $50,500. If the remaining 9,950 students pay the increase, revenue goes up to $10,049,500. The net increase is $49,500, which is short of the required $100,000. To obtain the desired $100,000 increase, tuition must increase by around 2 percent to offset the effect of decreased enrollment on tuition revenue. More generally, as shown in the chapter appendix, if the tuition elasticity equals −0.50, then the required percentage change in tuition per student to offset a decline in the subsidy is

$$(\% \text{ change in tuition}) = -2 \times [(1 - k)/k] \times (\% \text{ change in total subsidy})$$

If the shares of tuition revenue and the public subsidy are equal, a 1 percent decrease in the subsidy will require a 2 percent increase in tuition when the tuition elasticity of demand is −0.50. The larger the public subsidy share in the total budget and the more elastic the demand, the larger the required increase in tuition.

A Decline in the Subsidy in the Context of a Revenue and Cost Structure

Total cost consists of variable costs, which increase with enrollment, and fixed costs, which are independent of enrollment.[4] A more detailed discussion of cost will be presented in Chapter 5. The subsidy can be a direct grant to the university that offsets a portion of fixed costs, or it can be support per enrollment, acting as a direct offset to unit variable cost. In Figure 4.1, we plot the inverse demand schedule, which measures the relationship between tuition and enrollment. Higher levels of enrollment necessitate lower levels of tuition to induce more students to be willing to pay for education. If, for example, the university targets enrollment level E_A, then tuition T_A will induce E_A students to enroll. The figure also shows the average cost function per student.

The willingness to pay schedule intersects the average cost schedules at two points in Figure 4.1, where each point is consistent with tuition equaling

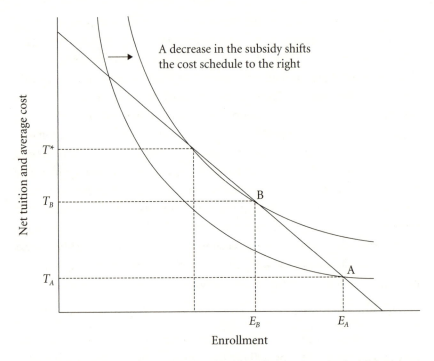

FIGURE 4.1 Tuition and enrollment adjustments when the subsidy falls

average cost. We will focus on point A, with E_A representing the larger break-even enrollment, arguing that the smaller enrollment, while meeting the break-even restriction, is not politically feasible. Suppose that the subsidy per student decreases. The university then faces an increase in cost per student at every level of enrollment. As shown in the figure, the average cost curve shifts to the right, leading to a new break-even enrollment, point B. At this solution point, enrollment is lower and both tuition and total university revenue are higher. With inelastic demand and a break-even requirement, a cut in the subsidy will lead to an increase in total tuition revenue. Specifically, Figure 4.1 has been constructed so that all tuition levels below a specific value of tuition T^* are associated with the inelastic range of the demand curve. In this case, the revenues are represented by areas. Area $T_B E_B$ is greater that area $T_A E_A$.

A graphical representation can help us to think about related issues. Reductions in subsidies act like increases in university costs, either fixed if the reduction takes the form of a fall in a direct appropriation, or variable if there is a reduction in subsidy per enrollment. An interesting situation occurs when subsidy declines lead to increases in average cost that shift the cost curve everywhere above the willingness to pay schedule. If this occurs, no tuition can be set that will permit the university to break even. Alternatively, moves that reduce variable costs reduce the average cost schedule at every enrollment. Other modifications involve possible shifts in the demand curve. One such shift concerns the discounting involved in determining actual (net) tuition. An important question might be whether there are ways to increase the willingness to pay for higher education at every enrollment level, which implies a shift to the right of the schedule. Differentiating the product in attractive ways can shift the demand curve, but it may also increase average cost if it is more expensive to provide a distinctive product.

The graphical representation in Figure 4.1 can be supplemented with a numerical example, which is provided in Table 4.1. Here, all the required preference and cost parameters are specified.

Case 1 is the initial situation. Case 2 describes a decline in the subsidy per enrollment from $5,000 to $4,500. In response to the decline, there is an increase in net tuition, a decrease in enrollment, a decrease in the total subsidy, and, in this instance, an increase in total revenue. Of course, obvious problems arise with the required adjustment to a subsidy decline if university governing boards balk at increasing tuition to a level necessary to achieve the new break-even point. In this example, a decline in the total public appropriation of 13 percent requires an increase in net tuition of 17 percent. But this tuition adjustment may be politically unpalatable. If the tuition increase is constrained below the required 17 percent, the university will not break even.

Example: The Tuition-Setting Process at the University of Texas at Austin

One example in which the tuition-setting process is clearly spelled out is provided by the University of Texas at Austin. This case is of particular interest because Texas, along with Florida, Louisiana, and Oklahoma, is one of the few states where the legislatures determine tuition. In Texas, tuition-setting authority was deregulated in 2003 and turned over to the governing boards of public colleges and universities. This delegation has allowed the separate institutions to forge independent tuition policies.

TABLE 4.1 Net tuition, enrollment, total revenue, and total subsidy under break-even constraint with two demand elasticities

	Maximum willing-ness to pay ($/FTE)	Variable unit cost ($/FTE)	Total fixed cost ($M)	Subsidy per FTE ($/FTE)	Tuition elasticity	Total enroll-ment (FTE)	Net tuition ($/FTE)	Total revenue ($M)	Total subsidy ($M)
Case 1	32,000	8,000	100	5,000	−.28	25,593	6,407	175	125
Case 2	32,000	8,000	100	4,500	−.31	24,401	7,598	185	110

NOTES: Specification used is a willingness-to-pay schedule, as follows: $T(E) = \alpha - E$, where T is net tuition, α is maximum willingness to pay, and E is enrollment; $C(E) = F + (c - s)E$ is total cost, where F is fixed cost and $(c - s)E$ is total variable cost. Subsidy per unit, s, reduces unit variable cost one for one. Break-even enrollment solves $E^2 - (\alpha + s - c)E + F = 0$. The smaller root of solution is eliminated as politically infeasible.

Willingness to pay, unit cost, the subsidy per FTE, and tuition are all measured in $/FTE, where FTE is "full-time-equivalent" enrollment. Revenue and the total subsidy are measured in millions of dollars. An elasticity is a unit-free number.

The University of Texas at Austin (UT), in response to deregulation, established the Tuition Policy Advisory Committee (TPAC), an internal group consisting of four students and five members of the faculty and/or administration whose responsibility is to develop tuition policy. The resulting policy seems apparent enough.[5] UT presents the details of its core budget, which includes a listing of ongoing and aspirational strategic priorities. Using information about the legislature's appropriation, a two-year estimate of endowment income, and some other relatively minor sources of income, the committee recommends a rate of tuition increase for a two-year period that will permit the university to break even and thereby maintain the acceptable components of the core budget. Tuition is determined by assuming that current enrollment will be unaffected by any increase. After the recommendation is finalized, UT's president reviews it, then holds a series of public meetings, and submits timely findings to the chancellor.

A few features have been added to the UT process to increase transparency for parents and students. Prior to deregulation in 2003, the university's base tuition mandated by the legislature was dramatically altered by the addition of numerous fees. This practice has since been eliminated by setting a "flat" tuition that includes all such fees so that students can know the true "list" price. Professional programs, including business and law, are allowed to select, within guidance bounds, their separate tuition structures, which are processed by central administration rather than by TPAC. These structures must be approved by the governing board. There are some relatively minor tuition differentials resulting from this process.

In a recent iteration, TPAC decided not to accommodate most of the strategic aspirations of the university, which would have required an 18 percent increase in tuition to fund this budget. Instead, the proposed tuition increase for 2010–11 was 3.95 percent. We can use the growth accounting relationship to illustrate how the percentage changes in tuition, public support and the academic budget are related in this example. The UT data indicate that about 50 percent of the core budget is attributable to tuition revenue ($k = 0.50$) and the decrease in the subsidy that was enacted is 2 percent. If we place these values in the growth accounting formula, it predicts that tuition will need to increase by 4 percent to break even, which is close to the percentage increase (3.95 percent) enacted by the legislature. Thus, it would appear that the Texas tuition process simply adjusts tuition, with some consideration for extenuating circumstances, to maintain the university's core academic budget.

An interesting feature of this cost-based tuition-setting process is the detail it presents in the discussion of program costs. This stands in sharp contrast to the university's avoidance of any attempt to measure and report demand-side factors that affect tuition policy. The welfare of students is discussed in general terms: "TPAC feels that its tuition recommendations are within what can reasonably be expected of students and parents financially, given the context of current economic realities, expectations of tuition affordability and the legislative policy constraints under which the University must operate."[6] In this process and in the accompanying statements, there appears to be an explicit assumption that the quality of education for a given enrolled population is both sacrosanct and being taken seriously. There is a certain basic appeal to an approach that starts each year by making minor adjustments to the previous year's budget that reflect recent cost conditions, and then seeks a tuition increment given the level of public support that will maintain the core budget.

Enrollment Determination When There Is Excess Demand

Price ceilings imposed by the legislature or regents can cause base tuition to be set below the market-clearing price. The result is excess demand, with more qualified students seeking public higher education than universities can afford to accommodate. Curiously, the desire to keep tuition low usually reflects arguments for increased access, but the actual result is a shortage of available slots and the need to ration access. A typical case develops when subsidy falls and base tuition rises to allow the university to continue to break even. With excess demand, the university can increase enrollment to generate the funds needed to replace the subsidy. But then a rule must be developed to determine who is admitted and who is rejected. A long-standing approach, which we adopt here, focuses on consumer surplus by first meeting the unsatisfied demand of those with the highest willingness to pay. In this case, enrollment is determined by supply rather than demand. As long as excess demand persists, the elasticity of supply replaces the elasticity of demand as the critical factor in determining enrollment response, with a more elastic supply implying a larger enrollment response to an increase in base tuition.

A numerical example illustrates the excess-demand case. We specify $q(T) = 20,000 + .55T$ as the positively sloping supply schedule. Net fixed costs inclusive of the direct subsidy are $500 million.[7] Break-even tuition is $T = \$17,027$, break-even enrollment is $q(T) = 29,365$, and elasticity of supply is .3. If the direct subsidy declines by \$50 million, break-even tuition increases to $T = \$18,295$, and enrollment increases to $q(T) = 30{,}062$. With a positive elasticity of supply and a higher base tuition, unmet demand will facilitate an enrollment increase. Essentially, to cover the increase in fixed costs associated with a decline in the subsidy, more tuition-paying students are admitted.

In California, and several other states, there does appear to be excess demand for subsidized public higher education, particularly for the very-high-research universities in the UC System. UC Berkeley and UCLA, for example, admit approximately 60 percent of eligible students. As public support falls and base tuition increases to accommodate university budgets, the queue of rationed resident applicants will shorten. However, with unmet demand, enrollment will increase as long as supply responds positively to higher resident tuition rates. If there are no supply responses to higher tuition from the universities (capacity constraints), enrollment will not change and the only result will be a direct substitution of tuition revenue for the public subsidy. The observation that higher tuition can be accompanied by higher enrollments is true when there is significant excess demand; indeed, this outcome is the standard prediction about what happens when an imposed price ceiling, in this case on resident tuition, is relaxed.

Tuition Set-Aside Programs

Why do universities continue to raise listed tuitions while at the same time engaging in active tuition-discounting programs? Part of the answer to that question can be found in developing a better understanding of the possible effects of tuition (price) discrimination practices, which are often characterized in public higher education as "high tuition–high aid" (Turner [2006]). These practices subsidize low-income (often resident) students by charging higher tuitions to high-income (often nonresident) students. The intended effects are (1) to increase overall student welfare, where the welfare gains of the low-income cohort must outweigh the welfare loss of the high-income cohort; and (2) to increase access for low-income students. The challenge is to do these things while maintaining a break-even university budget and avoiding any decline in the quality of education programs.

We illustrate a tuition set-aside program that allocates some percentage of total tuition revenue to need-based aid. Such programs are often mandated by governing boards as a way of rationalizing a higher base tuition. The scheme might work in the following way. The high-income cohort of students pays the full sticker price, with the resulting tuition revenue subtracted from a revenue target associated with the break-even requirement. A tuition discount to the low-income cohort is then determined so that the overall revenue target is realized. The modified revenue accounting relationship facing a public university with two sources of tuition revenue and a public subsidy is

$$T_1 E_1 + T_2 E_2 + S = F$$

For simplicity, all costs are fixed costs F. It is assumed that tuition revenue $T_2 E_2$ is determined for nonresident students to maximize obtainable revenue. Then the revenue that must be obtained from residents $T_1 E_1$ is that which permits the university to break even. This value is found by subtracting nonresident revenue and the appropriation S from fixed costs F. For any nonresident demand function, maximizing nonresident revenue when there are no variable costs requires selecting tuition so that the resulting elasticity of demand is unity. In effect, nonresident revenue is maximized when any further percentage increase reduces nonresident enrollment by exactly the same percentage, leaving nonresident revenue unchanged. If nonresident tuition is set at its revenue-maximizing level, when the public appropriation declines, then resident tuition must be increased to offset this decline in order to maintain the break-even requirement. Since increasing nonresident tuition lowers revenue, the other alternatives are to reduce base expenditures or change entry requirements.

While simple, the formulation just described provides useful insights. The target tuition revenue has to be increased to maintain the base budget if there is a decline in the state appropriation. Many universities have increased nonresident enrollments to offset subsidy declines, effectively increasing the share of nonresidents as a way to increase tuition revenue. This tactic might work but only for a short while. When a high tuition is charged to an identifiable cohort of students, say nonresidents, this market might be contested by rival universities that recognize a revenue opportunity. For example, given that Illinois residents can choose among Iowa, Wisconsin, and Indiana Big Ten public research universities, a successful move, say, by the University of Wisconsin to attract more Illinois residents will reduce demand for an Iowa or Indiana education. The result will be lower revenue available to Iowa from Illinois residents and the need to increase the tuition charged to Iowa residents to meet the target revenue level.

A tuition set-aside program acts like a tax placed on high-income students to accommodate a subsidy to low-income students; thus, it is essentially a high-tuition–high-aid program, which may or may not be revenue neutral. The effect of increasing tuition for one group in order to lower it for another depends on the relative tuition elasticities of demand of high- and low-income students. For example, if demand is inelastic for both groups, increasing tuition for the high-income cohort will increase its contribution to total revenue, while decreasing tuition for the low-income cohort will decrease its contribution. The overall impact on tuition revenue will depend on the combined net adjustment. It can be said, however, that the closer the tuition of the high-income group is to maximizing its total contribution, the less sense it makes to look to that group to provide additional tuition revenue to offset declines in the state appropriation—and the more vulnerable the school is to aggressive competitive moves by rival schools.

Other Factors Affecting Enrollment

To determine how total tuition revenue changes when tuition per student rises, it is important to consider other factors that influence the average student's decision to attend a university. In general, enrollment depends inversely on net tuition and directly on per capita income; it also depends on a variety of other factors, including population growth, demographics, family circumstances, unemployment rates, and future employment prospects. Net tuition refers to the price actually paid by the average student, which takes into account university scholarships as well as federal aid such as Pell grants. One important insight offered by a more complete enrollment demand specification is that enrollment can grow even when tuition is rising because population growth, income, or any number of other influences can exert a positive impact on it.

Simultaneous rising tuition and increased enrollment have occurred in several states, including California. University leaders often cite the strength of California's university system as the cause of enrollment increases in the face of increasing tuition, without giving credit to exogenous factors such as increases in federal grants and other forms of financial aid, high unemployment rates, and demographic changes. (Indeed, in 2010 a larger Pell Grant program served to offset tuition increases.) Absent these exogenous effects, increases in tuition will lower enrollment.

Those universities that face relatively inelastic demand can increase total tuition revenue by raising tuition and see only modest enrollment declines, but those universities that face elastic demand schedules will find themselves in a more challenging financial situation that cannot be resolved through tuition increases. Today, many public universities are relying on inelastic enrollment demand and supportive exogenous enrollment growth contributors to combat declining state support. This set of circumstances may not be permanent.

Frequent attempts have been made to forecast employment needs and to match predictions with the qualifications of labor-market participants. A McKinsey Global Institute report examines expected features of the U.S. labor force in 2020 and predicts a mismatch between attained college majors and projected employment demands; a shortage of 1.5 million college graduates; and a surplus of nearly 6 million people without a high-school diploma who will be unable to find employment (see Manyika et al. [2011]). The expected shortage in college graduates is compounded by the fact that there will be too many graduates with degrees in business and the social sciences and too few with degrees in the high-demand STEM (science, technology, engineering, and mathematics) areas and health care fields.[8] These predictions indicate that there will continue to be strong enrollment demand for higher education, although it will vary across fields.[9] The projections also suggest opportunities for public research universities to increase value through improved program alignment.

Summary and Conclusions

Large percentage increases in tuition are always of concern to families worried about the cost of higher education and to legislatures that attempt to maintain a low-cost option for residents. In this chapter, we demonstrated that large percentage increases in tuition are necessary to maintain current university budgets in response to decreases in the public subsidy. We also argue that gifts and entrepreneurial programs, while helpful, are unlikely to generate sufficient revenue to fill the void created by the loss of subsidies. With tuition increases as a plausible response, university administrators sometimes overlook the negative effect of net tuition increases on student demand. Tuition elasticity plays an important role in determining the percentage increase in tuition necessary to offset subsidy reductions. The more sensitive is the demand elasticity, the higher the necessary increase. If demand is elastic and other factors affecting enrollment are fixed, then it is *not* possible to increase tuition revenue by increasing the tuition rate. It appears that many universities are relying on inelastic enrollment demand and exogenous enrollment growth contributors to combat declining state support. Futile attempts through lobbying to restore the subsidy in the face of declining state budgets postpone necessary acceptance of the new financial reality.

Our analysis in this chapter makes the simplifying assumption that what the university is attempting to do in setting tuition is to maintain its existing instructional budget. This goal, while plausible for those who hope normal times will return, cannot be a permanent remedy. Throughout, we argue that strategic planning means facing program scope issues and that resulting decisions may change instructional budgets. Still, to understand the operation of the public university, it is important to have a well-articulated set of goals. In Chapter 9, we will develop the case where a public university selects both the tuition and the quality of education to maximize student welfare, with the university constrained to break even. The subsidy is justified in this case as a way to mitigate pricing power that reduces welfare, making it possible to discuss and evaluate both the benefits and the cost implications of providing a subsidy to higher education.

Appendix: A Break-Even Formulation for Tuition Setting

The basic concepts can be presented in a straightforward framework; doing so illustrates some of the implications discussed in the text and allows us to derive more specific conclusions. The budget constraint is

$$B = R + S$$

The growth rate of the budget dB/B is a weighted sum of the growth rates of tuition revenue dR/R and the subsidy dS/S:

$$\frac{dB}{B} = k\frac{dR}{R} + (1-k)\frac{dS}{S}.$$

The weights k and $1 - k$ are the relative shares of tuition and the subsidy in the total budget. This linear approximation allows us to think of the relative weights as being constant.

To determine by how much tuition revenue will rise as the subsidy falls, we assume that the university takes the subsidy as given and sets tuition to meet a fixed budget. In this case, setting $dB/B = 0$, to maintain the total instructional budget in the face of a change in the subsidy, tuition revenue must change according to the following expression:

$$\frac{dR}{R} = -\frac{(1-k)}{k}\frac{dS}{S}.$$

The implications of this relation are discussed in the text.

To see the importance of elasticity of demand, we expand the formulation just given by separating the revenue response into a tuition response and an enrollment response. Tuition revenue is defined as net tuition per enrollment T multiplied by total enrollment $R = T \times E$.

Net tuition is the "sticker" price minus various discounts and allowances (usually financial aid and scholarships), which are often significant. In growth-accounting terms, the revenue expression is

$$\frac{dR}{R} = \frac{dT}{T} + \frac{dE}{E}$$

In setting tuition, it is important to consider the factors that determine the average student's decision to attend the university. We assume that enrollment measured relative to total population depends on exogenous factors, net tuition, and per capita income according to the following relationship:

$$\frac{E}{N} = AT^{-1/2}\left(\frac{Y}{N}\right).$$

Here E is enrollment, N is population, and A represents other (exogenous) contributors to higher enrollment per capita; T is net tuition, and Y is state income.[10] The relationship implies that as net tuition rises the fraction of population enrolled falls. This enrollment-demand expression presumes that the tuition elasticity of demand is −0.50, which implies that a 1 percent increase in net tuition lowers enrollment by 0.50 percent; demand is inelastic. The relation also predicts that as income rises so does the fraction of population enrolled. We presume the income elasticity of demand to be unity, which implies that enrollment rises at the same percent as income. These are reasonable estimates, and they also simplify subsequent calculations.

Expressing the relation in percent changes, the growth-accounting relationship for this enrollment expression becomes

$$\frac{dE}{E} = \frac{dA}{A} + \frac{dY}{Y} - \frac{1}{2}\frac{dT}{T}$$

Enrollment growth depends positively on growth in the index of other contributors, positively on income growth, and negatively on tuition growth. Enrollment growth can be positive even in the face of tuition increases if growth in other contributing factors and income offset those increases by half. Inserting the just given formulation into the expression for the growth rate of tuition revenue provides the budget-growth accounting expression

$$\frac{dB}{B} = k\left[\frac{dA}{A} + \frac{1}{2}\frac{dT}{T} + \frac{dY}{Y}\right] + (1-k)\frac{dS}{S}.$$

The first expression is the growth of tuition revenue weighted by the share of tuition revenue, and the second expression is the weighted growth rate of the subsidy. The growth rate of tuition revenue is thereby decomposed into its contributing factors.

This model can now easily be solved for the growth rates of enrollment and net tuition that will support a break-even instructional budget ($dB/B = 0$) in response to a decline in subsidy growth:

$$\frac{dE}{E}^* = 2\left(\frac{dA}{A} + \frac{dY}{Y}\right) + \frac{(1-k)}{k}\frac{dS}{S} \text{ , Enrollment growth}$$

$$\frac{dT}{T}^* = -2\left(\frac{dA}{A} + \frac{dY}{Y}\right) - 2\frac{(1-k)}{k}\frac{dS}{S} \text{ , Net tuition growth}$$

For example, if the share of tuition revenue k is 40 percent and the combined growth rate of income and other factors contributing to enrollment growth is 5 percent, then a 7 percent reduction in the subsidy requires an 11 percent increase in tuition. In this case, enrollment declines by 0.50 percent. In general, the larger the decline in the subsidy and the smaller the combined growth rates of other contributors and income, the larger the increase in tuition required to maintain the instructional budget.

The critical preconditions in these calculations are that the tuition elasticity of demand, which we take as −0.50 and the combined growth rates of the contributors that are independent of tuition. If demand becomes more responsive to increases in tuition, larger net tuition increases are required. If tuition demand is elastic, then an increase in net tuition will *decrease* tuition revenue, if all other factors remain constant. During the Great Recession of 2008–2010 both income growth and subsidy growth were negative. These two factors, which contributed to large tuition increases, were partially offset by increases in federal support (e.g., Pell grants) and increases in college participation rates associated with poor labor-market employment prospects.

5   Basic Financial Structure
of Public Universities

A government which robs Peter to pay Paul can always depend
on the support of Paul.

      —*George Bernard Shaw*

Complexity of Public Research Universities

Public universities are complex financial and organizational entities that provide a wide array of academic programs and community services. The scope
of their activities includes educational programs and academic research as well
as various enterprises, including hotels and restaurants, hospitals and clinics,
sporting events, and economic development initiatives. Revenues derive from
a mix of public and private sources: tuition and fees, state subsidies, federal
grants and loans, sales of services, and private gifts. This multifaceted, interconnected system of activities and financial flows leads to perceptions and popular press interpretations of public higher education that are often distorted
and sometimes incorrect. There can be confusion and disagreement about the
primary missions of public research universities, even among those providing
products and those responsible for governance and oversight. Are universities
supposed to provide enhanced access to job markets? Do they have a major
role to play in economic development? Is their research mission overrated and
underappreciated? Is the main purpose the provision of big-time sports?

Beyond mission confusion, the financing of public universities appears to
be a mystery to many. Since public universities receive a diminishing fraction
of their total revenues from taxpayers, both the extent and the coverage of
the public subsidy are either overestimated or misunderstood. There are frequent statements made that treat increases in tuition as increases in the unit

cost of education rather than as the principle response to a decline in state revenue.

The lack of understanding about the value of public universities and how they are financed leads to distorted decisions both by state legislatures in their allocation to higher education and by universities themselves in reacting to the changing financial environment. The purpose of this chapter is to provide a framework for assessing the implications of the changing sources of revenue and the increasing competitive pressures facing public higher education. To help focus the discussion, we provide an overview of some of the main points that are developed in this chapter.

- Public research universities provide a mixture of subsidized and nonsubsidized programs. Subsidies support mainly traditional core educational and research programs. The nonsubsidized programs—the so-called "enterprises"—are typically independently organized and produce health care, student housing, occasionally athletics, some research outputs, distance-education programs, and a few professional graduate programs.

- State subsidies have typically provided unrestricted operating support and occasionally are assigned to directly support enrollments.

- Declining state subsidies and offsetting increasing tuitions combine to threaten the financial base traditionally used to support research.

- When research and instructional activities are complementary, it is impossible to eliminate one without adversely affecting the other.

- Once programs are in place and faculty are tenured, awkward problems arise because many costs are fixed, with a high proportion of those being sunk; these specialized inputs have limited alternative uses.

- University budgeting models that attempt to sustain long-standing cross-subsidies have been disrupted by changing demand patterns. Increasing misalignment of budgets can lead to poor decision making, inefficient allocation of resources, and the failure to strengthen and develop programs that are attractive to students, taxpayers, and society.

- As competitive pressures increase, academic instruction and research programs that lack a viable financial model and are not critical will have to be downsized or even eliminated.

Output Mix

Public universities offer a range of products and services that provide some measure of shared value to society, taxpayers, and students. These value propositions are changing, primarily because of external changes in the willingness-to-pay patterns of participants. As enterprise activities increase to help defray the loss of subsidies, the traditional mission that focuses narrowly on teaching, service, and research no longer describes much of what a university produces. To help classify this expanding array of products and activities, McPherson and Shulenburger (2010) define two encompassing segments of public universities: "education" and "enterprise." The education segment includes instruction and research. Instruction involves academic programs, courses, and advising and placement. The primary sources of education revenue are tuition and fees, the state appropriation, funded research, and private support.

The enterprise segment consists of all programs and activities that raise their own revenues, incur their own costs, and are organized more like independent private business units, either as profit or cost centers. These auxiliary enterprises and clinical services involve the direct delivery of an increasing variety of noninstructional products to diverse fee-paying consumers. Often fees are collected to support these services, but they can be internally taxed. The education and enterprise segments are thus differentiated by their respective governance and funding structures, their incentive systems, and the degrees to which they are regulated and subsidized.

One weakness of the two-way classification of products is that it fails to take into account differences in the degree to which the products of public universities are both subsidized and organized. Failure to recognize these differences makes it more difficult to understand and interpret the implications of the changing financial picture. To develop a more comprehensive structure, we separate the education component into three categories: instruction, research, and enterprises. To further identify the organizing structure, we consider two discrete organizing types: subsidized and independent. This organizing framework is depicted in Figure 5.1, which presents examples of an activity or program in each of the six cells.

The funding for many instructional programs relies on a combination of tuition revenue and public subsidy. Often entry criteria and tuition rates are determined by an external governing board and by faculty governance

	Instruction	Research	Enterprises
Subsidized	Undergraduate Engineering Dentistry	Humanities Social sciences Arts	Indigent patient care
Independent	Executive MBA	Basic sciences	Athletics

FIGURE 5.1 Product classification for a public university

processes. We refer to these programs as "regulated subsidized instruction." In contrast, some undergraduate and graduate professional programs are funded largely by the tuition they generate. They occasionally have more discretion in determining their entry requirements and tuition. We refer to these instructional programs as "independent instruction." Obviously, these classifications are a matter of degree. Low-level undergraduate instruction in the aggregate is often close to being self-supporting, but it usually has limited control over entry standards and tuition rates. An undergraduate English major is ordinarily charged the same tuition as an undergraduate chemistry major, even though there is a big difference in the cost of their respective majors.

Similarly, research programs can be separated by funding and control. "Indirectly funded" academic research includes activities supported by block grants (usually state appropriations) or by internally cross-subsidized funds from instructional and clinical revenues. Faculty research in many departments in the arts, humanities, mathematics, and social sciences falls into this category. "Directly funded" research includes specific-purpose projects, activities, and institutes that are supported, at least partially, by government grants, private sources, or private donations.[1] Faculty who write grant proposals and receive funding from NIH, corporate-sponsored research projects, and private gifts dedicated to specific areas such as cancer or, less likely, opera, fall into this category. We see directly funded research as exhibiting a degree of enterprise independence. Among the enterprises, health care for the indigent is an example of a regulated activity where patient access criteria and fees are externally determined. Athletics at a few major public universities are independent enterprises.

Funding sources for this array of products are changing. Tuition revenue in support of instruction is increasing, clinical revenues in health care are increasing, state appropriations per student are declining, federal support for research is increasing, albeit slowly, and private donations are increasing. The impact of private donations varies across programs, with significant support going to the professional schools (e.g., medicine and business), to athletics, and to student scholarships, and with less typically going to the humanities and the arts. These shifts in level, focus, and sources of funding are straining the current system, which is reliant on state funding to support a complex pattern of cross-subsidies.

As much as 75 percent of total costs at major public universities are for faculty and staff. Only 10 to 15 percent of employees at a major public university can be identified as traditional tenure-track, yet these are among the key resources in (and costs of) both instruction and research.[2] Many faculty costs are fixed, and many of these are sunk, where there is little potential for their redeployment. Special-purpose tenured faculty in one academic area cannot easily apply their knowledge or skills to other areas. These individuals have made relationship-specific investments in specialized areas of instruction and research, and there is usually a substantial difference between their value in the primary area and that in the area of their next best use. The same challenges arise when attempting to redeploy physical space and facilities. Areas such as dedicated laboratories and certainly football stadiums have but one use.

With some variation, traditional tenure-track faculty at major research universities who teach and engage in indirectly funded research typically report that 40 percent of their time is spent on teaching, 40 percent on research, and 20 percent on service. Service usually includes a mixture of commitments allocated to both internal and external instructional and professional activities.[3] Both teaching loads and compensation are influenced by external market conditions, which determine the levels of support required to attract and retain faculty. Market pay scales are well known and well considered. Few tenure-track faculty members in the traditional areas of liberal arts, business, education, and law devote 100 percent of their time to research. However, in engineering and some of the health care fields, which emphasize directly funded research, it is more common for some faculty to devote more of their time to research, even up to 100 percent. They are often required to raise external support to cover as much as 60 percent of their compensation from grants, with the remaining 40 percent devoted to instruction and service covered by institutional funds.

Relationships Between the Public Subsidy and Core Programs

Most internal and external subsidies are allocated to the academic core and to overhead costs. It is useful to consider why the university as a whole receives a subsidy and then to consider why certain internal programs are cross-subsidized and others are not. There are many answers to the question of why there are subsidies for higher education, and we address this at length in Chapter 7. The standard claim is that higher education provides benefits to society that exceed private benefits accruing to individuals. Frequently cited social benefits include enhanced participation in the political system, greater aggregate productivity, more tolerance for diverse groups, a healthier population, and reduced criminal activity. The most important nonappropriable social benefit is that associated with basic research (Scott et al.). These social benefits cannot be captured by public universities.[4]

When social benefits are significant, taxpayer support is necessary to encourage more students to acquire higher education and more researchers to engage in basic research. Thus, subsidies are used to guarantee an educated and productive workforce, particularly in the high-cost areas of science, engineering, and medicine. Without a subsidy, too few students would choose to study in these needed areas because of uncertainty and limited access to funding.

A second rationale for the subsidy draws on an analogy to public utilities and seems to apply well to the emergence of public universities in the nineteenth century when there was little, if any, private-sector competition. After a state legislature granted an exclusive franchise to provide a range of educational products, a combination of public support and regulated tuition was employed to control the tuition rates that would be required to cover all costs. In effect, charging monopoly prices for public education was not seen to be an acceptable outcome, just as it was seen as unacceptable to permit public utilities to charge monopoly rates after being granted an exclusive regional franchise.

In our view, external public subsidies can be justified for activities like research when social benefits exceed private benefits. In addition, efficient market-based outcomes may not provide sufficient access, especially for residents who are capable but cannot afford to pay. A subsidy can also be beneficial to offset adverse effects of large fixed costs. In these cases, its desirable effects are to expand outputs and enhance social welfare.

Moving from external to internal issues, why are some internal programs subsidized when others are not? Here it must be recognized that there are vast differences in programs costs within a public university, with only limited tuition variation. Some instructional programs have high setup costs that are independent of enrollment. Charging sufficient tuition to cover them would be both prohibitive and judged by some to be unfair. With restraints on tuition, internal subsidies achieve a break-even budget by transferring revenues from low- to high-cost programs. Within universities, the one-size-fits-all tuition policy and the considerable variation in program costs, leads the internal budget allocation process to direct subsidy and tuition revenues to support high-cost programs. The efficiency implications of internal cross subsidies are harder to rationalize than is the overall subsidy. These issues will be taken up in more detail in the following chapters.

Teaching and Research: Substitutes or Complements?

The other defining feature of the academic core is the high degree of interdependence between research and instruction. Attempts to examine the instructional components while ignoring the research components can be misleading, if not futile. Any strategic discussion of the finances of public research universities must address the cross-subsidy relationships that exist between instruction and research and the financial models that can sustain these activities.[5]

One can usefully think about research universities as using the inputs of faculty resources to jointly produce instruction and research outputs. A critical issue concerns how the proportions of instruction and research output can be varied in response to changes in consumer preferences and in the public subsidy. For example, if demand for courses in a particular area falls, to what extent can instruction be decreased without adversely affecting research? If the size of the faculty is allowed to decrease, both instruction and research output will decrease as well. To illustrate the implications of the joint production of teaching and research, we first consider a case where instruction and research outputs are produced by the research university in fixed proportions, using a specialized input called "faculty."

Picture the faculty as allocating 60 percent of its time to teaching and 40 percent to research, with this proportion remaining fixed regardless of faculty size. In this case, the compound product of the university is a "tightly bundled" combination of instruction and research. Changes in faculty size affect the level of output, but the proportion of time allocated to research and teaching is fixed. When an academic department hires faculty with particular research expertise, the courses and programs in that area develop around that expertise. The typical organization of academic departments centers on research disciplines, such as economics or biology, rather than on teaching categories, such as general education requirements or upper-class or elective courses. The interdependence of instruction and research with fixed proportions actually makes it impossible to separately identify the costs associated with each.[6] While consumers may exhibit varying willingness to pay for instruction and research, these preference patterns do not alter the proportions in which the two products are supplied. In this setting, a reduction in the willingness by consumers to pay for research leads to a decline in the price of the compound output and to a proportionate decline in both instruction and research. A reduction in the public subsidy to support instruction reduces instruction and research but maintains their proportionate relationship. In a fixed-proportion situation, the university shrinks in overall size if revenues decline but the proportions in which their products are offered remain the same.

A fixed-proportion view of the university provides an extreme, but useful, characterization of the outputs of a research-intense faculty, which is generally made up of tenure-track and tenured professors. In the fixed-proportions case, no substitution of instruction for research is possible. More realistically, the possibility of varied proportions arises by including part-time faculty, lecturers, and clinicians whose primary function is instruction or the delivery of health care. If the proportions of the outputs of a major research university can be varied in response to changes in demand patterns, say by substituting lecturers for research faculty, the new mix of a given number of faculty members can produce different proportions of instruction and research. As more instruction and less research are produced from a fixed faculty input, an increasing amount of research is then sacrificed for each additional unit of instruction. Here, in contrast to the fixed-proportions case, changes in consumer preference may lead to adjustment of the output mix. If the price of teaching relative to that of research increases enough, the university may be induced to switch to a more teaching-intense delivery.

A decrease in the level of public support for research leads to a reduction in research output as faculty resources are rationally realigned to favor instruction.[7] Thus, with variable-proportions. of instruction and research, changes in the level and composition of the public subsidy lead major research universities to adjust their product mix. Accordingly, as the subsidy falls and tuition revenue rises, it is not surprising to see universities using additional part-time faculty to increase the proportion of instruction.

Interdependencies can also appear on the demand sides of public higher education. The decision to alternate between teaching and research can be influenced by the often asserted demand-side complementarity between the two activities. Specifically, the argument is often made that faculty involved in active state-of-the-art research add value to the teaching mission. This claim is undoubtedly true in graduate and Ph.D. education, where research competence clearly enhances instructional quality. Nevertheless, the claim of demand-side complementarity is perhaps less valid when applied to undergraduate instruction, where students face a wide range of instructional delivery systems as well as variously prepared and credentialed instructors.Both production technology and demand preferences affect the extent to which major research universities can adjust to a permanent decline in public support. Facing a fixed-proportions technology and elastic demand for the compound instruction-teaching output, a permanent decline in public support implies a decline in size for public research universities but retention of their uniquely defined product mix. Alternatively, under a variable-proportions technology, a decline in public support implies an output mix that favors increasing instruction relative to research.

Financing Research

Research is the differentiating feature of very-high-research universities, and it helps to explain traditional aspects of public higher education. For example, a sophisticated argument supporting tenure is that faculty in specialized disciplines support hiring strong research-quality colleagues because tenure protects existing faculty from being replaced by them.[8] The established patterns of research financing presume a predictable flow of funds that derive from teaching and clinical services activities, where the public subsidy is an important contributor of unrestricted block funding for research support.

The greatest threat to the positioning strategy of public very-high-research universities is the increasing reliance on tuition revenue, which is directed at the support of instruction, not research. To offset the decline in public support, universities have increased tuition significantly, and those with medical centers have also pressured their medical faculties for higher clinical revenues.[9] So far, federal funding for research continues to grow slowly, and public universities have continued to be competitive in pursuit of federal grants relative to even the best private universities.

To meet teaching and clinical needs, the shift in focus of financial support toward instruction has led to an absolute and relative decline of tenure-track faculty, which has been documented by Ehrenberg (2011). The protection of faculty by tenure is shrinking in public universities because the proportion of tenured to nontenured faculty is shrinking. Those who pay for instructional and clinical services, and even those who benefit from them but do not pay, are usually not interested in seeing tuition and clinical dollars diverted from instruction and clinical care to academic research. It is difficult in an environment where students are paying more, and there are more students to educate, to continue to maintain the teaching-load reductions that support academic research. It is also difficult in specialty-care medical environments to provide distinctive, expensive clinical services whose costs cannot be passed on to consumers and are not state subsidized.

The modest inclinations of state governments to support academic research and graduate programs when the recipients of this support often leave the state have created a research-funding crisis for very-high-research public universities. The change has been dramatic.[10] Tightened financial constraints on research funding have led some to call for an immediate examination of alternatives. Recognizing the social benefits of basic research, Courant et al. (2010) argue for expanded federal funding to offset the decline in state support. This appears to be an increasingly unlikely outcome in the United States as the federal deficit grows at an alarming rate.

Unfunded Mandates

One factor that places stress on public universities is the growing impact of unfunded mandates. For example, public universities are required to "set aside" a portion of tuition revenue to support needy applicants. This needs-based funding may be as much as 25 percent of tuition revenue, as it is in the University of California system; its impact is to lower the net tuition of low-income students. The University of California has instituted a program that provides free tuition for all accepted students whose family income is below a base level. Baum, Lapovsky, and Ma (2009, 12) report that the average net tuition and fees paid in four-year public universities in 2007–08 by the lowest quartile income group of students was zero.

In effect, while legislatures are cutting back on public support, they and university-governing bodies continue to impose unfunded mandates that require providing access to those with limited ability to pay. What is actually happening with subsidized education contrasts with the story that is usually reported in the press, which focuses on rapidly increasing listed tuitions and their adverse effects on the entry decisions of low-income applicants.[11] Press coverage of tuition that, mistakenly, claims students face runaway cost increases fails to take into consideration patterns of mandated tuition discounting.

The same unfunded mandate issue holds for public university hospitals that are required by statute to accept all indigent patients. Since reimbursement from Medicaid is not sufficient to cover delivery costs, and tax-exempt hospitals have minimal requirements to provide care to those that cannot pay, indigent patients are increasingly referred to hospitals and clinics run by public universities, which cannot refuse care. Finally, state monies allocated to Medicaid are apparently drawing funds away from educational support.[12] Thus, higher education financing may be hit twice: by lower state subsidies and by additional costs imposed to meet the indigent-patient mandate.[13] But, not all mandates impose costs. The increasing pressure on public universities to accept community college graduates through articulation agreements is a policy that reduces revenue.

Enterprises: The Growing Periphery

Universities run an array of independent enterprises, including hospitals and clinics, athletic programs, housing and food services, extension programs, direct sales of products and services. These enterprises capture their revenues and are responsible for their expenditures. They do not depend on either state appropriation or student tuition, and their growth and vitality are usually deemed desirable from a local and regional economic perspective. Often, university enterprises are subject to market competition, which promotes both efficiency and innovation. Even some academic and research programs fit the enterprise framework. In some ways, these enterprises provide a budgeting template for other university units.

As tuition revenue increases, lower-cost undergraduate programs in business and liberal arts are effectively achieving enterprise status, whereby the tuition revenues they generate approach instructional expenditures. Indeed, the reasons for the extensive expansion of business programs across the globe include their attraction for students, their low setup costs, their use of adjunct faculty, and their potential as generators of net revenue. This same claim can be made for a number of popular programs in the liberal arts, the social sciences, communications, journalism, and some area of the humanities, including English and history. If their revenue is not used to offset declines in public support, such programs have the potential to be both high quality and self-supporting in a high-tuition–low-subsidy environment. The apparent problem, then, is their widespread use as providers of cross-subsidy funding for high-cost programs that currently rely on public support. As will be discussed in Chapter 6, continued cross-subsidy from low- to high-cost programs is a significant strategic issue that becomes more threatening in a tuition-driven environment.

There may be a lack of appreciation for the growing role of enterprises, particularly academic enterprises, in public universities. These units have more options in the fees they can charge, and they have the potential for greater decision-making autonomy. It is difficult to explain why university leadership focuses so intently on subsidizing core academic programs and pays much less attention to the financial and strategic implications of the often larger enterprises. Part of the answer relates to the expertise of university administrators. Also, leadership may judge the academic programs to be more important for the overall reputation of the university.

Summary and Conclusions

The shifts in demand and financing sources stress current funding patterns and threaten research. The implications of the discussion in this chapter follow:

- Universities produce instruction, research, and a wide variety of enterprise goods and services complementary to educational activities. The demand for each of these is shifting. Traditional funding sources—tuition, state and federal subsidies, independent revenues from enterprise services, and products and gifts—are also shifting rapidly. The result is that the long-standing pattern of internal cross-subsidies is under increasing stress.

- A major responsibility of top leadership is to assess the external environment of the organization and then communicate its implications to internal constituents. An important message is how these changes may affect patterns of internal cross-subsidy. Recognition of changing environmental forces lead to conversations that precede adjustment in strategy and policy.[14]

- Because research and teaching outcomes are interconnected, it can be difficult to react to a change in the proportion of funding sources by adjusting teaching relative to research. Lowering the number of research-oriented faculty can decrease both research and teaching output.

- When the subsidy declines, universities may respond by changing how they deliver academic programs. Alternative balances of tenured, tenure-track, and non-tenure-track faculty and new delivery formats have quality implications.

- The traditional missions of teaching and research are being diluted as diverse enterprise activities expand in size and relative importance.

Chapter 3 emphasized that a public research university, whatever its strategic intent, makes decisions in several areas: *quality* standards; program *scope*; *organizing structure*; and *tuition-setting* strategy. It appears that, as demand and finances shift, now is the time for public universities to narrow their scope of activities and to focus on programs and research activities that provide selective differentiation and distinction. No institution can survive if its credo is "We do everything for everybody," but public universities have made a gallant effort. Areas that do not generate sufficient enrollment, research, or external funding to sustain operation need to be re-evaluated in terms of their centrality to the mission; this means that some traditional programs will inevitably be eliminated. The basic prerequisite of a sustainable strategy is the presence of a fully supportive financial model, and this is a duality that can no longer be ignored. A new decision model not only will accommodate downsizing or elimination of nonsustainable programs and majors, but also will allow identification and evaluation of relatively new, but promising, program options that can attract financial support.

6 Two Prominent Models for Resource Allocation

Central-Administration Management and Responsibility-Centered Management

In finance, everything that is agreeable is unsound and everything that is sound is disagreeable.
—*Winston Churchill*

An Overview of Budget Models

In this chapter, we examine and contrast two budget models to allocate revenues, costs, and subsidies, and we present examples of their implementation at prominent public universities. Whichever system is used, we argue that it is hard to hold units accountable for their decisions unless they have accurate financial information, measurable goals, and a clear understanding of what is expected of them. In both models, we illustrate the misallocation of resources and the misunderstandings that are common when there is a lack of accurate decision-making information.

Historically, most universities made allocation decisions within the educational core by utilizing a framework referred to as *central-administration management* (CAM). In this framework, tuition revenue and the state appropriation flow to the university's central administration, which then allocates funds to strategic initiatives and to the colleges. CAM's allocation procedures vary considerably in their formal transparency. A second framework, referred to as *responsibility-centered management* (RCM), is widely applied by universities to nearly all of their enterprises but until recently was less commonly used within the academic core. Under RCM, formulas are developed to govern the flow of funds directly to the units generating the revenue and then to assess taxes to cover the unit's share of centrally borne expenditures.

CAM and RCM are sometimes combined; for example, RCM can be used between the central administration and the colleges, with CAM implemented between the colleges and the academic departments. A hybrid process raises some interesting issues. Where should RCM end and CAM begin? Should RCM stop at the level of the dean, or should it continue to the departments? Political and economic issues can arise, especially if each level of the organization prefers autonomy for itself but discretion over others.[1] Under both models, resources originating from private fund-raising are typically assigned to the decentralized units, and these resources may or may not be taxed by the central administration.

An increasing number of private and public universities have adopted or are adopting RCM.[2] Although the choice of framework for resource allocation provides a mechanism for implementing selected goals and objectives, it does not solve the strategic problems confronting universities. The changing environment requires that choices be made. Ideally, subsequent budget allocations reflect the strategic emphasis of the university, with the financial structure providing a transparent monetary-based representation of programs that are important and those that are not.

In practice, there are relative strengths and weaknesses in each system. Under CAM, budget adjustments can be made centrally to better reflect perceived permanent shifts in institutional priorities, student needs, and societal preferences. But CAM is commonly criticized for its lack of transparency. The absence of clear rules to link revenues generated and resources allocated to a unit inhibits the development of incentives that reward cost control and revenue generation. When subsidies are plentiful and predictable, a lack of transparency is less critical than when the university's resource base depends on market forces. The intent of RCM, on the other hand, is to align incentives by encouraging both revenue enhancement and cost reduction, but the resulting independence risks misalignment with university strategy by freeing units from their accountability to the central administration and from administrative oversight We will also argue that both CAM and RCM can be implemented in a way that perpetuates nonsustainable cross-subsidies.

One critical factor in distinguishing CAM from RCM is not whether revenues flow to the central administration or to the unit generating them, but whether the actual allocation rules differ. The most specific and widely employed rules are usually those for the distribution of tuition revenue and indirect cost revenue. A number of measurement problems arise when assigning tuition revenues to specific units, especially when RCM implementation becomes more decentralized. One example is course ownership, which requires the imposition of institutional constraints. Should the business school be restricted from teaching statistics or the engineering school from teaching physics? If the allocation rules for these revenues and for the public appropriation are clear, or at least accepted, and if they track revenue sources, there may be little *conceptual* difference in the resource allocations as between the two frameworks.

The acknowledged *practical* advantage of RCM is the transparency of the relative weights (prices) assigned to various programs. These weights reflect the institution's strategic choices. Given the assigned relative weights in RCM, those who run the units are aware of the trade-offs they face in the budgeting process if they know both relative costs and revenues. This is not always the case with CAM, where a common complaint is the lack of budget transparency, especially on the revenue side.

The most significant challenge for either system is how to provide continued support to units that would fail without a subsidy. In all public universities there is a complicated pattern of cross-subsidy. Subsidies that cover high fixed program costs can be welfare enhancing. Moreover, they are needed when strategically identified programs are constrained to charge tuitions to cover only variable cost. But subsidies that provide traditional support or that allow departments to make wasteful choices lead to inefficient uses of resources and adversely affect enrollment patterns.

How subsidies are determined and then incorporated into the financial structure is important. Some colleges and programs require little public support, while others depend on it. This pattern of self-sufficiency and dependency cannot be ignored. The challenge, therefore, is not deciding which financial model to adopt but rather whether and how cross-subsidies are assigned. Either CAM or RCM should address identified goals and programs of distinction. This returns us to the familiar questions: In what areas will the university excel? In particular, which programs will the university not offer? A good strategic analysis will guide resource allocations to certain areas while deflecting them from others, regardless of the budget model chosen.

Fundamentals of CAM

One optimistic way to view CAM is as a mechanism for allocating funds that support the university's academic vision. A vision is developed for a system of highly interrelated units, and the central administration allocates tuition revenue, the public appropriation, and research funds accordingly. There is conceptual appeal to a centralized approach, especially when changing environmental factors require immediate strategic attention, and when there are spillovers across academic units that can be internalized by a central authority. Indeed, for all applications of budgeting that we consider, there is always a central capture of funds that is applied to institutional initiatives. Once these funds are centrally absorbed, what remains is allocated to the various academic units, usually on the basis of historical precedence.

The public subsidy in the CAM process is usually allocated to the higher-cost units, whose tuitions are constrained. Some colleges generate more revenues than their direct General Education fund (GEF) allocation; some, significantly less. The GEF includes the state appropriation, tuition revenue, indirect-cost recovery revenues, and other minor contributions. After measuring annual revenue and indirect-cost recovery for each college, the *net* contribution to the GEF (GEF revenue minus GEF expenditures) can be positive or negative.[3] One goal of the central administration in developing these net measures is to allocate funds within CAM in a way that considers differences in contributions across colleges and thereby provides some financial incentives to the units to adjust to changes in demand and cost.

While there is predictability, if not inertia, in most CAM allocation processes, considerable effort is spent by the deans of revenue-contributing colleges to convince the provost to treat them differentially. Liberal arts and business deans traditionally appeal for a larger allocation when growing enrollment and tuition revenues increase their net contribution to the GEF. Health science deans seek a greater share of indirect-cost recovery. The subsidized units make their appeal based on the criticality of their contribution or on the visibility of their excellent reputation. The provost usually argues that all of the resources at his or her disposal have been allocated. That resources are spent on influence seems to be a defining feature of a CAM system that involves innumerable cross-subsidies. This influencing behavior may not make that much difference in the final allocation, but we cannot really know what might have happened in the absence of rent-seeking behavior. This point is made by Johnson and Turner (2009) in trying to explain the fact that academic disciplines with low student demand often are able to sustain high faculty-to-student ratios.

Fundamentals of RCM

RCM is purportedly based on the principles of activity-based accounting and involves establishing budgeting conditions so that the revenue and costs associated with teaching, research, and service are assigned to the areas that are responsible for generating them. The basic goals of RCM are to instill local ownership, to increase budget transparency, and to provide responsibility centers (RCs) with incentives to increase revenues, improve productivity, and reduce costs. Because of a historically large state subsidy and the prevalence of large cross-subsidies across academic units, academic programs do not commonly use RCM to guide their budgeting and resource allocation decisions. On the other hand, the university's enterprises routinely use it. In response to significant declines in the subsidy and changing patterns of demand, the list of universities that have either adopted or that plan to adopt RCM is growing. The use of RCM for specific programs, especially part-time master's degrees and distance education, is also becoming more prevalent.

The RCM framework is intended to promote more efficient outcomes by allowing market forces, subject to institutional constraints such as course ownership and quality, to influence allocation decisions.[4] A useful way to gain insight into both how this model can work and the challenges it presents is to examine an isolated instructional or research program that operates as an independent unit. Our example is a professional graduate degree program, which many universities offer at off-site locations to working students. This type of instruction is sometimes referred to as "off-book", which means that it is financially self-reliant and does not require a subsidy.[5]

For many off-book programs, tuition rates and fees, while influenced by market conditions, are set independently of the university's base tuition structure. Changes in demand and cost will lead to changes in tuition. In particular, high tuitions are associated with high willingness to pay and high costs of delivery. All of the program's associated expenditures, including salaries for faculty and staff, supplies, utilities, and rents are assigned to it. Products and services not provided are typically purchased in markets. The university and college impose quality constraints and entrance criteria, and they impose taxes or charge overhead for various central services. While there may be sticky issues regarding internal transfer prices and "franchise" fees, the administration of an off-book program is primarily charged with running the operation to manage revenues and to control expenditures effectively.

It is not much of a stretch to claim that an acceptable goal for an off-book graduate program is to maximize profit, subject to quality standards. Presuming that centrally administered taxes do not expropriate the net revenue, positive changes in market demand will lead to increased enrollment, expanded margins, and increases in spending on faculty and staff. Decreases in market demand will have the opposite effects. In this way, the incentives for running an off-book program are properly aligned; the program seeks ways to both innovate and improve performance with a goal of outperforming the competition. In an off-book instructional program, there is no subsidy-supported sense of entitlement, there is modest dependency on the political preferences of a state legislature, and, importantly, there is direct accountability to both students and their employers, who often pay the tuition. Still, there is a problem if independent programs view themselves as disconnected from university governance structures, with little accountability to broader measures of access, quality, and distinctiveness. Moreover, students do not always know what is best, and the latest fads are frequently not what should be taught in programs that are intended to develop sound learning foundations.

This description of an off-book graduate program can be applied to an independently funded research program as well. The faculty and staff of an independent research center compete, often in national arenas, for grants that are peer reviewed and allocated to the most successful applicants. Direct and indirect expenditures associated with the center are allocated to research activities, with the participants held accountable for sustained performance. The motivation is to acquire grant income consistent with the vision of the university and to achieve an acceptable level of financial performance. If grants cannot be consistently obtained and costs cannot be controlled, the research center should be allowed to close. Admittedly, allowing the failure of a single research activity conducted by a few faculty is a less significant issue than permitting the same to happen to a large multi-investigator research center made up of tenured faculty that is as large as that in many colleges. For this reason, the decision to create a new research center or college is critical and has long-lasting financial implications. With the recent financial crisis, we have become painfully aware of the consequences of being "too big to fail."

In the off-book model, both instructional and research programs are self-contained; if a program is not financially solvent or if its quality suffers, it can be downsized or eliminated with little impact on other programs. If the benefits and costs of an "on-book" undergraduate major in one area were totally independent of other majors, it too could be organized as an "off-book" responsibility center. Then, if the willingness to pay of taxpayers, donors, and students were insufficient to cover the cost of delivering the program, it would be easier to reduce or eliminate it. But on-book programs are usually not isolated entities, and the interconnection between programs poses a significant challenge when implementing RCM. Interdependencies exist both in the way products are viewed by consumers and in the way they are produced. For example, courses in physics and mathematics are complements to a major in engineering. Complementarity such as this exists among many areas, including the primary activities of teaching and research. The existence of joint products makes the establishment of independent resource centers more difficult.

Apart from program interdependencies, another issue is the alignment of tuition and cost. Most off-book programs can set tuition to align with costs and willingness to pay, but on-book programs must mostly align with the tuition established university-wide. A differentiated tuition structure is rarely available even where there are major differences in program costs and willingness to pay. Because the long-standing belief in higher education is that charging students different tuitions based on different program costs limits student choice, differential tuition by program is resisted. If tuitions matched costs, the high tuition and fees required by many academic programs could cause them to disappear or cause shrinking enrollments and limited access, particularly for low-income students. For example, if tuition were set at full cost, there might be decreased demand for programs such as dentistry, medicine, and veterinary medicine. Therefore, rather than match tuition with cost, public higher education chooses to adopt a somewhat altered version of one size tuition fits all. This can lead to distortions in program enrollments and to an inefficient utilization of resources, but it does have some appeal to fairness criteria.

Beyond the ability to adjust tuition, off-book programs can negotiate freely with internal and external suppliers for services and products they do not provide themselves. It is difficult to imagine that this practice could be adopted for most on-book programs. Universities provide many services centrally, and they draw on tuition revenue and the subsidy to pay for them. Agreeing on the internal transfer price for these services without a relevant market to determine their value is difficult, and negotiations can become contentious. The RCM model cannot reach its potential unless there are good transfer prices for centrally provided services.

In discussions of enterprise net revenues with a number of administrators, the subject of revenue expropriation often surfaces. One of the driving forces for RCM may be the desire by some units in public universities to impose restrictions on the administration's ability to tax certain programs and use the revenue to cross-subsidize others. One suggestion is to establish a condition such that no RC will receive less than the tuition revenue it generates. Thus, just as taxes can thwart the growth of enterprises, cross-subsidies can penalize efficient RCs in favor of inefficient ones. To put the matter into one context, nonresident students are increasingly being recruited to replace revenue lost through declining state support. Heavily taxing RCs that can recruit nonresidents may be a poor way to implement a budgetary process that is intended to provide the right incentives.

How should funded research be supported in an RCM system? If research revenues are sufficient to cover all expenditures, allocating revenues to the generating faculty makes sense. But if the subsequent indirect cost recovery rate is not sufficient, which is often the case, the research activity must either be subsidized or not be undertaken in the first place. Note that the subsidy choice is made as part of the initial research project decision. There are no special issues raised by start-up costs, which can be assigned in the RCM process to the initiating RC as an expense to be covered by future research revenues.[6] A typical example is a project where indirect costs are estimated to be 60 percent of total research expenditures and the negotiated recovery rate is estimated at 50 percent. Thus a subsidy of 10 percent is required, so the RCM allocation to research consists of all funded research revenue plus 10 percent. The entire 10 percent might come from central resources or there might be sharing between central administration and the RC. Interestingly, we have not been able to identify any cases where it is recognized that research is typically being subsidized in implementing RCM.

Choosing Between CAM and RCM

Before examining several practical implementations of CAM and RCM, it is helpful to look at a simplified representation of what these budgeting frameworks are trying to achieve. One way to think about internal cross-subsidies is to represent the relationship between tuition, subsidy, and cost for two distinct programs. If programs are to break even, tuition plus subsidy in each one must equal unit cost:

$$T_1 + s_1 = c_1 \text{ and } T_2 + s_2 = c_2$$

Here c_1 and c_2 represent the cost per student in each program, T_1 and T_2 are tuitions, and s_1 and s_2 are individual program subsidies per student; students can enroll in only one program. If the tuitions are comparable, the program with the highest unit cost receives the largest subsidy per student to break even. When the subsidy declines, total tuition revenue is increased relative to subsidy revenue.

The tradition of charging a common tuition to students participating in programs with different costs, combined with a shrinking subsidy, leads to a perverse resource allocation pattern in which low-cost programs increasingly support high-cost programs. As this process continues, the resulting allocation between low- and high-cost programs becomes more distortive and, arguably, more unfair. A decision to offer a high-cost program that cannot charge the tuition required to cover its full cost has lasting implications. Creating a new college when subsidies are generous commits future generations of university administrators to providing an annual subsidy to that college if its cost cannot be covered by tuition.[7] Once the program is in place, this annuity is impossible to discontinue. It is one thing to add a high-cost program; it is another to restrict the price that can be charged for it. Nevertheless both situations are common, and they are what provide the initial conditions that ultimately limit leadership's ability to introduce new strategies.

The cost of a program can depend on the way it is financed. While it is possible to choose to provide a high-cost subsidized program, when the subsidy wanes most universities recognize the problematic nature of underwriting high-cost units at the expense of low-cost units. To continue to break even under a lower subsidy, the high-cost areas may have to adjust their expenditures, possibly by providing more instruction with lower-cost faculty (lecturers) and by eliminating low-enrollment courses. These adjustments do happen, but one issue is whether selection of the budget model makes a difference.

We can highlight many of the implications of the CAM and RCM models by expanding the tuition-setting framework developed in Chapter 4 to consider multiple academic programs. We examine a case of two units with different costs of instruction. The break-even budget constraint for the university states that tuition revenue plus subsidy must cover costs:

$$B = T_1 E_1 + T_1 E_2 + S - c_1 E_1 - c_2 E_2.$$

Here, E_1 and E_2 are enrollments. There are two alternatives to consider for determining T, S, and E. One is to presume that that subsidy is the result of an external legislative decision and that the university governing board selects tuition rates to facilitate a break-even budget. The other is to start with determined tuition rates and then require the subsidy to adjust. For example, if each tuition is set to equal the unit cost of the program, no subsidy is required. We follow closely the approach taken in Chapter 4 and develop a solution where a common tuition is selected to permit the university to break even, conditional on receipt of the public subsidy.

Given individual demand curves that link enrollments to tuition, we can solve for the single tuition that meets this break-even condition, which we call T^*. The resulting tuition rate depends on the size of the subsidy—the higher it is, the lower the tuition. Via the demand functions, enrollments E_1^* and E_2^* depend on the subsidy, tuition, and all other factors that independently affect enrollment. The implied rules for allocating budgets to each unit ensures that each unit covers its cost and also that the university breaks even. These allocations are $A_1^* = c_1 E_1^*$ and $A_2^* = c_2 E_2^*$. If enrollments increase or decrease because of population or income growth, these changes can be incorporated into the budget allocations. If the subsidy declines, the budget allocation can be appropriately adjusted.

Equivalent allocations of the budget can be obtained under either CAM or RCM. Under CAM, the break-even condition implies that units receive their allocations from the administration equal to A_1^* and A_2^*; the rule that generated these A's is not apparent. Under RCM, they receive the tuition revenues they generate, which are determined by the equivalent rules $c_1 E_1^*$ and $c_2 E_2^*$. With RCM, it is clearer to the units how changing costs or enrollments change allocations.

It is useful to consider a numerical example to illustrate the implications of the two budget models when the subsidy declines. Our intent is to describe a typical situation faced by the majority of public universities, where different programs entail different unit marginal costs. We look at three scenarios: a subsidy and common tuition, no subsidy and common tuition, and, finally, no subsidy but differential tuition. In Table 6.1, we illustrate these cases for two academic programs: A has a marginal cost per student equal to $10,000, while B has a marginal cost of $15,000. In scenario 1, which is displayed in the top section of the table, the subsidy is set by the legislature equal to $100 million. The break-even tuition is $10,000, and the budget allocations are $200 million and $300 million, respectively. These specific allocations can occur under either CAM or RCM. The most significant observation in scenario 1 is that the entire public subsidy is used to provide enhanced access to students in the high-cost program: every student in program B pays tuition that is below program cost. The last column, social welfare, is defined as the total monetary benefit in excess of tuition expenditure that students receive (net consumer surplus) minus the cost of the subsidy.[8] The social welfare in this scenario is $33.30 million.

In scenario 2, we examine the case with a common tuition and no subsidy. This scenario permits us to consider the impact of a subsidy reduction. To break even, tuition increases from $10,000 to $12,500. The budget allocation to program A is less than the revenue it generates, with the remainder used to subsidize program B. When students in a low-cost program subsidize those in a high-cost program, administrators of the low-cost program become concerned about the tax imposed on them, which they can see if RCM is used.[9] Interestingly, social welfare increases in scenario 2 over that in scenario 1. While students are all paying a higher common tuition, which reduces their net benefits, this private reduction in benefits is more than offset by the fact that taxpayers are not paying the $100 million subsidy.[10]

In scenario 3, while the subsidy remains at zero, tuition for each program is set differentially to cover cost. Enrollment increases in the low-cost program and decreases in the high-cost program. Because prices reflect marginal costs, economic efficiency is achieved and social welfare is the highest in this scenario. This case mirrors the off-book program example, where tuition differentials reflect program costs. One implication is that high-cost programs attract fewer students. The example just given makes no assertion about the fairness of scenario 3 relative to the other two scenarios, but only that it works to align students' willingness to pay with program costs.

Table 6.1 may help to explain both the observed uses of the public subsidy and the benefits of differential tuitions. With differences in unit costs across programs and a common tuition, scenario 1 shows that the purpose of the subsidy is to accommodate tuition discounts to students in high-cost

TABLE 6.1 Subsidy and differential-tuition interactions

Program scenario	Tuition ($/FTE)	Cost per student ($/FTE)	Enrollment (FTE)	Total tuition revenue ($M)	Total subsidy ($)	Total allocation ($M)	Social welfare ($M)
1 (COMMON TUITION/PUBLIC SUBSIDY)							
A	10,000	10,000	20,000	200	0	200	—
B	10,000	15,000	20,000	200	100	300	33.3
2 (COMMON TUITION/NO PUBLIC SUBSIDY)							
A	12,500	10,000	12,500	156.3	0	125	—
B	12,500	15,000	12,500	156.3	0	187.5	52.1
3 (DIFFERENTIAL TUITION/NO PUBLIC SUBSIDY)							
A	10,000	10,000	20,000	200	0	200	—
B	15,000	15,000	5,000	75	0	75	70.8

NOTE: A and B are distinguished by the marginal cost per student, with A having a marginal cost per student of $10,000 and B having a marginal cost per student of $15,000.

programs. The benefits associated with differential tuition are evident by comparing scenarios 2 and 3. In scenario 2, with a common tuition, students who are willing to pay more than full cost to enroll in the low-cost program are not provided access, while those in the high-cost program enjoy a tuition that is less than full cost. Given the pattern of demand, too few resources are devoted to the low-cost program and too many are devoted to the high-cost program.

While we have made no attempt to include the social benefits (positive spillovers) of higher education, if those benefits exceed private returns they can be added to the private benefits reported. Claims about a loss in social welfare when public funding falls must be able to assert that social returns exceed the gains to taxpayers associated with a decrease in the subsidy. The basic question then becomes whether the subsidy's incremental external social benefit is sufficient to offset the private efficiency loss associated with charging some students more and some students less than what their programs cost. We consider this issue further in Chapter 7.

Without tuition discretion and the authority to purchase services and products from the most preferred sources, it is not immediately apparent why RCM is preferred over CAM for distributing revenues. We have suggested two reasons. One involves the attractiveness of knowing the relative weights assigned by the central administration to university programs. Another might be that decentralized organizations under RCM are less affected by "influence costs." In a CAM model, time is wasted at all levels in attempting to influence the opaque allocation. Once transparent allocation rules are established in an RCM model, much of this lobbying time is unnecessary, although there still may be considerable initial lobbying regarding rule specification.

Finally, a conceptual advantage of RCM stems from the fact that tuition revenue is becoming more important. Adopting RCM is a precursor to installing a budgetary process that facilitates greater tuition discretion for individual colleges. If governing bodies allow more tuition discretion to combat declining government support, then it is easier to implement a tuition-setting approach using an RCM structure. In this way, some will favor RCM because it is a better way to price academic programs, one where the allocation of resources is directed by consumer choice and conditioned by program costs. With RCM, there are relatively minor problems associated with allocating tuition revenue and funds from research grants to the RCs that generate these revenues. Some difficulties also arise in funding various cost centers that provide central services, but these costs can be allocated to users across the university, albeit imperfectly.

Examples of Implementing CAM and RCM

How are budget models implemented in practice? For both allocation models, a portion of tuition revenue and appropriation funds are captured by the central administration to effect institution-wide strategic initiatives. Questions and criticisms are always raised about the existence, or lack, of constraints on the size and purposes of these funds. We will review five examples of the budgeting process. The first is a CAM model used at the University of Iowa. The next three look at different ways of moving a major research university budgeting process to an RCM system using the University of Minnesota, Iowa State University (ISU) and the University of Florida (UF). The final example directly compares an off-book RCM program with a comparable on-book CAM program, at the University of Iowa.

CAM at the University of Iowa

A description of the CAM process at the University of Iowa (UI) may help to clarify how this system works. There are ten academic colleges (Business, Dentistry, Education, Engineering, Law, Liberal Arts and Sciences, Medicine, Nursing, Pharmacy, and Public Health). Their funding comes from the central administration through allocation of the GEF, whose three components are the state appropriation (40 percent), tuition revenue (40 percent), and indirect-cost recovery revenues (20 percent). While there has been a permanent change in the composition of Iowa's GEF, with tuition revenue rising relative to state support, overall it had grown steadily until the Great Recession placed the annual budget under stress.

The CAM process begins with the legislature and the governor determining the public subsidy. An independent board of regents then sets the base level of undergraduate tuition for residents and nonresidents, applying the same tuition and entry criteria to Iowa's three distinctly positioned public universities. Most GEF funds are allocated centrally by the provost's office to the various colleges and, since any annual allocation lapses, these funds are spent. The historical formula employed by the provost to allocate funds basically consists of adjusting the prior year's allocation to include the university average salary increment. So, if the average salary increment is

4 percent, a college's GEF allocation increases by 4 percent. For lean years, percentage reductions in the GEF are both absorbed centrally and assigned across the board. This path-dependent budgeting process is applied across all university academic programs almost regardless of student enrollment, shifting costs, or changes in technology. Until recently, its application appeared to have had little to do with high-level strategic goals, competitive market conditions, or other financial contributions of the separate units. A recent new emphasis involves the central direction of research initiatives that focus on interdisciplinary "cluster" hiring.

Looking at the data for the University of Iowa in Table 6.2, the pattern of large subsidies accompanying high unit costs is apparent. Tuition revenue is calculated at the course level for individual students who can pay a variety of rates depending on their classification (resident, nonresident, college, program affiliation, etc.). To adjust for differences in college size, tuition revenue is divided by the total number of student credit hours (SCH). In parenthesis, we measure net tuition per SCH (gross tuition minus student financial aid divided by SCH). Total cost is calculated as direct cost plus indirect cost (net of indirect-cost recovery associated with funded research) divided by SCH for each college.[11] The subsidy per SCH is the calculated difference between cost per credit hour and tuition per credit hour, which assures each college of a break-even result.

The subsidy to each UI college tracks unit cost, with the higher-cost colleges receiving the larger subsidy per SCH. One explanation for this pattern is a simple scale argument. If tuition equals marginal cost, or if it is identical across colleges, then the subsidy flows to units with the highest fixed cost per SCH. Thus, those colleges with either high fixed cost or low SCH receive the larger subsidy per SCH to break even. Sustainability of the pattern is a key issue as state support declines.

A major move to eliminate even partial dependency on the GEF is viewed as a momentous decision. The Iowa Athletic Department was given four years to become financially independent, which it became in 2007 with minimal disruption under committed leadership. Arguably, among the subsidized academic areas this significant partial step toward RCM implementation can take place only under special circumstances. But athletics demonstrates that a large unit, with an annual budget of over seventy million dollars, can be organized effectively and operated around an independent budget. This is an

TABLE 6.2 Relationships between tuition, subsidy, and unit cost in colleges at the University of Iowa

	Tuition per SCH ($/SCH)	Subsidy per SCH ($/SCH)	Cost per SCH ($/SCH)	Total semester credit hours
Dentistry	492.30 (398.80)	1,1711.10	1,663.40	15,743
Medicine	693.20 (470.90)	1,001.00	1,694.20	43,176
Engineering	388.10 (299.80)	549.80	937.90	25,163
Nursing	425.90 (314.50)	333.90	759.80	14,415
Education	341.60 (257.50)	371.40	713.00	29,476
Law	690.90 (543.40)	343.90	1,034.90	17,422
Pharmacy	644.90 (549.50)	269.10	913.90	13,383
Liberal arts	358.20 (288.10)	71.90	430.10	422,439
Business	377.90 (313.10)	34.20	412.10	86,182

SOURCE: Data obtained from Information and Resource Management (IRM), Office of the Provost, University of Iowa. These data and their interpretation were developed independently by the authors and are not the official listings of the Office of the Provost.

interesting case study because most of its programs are totally subsidized by the revenues from two sports, men's football and basketball. Thus it is possible to develop enterprise status for a program that itself features complex internal cross-subsidies.

RCM at the University of Minnesota

The University of Minnesota has had an RCM program in place since 2006.[12] The intent of the program, referred to as "Incentives for Managed Growth," is to improve transparency and accountability, reveal the patterns of cross-subsidy, and link unit performance to results. Revenue for each RC is composed of tuition revenue, the state subsidy, fundraising proceeds, and fees from entrepreneurial programs. Tuition revenues (100 percent) and indirect cost recovery (50 percent) are assigned to originating units. Direct operating costs and overhead are charged to the units, which are also responsible for employee benefits and the incremental cost of merit increases. There are seven shared-cost centers ("cost pools"), including energy, space, financial aid, student services, registrar, legal, and administrative services. The state appropriation, however, is centrally administered (CAM), so the model is a hybrid. There are a number of centrally funded presidential initiatives, and there is a growing internal revenue-sharing program that supports common initiatives. The tax supporting this program was 8.5 percent in 2006.

The critical determinant of the on-book annual budget is assignment of net marginal revenue, which is measured as

> Net marginal revenue = change in tuition revenue + change in subsidy – changes in merit pay for current employees (no account is taken for new hires) – change in expenditures of the seven cost pools.

If the intent is to achieve a break-even outcome for a unit, the associated change in the subsidy can be determined by solving the equation so that net marginal revenue to zero.

Implementation of the RCM depends on what forces initiate the change in revenue. Suppose there is a decline in the state appropriation. With a common tuition charged across all academic units, tuition revenue must increase to maintain a break-even budget. If demands across units are inelastic, an increase in base tuition will increase tuition revenue and reduce enrollment. These responses reflect what happens when public support declines with a common tuition and a break-even requirement under inelastic demand. In particular, the increases in unit tuition revenues are not the result of entrepreneurial efforts, but rather, the result of an increase in base tuition required by the reduction in the subsidy.

The relevant case from the perspective of performance incentives develops when a unit engages in entrepreneurial activities. When a unit expands program enrollment, it requires incremental revenue to cover the associated incremental costs. If incentives are to align properly, the subsidy should not be cut, because the unit has been successful in its revenue enhancing activities; otherwise, the RCM exposes itself to the same influence-cost behavior that characterizes a CAM. The basic issue is the tax imposed on the entrepreneurial outcomes of the units.

Over the five years from 2006, the budget of the Carlson School of Management at the University of Minnesota (approximately $90 million) went from $17 million of state support and $15 million to the cost pools to $2 million in state support and $22 million to the cost pools. The key issue is whether the reductions in state support were accommodated by increases in tuition revenue that were *not* accompanied by enrollment increases, or, whether the successful entrepreneurial efforts of the college adversely impacted by subsidy reductions were used to accommodate less entrepreneurial units in the university. A lack of transparency in the central allocation of the subsidy can thwart the effectiveness of the process. It is important for a transparent RCM to distinguish situations where there is entrepreneurial activity from those where tuition revenues increase because the subsidy declines. One way to provide this assurance is to link some portion of the allocation of the subsidy to enrollment.

RCM at Iowa State University

It appears that the only way to broadly implement RCM is through a university-wide initiative. Such a move was recently made at Iowa State University, whose model identifies specific formulas for allocating tuition revenue and indirect cost revenue to the contributing RCs. The stated intent is to facilitate better decentralized decisions and to provide explicit incentives for expanding revenues and cutting costs. Apart from adjustments for supporting mandated tuition set-aside programs, the various RCs capture most of the tuition revenue they generate and retain a major share of the indirect-cost revenue associated with funded research. In turn, the RCs pay all of their direct costs and are required to pay a range of fees for numerous beyond-basic shared services.

While various formulas govern the assignment of tuition revenue and research-related expenditures to cover indirect costs, the state appropriation is still collected and allocated by the central administration. Portions of the state appropriation are assigned to the various RCs based on their enrollments, but the largest portion is retained centrally going to cover an array of unassigned fixed costs and all central administration overhead; most important, this portion is used to maintain historic cross-subsidies. Effectively, once tuition revenue is assigned to the RCs, it can be determined centrally how much of the public appropriation is required to meet the current year's budget target for the overall university. In this sense, the budgeting process does not differ in significant ways from CAM.

How is a shift in student demand accommodated in the ISU structure? As previously noted, when demand for an off-book program declines, the program has to adjust. What happens when there are changes in demand for on-book programs under RCM? For example, if demand for engineering increases while that for business decreases, both units receive a formula-determined amount of tuition revenue. What then happens to the allocated subsidy? Does the amount of subsidy allocated to engineering decrease, since that program now has additional tuition revenue, while that allocated to business increases? This is the kind of response that condemns CAM, and it can also eliminate the effectiveness of RCM. Indeed, all of the positive benefits of RCM can be undermined by a continued allocation of the public subsidy that reinforces the historical pattern of cross-subsidy regardless of entrepreneurial efforts or changes in demand. This is especially true if units that enjoy expanded tuition revenue are implicitly taxed by reallocation of the subsidy to support units with contracting tuition revenue. Thus, the downside of the ISU "hold-back" approach is continued effort by the deans of both engineering and business to influence the outcome, one encouraging the administration to respect the voice of the market and the other encouraging the opposite.

At ISU, indirect cost recovery funds (IDC) were historically distributed as follows: 15 percent to the principal investigator, 20 percent to the Overhead Use Recovery Fund, and 65 percent to the GEF.[13] Presumably, the internal cross-subsidy of research expenditures that exceeded the IDC contribution was handled by CAM. The newly implemented distribution under RCM is 15 percent to the principal investigator, 20 percent to the Overhead Use of Facilities Fund, 10 percent to the Office of the Vice President of Research and Economic Development, 10 percent to grant management, and 45 percent to the initiating RC. There is no statement concerning sources of additional subsidy to support research, either from the central administration or from the host RC. Does this RCM allocation to support research stimulate entrepreneurial activity while providing a transparent allocation? Certainly, the adoption of RCM does not greatly affect the principal investigator. Indeed, it might adversely affect the host RC if the subsidy required to support research expenditures were to be internally provided.

RCM at the University of Florida

RCM was recently adopted at the University of Florida with the following goals:

- To provide decision makers with increased transparency into the university's finances.
- To foster an information-rich discourse on college priorities and budget matters.
- To create appropriate incentives that advance the university's Strategic Work Plan.

- To allow RCs to keep the revenues they generate.
- To recognize differences in costs of teaching.
- To align responsibility and authority over fiscal matters.

Florida goes much farther than many universities to make the allocation of private and public revenues transparent. To address the cross-subsidy issue, the initial allocated budget has been constructed to mirror the cost structure of the previous budgeting system. Data from the previous budget is used to develop normalized cost-per-student credit hour weights for discrete undergraduate and graduate programs for each of the identified RCs. Selected normalized weighted costs of delivery are presented in Table 6.3.

The administration uses the weighting system to arrive at specific budget allocations. Using these cost weights, the state appropriation and tuition revenue are allocated to the various RCs using a formula that weights SCHs at 70 percent and the number of majors at 30 percent. The budget process involves identifying the SCHs for each classification and multiplying the number of credit hours by the cost per SCH. For example, an SCH in a lower-division course in business is weighted at 0.98, while an SCH in a Ph.D. course in business is weighted at 22.06. This weighted cost structure is used to allocate

TABLE 6.3 Relative normalized unit costs of delivery in colleges of the University of Florida

	Lower	Upper	Graduate level I	Graduate level II[a]	Graduate level III[b]
Fine arts	3.97	5.57	18.45	18.47	—
Liberal arts	2.16	3.36	11.28	13.31	—
Medicine	—	8.84	9.07	18.10	44.17
Dentistry	—	9.21	5.26	—	23.68
Veterinary medicine	—	7.92	4.52	14.20	27.14
Law	—	—	7.92	7.94	—
Business administration	0.98	1.63	6.97	22.06	—

SOURCE: University of Florida (2011). Selected weights identified by the authors.
NOTE: Weighted cost of delivery is the cost for instructional mission, departmental research, public service, and administration.
[a] Ph.D. courses
[b] Clinical-level courses

both tuition revenue and the state appropriation. In addition, all indirect-cost recovery from funded research is assigned by formula to the unit generating it. Each center is required to pay all of its direct costs, and a proportion of its expenditures is allocated ("invoiced") to cover the costs of various cost centers, such as student services and central overhead. The RCs also pay for their utilities and utilized space based on another set of specific formulas.

Given the system of cost weights, the individual centers are expected to make their own decisions regarding what programs to enlarge and what programs to cut. If subsequent productivity enhancements lower the actual weight associated with a particular program, the budget allocation is still assigned using the initial weights, so there are built-in incentives to reduce delivery costs. A number of oversight boards and commissions monitor the progress of the new budgeting process. There is an acknowledgment that the selected rules may contain unanticipated flaws and will have to be adjusted.

How does an RC use the unit cost values to make program trade-off decisions? One problem with the Florida RCM allocation is that it provides incentives to the RCs to reallocate using relative costs while not holding the units accountable for relative tuitions. Consider the perspective of the University of Florida's Business School. Given its RCM cost values, it will be necessary to add 22.51 (22.06/.98 = 22.51) undergraduate credit hours to equal the assigned revenue received from one graduate credit hour. Thus, it appears that the school is provided with an incentive to expand graduate education, where unit cost is high, and to contract undergraduate education, where unit cost is low. From the Business School's perspective, this response makes sense. From the university's perspective, it may not. For the university, expansion of high-cost programs makes financial sense only if incremental tuition revenue is sufficient to cover incremental costs. However, this is surely not going to be the case for the Business School since tuition for the high-cost program would have to be orders of magnitude (22.51) higher than that for the low-cost program to support the reallocation. In fact, tuitions for graduate programs at Florida are only about 2.7 larger than those for undergraduate programs.

The standard efficiency argument is that tuitions should approximate the marginal costs for each program. For programs like English or history, the weighted cost per student is relatively low, while programs in the fine arts cost more to deliver—teaching oboe at the upper level tends to be done one on one. Theater majors also are high cost. At the University of Florida it costs 1.84 times more to provide an average credit hour for a lower-division fine arts course than for a liberal arts course; upper-level courses cost 1.66 times more, and graduate costs are even higher. Charging tuitions high enough to cover costs in fine arts programs would result in prohibitive prices for many students. It is unlikely that art majors would pay tuition that is 1.66 times more than that for history majors.

The high cost of medical, dental, veterinary, nursing, and law majors raises the same issues. The University of Florida reports that the weighted cost of a credit hour of clinical education in medicine is 34.17, veterinary medicine is 27.14, and dentistry is 23.68; this compares with the weighted cost of a credit hour of a Ph.D. in liberal arts of 13.31. Would future physicians be willing to pay 2.57 times the tuition per credit hour of a Ph.D. candidate in mathematics? Given their future incomes, it is possible, but universities need to recognize the enrollment implications of such policies.

Are there clear advantages to RCM at Florida? The rules for allocating tuition and the state subsidy, while somewhat arbitrary, are apparent to all, as are the rates imposed for supporting the various cost centers. The system does impart a sense of transparency and also some sense of local autonomy. There is the question of whether everyone will come to understand the implications of the particular rules and reimbursement formulas, but it appears that having the rules laid out for all to see dominates a CAM, where it is impossible to observe the effects of others' influencing efforts. In this regard, there still exists an autonomous Strategic Fund, which is centrally controlled and allocated. The relative importance of this fund will matter going forward.

As with the ISU example, it appears that the Florida implementation intentionally built in from its inception the entire history of past budgets and subsidies. Taking that history as the initial state of the system as reflected by the relative cost weights assigned to each program, Florida will begin to allocate future revenues, both public and private, on the bases of these weights. In this way RCM will lead initially to the same general allocation of resources that previously occurred. Colleges and programs with high unit costs, for whatever historical reasons, are rewarded in the RCM allocation relative to colleges with low costs. It may be that this is intended, but this choice makes sense only if the cross-subsidies reflect prior strategic emphasis. It might be both possible and sensible to periodically recalibrate the cost weights. Then changes in market demand and cost patterns can be included in a gradual way and the units will have time to adjust. Indeed, there is some discussion in both ISU and UF published statements that the allocation rules and cost assignments need to be revisited periodically. At the University of Michigan, for example, the RCM process examines the basic allocations every few years.

There are many similarities between Iowa State and Florida in their adopted systems, but there are also major differences in the ways the two universities address the cross-subsidy issue. ISU allocates most tuition revenue and IDC to the generating units, allocates a portion of the public appropriation in the same manner used to allocate tuition, and then holds back a major portion to sustain the traditional pattern of cross-subsidy. In contrast, Florida computes weights to reflect the relative costs of the various RCs and then allocates tuition revenue and the state appropriation based on a weighted combination of SCH and relative program costs. Both of these methods have the effect of initializing within the new RCM the prior structure of cross-subsidies.

Inherited initial system conditions can matter a great deal. Would anyone facing a blank sheet of paper design the current pattern of cross-subsidy that exists in most public universities? What both ISU and UF have done in moving to RCM is respect the inherited pattern of cross-subsidy while also attempting to build into their budgeting processes greater transparency, local accountability, and better aligned incentives. Because, in both systems, a major component of the public subsidy is held back, it remains to be seen what effects the new budgeting processes will have on reducing the cost of influencing behavior. The University of Florida RCM does provide a more transparent and less discretionary allocation of the subsidy to the RCs.

Measurement of Unit Cost: Law Versus Business at the University of Iowa

The way cost is measured can be a critical issue in the development of RCM, as illustrated in the University of Florida case. In Table 6.2, the unit cost of a University of Iowa academic program is obtained by dividing the GEF allocation plus the assigned indirect expenditure for each college by student credit hour; this approach effectively yields unit cost by dividing the operating budget by SCH. An alternative is to directly measure all expenditures, such as salaries, general expenses, utilities, and space, to determine total expenditure and then divide the total by the number of student credit hours. These two approaches to cost measurement can provide different estimates: the first includes the subsidy; the second does not.

We compare the MBA-PM program at UI's Tippie College of Business, which is off-book and does not receive a subsidy, with its College of Law, which is on-book and does receive a subsidy. Both programs have similar enrollments; both charge similar tuitions. For FY10, net tuition per SCH for the MBA-PM program was $598; that for the College of Law was $543.40. The big difference between the two programs is in cost per semester hour. Direct expenditures (salaries, general expenses, and some transfer adjustment) for the MBA-PM program for FY10 imply a cost per SCH of $339.40.[14] All expenditures are allocated, and there is no subsidy. The unit cost for the College of Law, computed as direct plus indirect expenditure divided by SCH, is $1,034.90. These are two professional graduate programs; both are taught by comparatively credentialed and compensated faculties within the same university. What accounts for the almost $700 difference in the cost per SCH between the two? One answer is the presence of historic subsidies.

There is no subsidy for the MBA-PM, while there is a $343.90 subsidy *per SCH* for the law program (see Table 6.2). The presence of the subsidy apparently shapes the different programs' delivery mechanisms.[15] The unit cost differences between two similar programs reflect past decisions about the way the two faculties provide instruction. The MBA-PM core courses feature large-enrollment classes (35 to 70 students); multiple faculty members teach different sections of the same course, and courses are facilitated by an administrative staff. The large first-year law courses are offered in small sections (20 students), with the same faculty teaching several sections of the same course. The MBA-PM limits the number of electives, even though the program faces pressure from students to increase them. Large-enrollment electives are offered by a mix of permanent and adjunct faculty. The law program provides a large number of small enrollment second- and third-year electives. These are often highly specialized to suit the teaching and research interests of senior faculty and are a way to attract distinguished faculty.

The law program also requires specialist-provided writing experiences. The oft-heard claim, pertaining to medicine, dentistry, mathematics, languages, and other programs, is similar to that offered to us by a law program colleague: "Some colleges . . . have their own unique pedagogical models that are essential to the training in their discipline. Tough analytical thinking and writing is at the core of law. Teaching these skills requires a different scale of education in law than is needed elsewhere . . ." The point, however, is that such choices are also influenced by the way programs are financed, with continued subsidy providing options not available to nonsubsidized programs.

Does one method of instruction dominate the other? Certainly, the business program faculty would prefer small-enrollment courses in areas of their special interest. These are not offered because they are both strategically and financially infeasible. There is no subsidy available to support them. Are there major outcome differences between these programs? Nearly all MBA-PM students are employed, they are well paid, and, for many, tuition is reimbursed by employers. The employment results at graduation for law students have been uneven at best, especially during the Great Recession. Arguably, it is not the case that law professors are more productive scholars than business professors, and the two colleges are similarly evaluated by national rankings. What does seem clear is that the law program provides a particular kind of instruction because it is subsidized. Ironically, it is subsidized because it has high costs. The MBA-PM program is what it is primarily because it is not subsidized and is therefore governed by a different objective in its use of resources.

Effectively, what many budget allocation schemes, whether centralized or decentralized, do is build the inherited cost structures into their initial conditions. In our opinion, it would be more effective to measure costs directly through a process of activity-based accounting and then link subsequent budget allocations to comparatively measured costs. There is nothing in principle wrong with a separate allocation to support strategically identified tuition-constrained programs, or research activities, possibly basing the allocation on some transparent index of research productivity.

Summary and Conclusions

A critical component of an improved organizational structure is the transparency of the budgeting system, regardless of whether CAM or RCM. Academic units will have difficulty being accountable for their choices if they do not have accurate financial information, measurable goals, and a clear perception of what is expected of them. A lack of accurate information leads to both misallocation of resources and misunderstandings. While some academic organizations suffer from a lack of financial accountability, there are many units that have viable, robust financial models, including arrays of enterprises that do not depend on either tuition or public support. These units should be expected to perform effectively and to price their services accordingly. Central university administration should set a reasonable overhead charge for the "standalone" units and not tax them excessively.

For many universities, the first step may be to develop a transparent template of finances across all units. This template should identify both the sources of earned revenue (tuition, indirect cost recovery, and private donations) and all operating costs (facilities, centrally provided services, and employee benefits). Subsidies should be made a clear part of this information set. For each unit that cannot "carry its own weight," leaders can develop a clear rationale and defense for any long-term subsidy based on the university's mission. Goals set for them can be consistent with the university's academic standards. To sustain high-cost programs, someone has to be willing to pay for them. The traditional option is to rely on the state subsidy, using the argument that, for example, the arts and medicine are highly valued by society. Another possibility is that private donors will support such programs; however, the tradition of doing so is not always present. Internally cross-subsidizing programs where there is a lack of willingness to pay is least attractive because it imposes taxes that adversely affect incentives.

It should also be noted that the costs of providing programs are not independent of the way the programs are financed. Some interesting questions are these: What will high-cost professional programs do if their subsidy support is reduced? Will they explore alternative ways to deliver their product such as web-based courses or other alternatives to traditional didactic instruction? If the subsidy support declines for medical students, will universities expand lower-cost physician assistant programs? Will they increase tuition?

If the established pattern of cross-subsidy in public higher education is maintained, there is no clear dominance of either CAM or RCM. The RCM framework has the potential to achieve an improved allocation of resources, but there are a number of challenges to its implementation. These include

- The difficulty of establishing tuitions to reflect differential costs across programs, with the inability of certain programs to raise tuition enough to cover full costs.
- The difficulty of establishing effective rules for allocating common revenues and block grants (state appropriations) and common costs that mimic the incentive structure and performance criteria of independent instructional and research (off-book) programs.

- The realization that some subsidies will continue to be necessary and that decisions about allocation rules, tuition setting, and subsidies can be made based on the university's strategy and value proposition.
- The risk that units will become "too" independent, with a misalignment of strategy between individual units and the university.
- The challenge associated with setting the appropriate tax for each unit in a systematic and predictable way to reflect efficiency and the value proposition of the university.

The main conclusion from our discussion is that the university's most important task is to chart its strategic course based on the determination of its value proposition and the distinctive niches it wishes to serve. The financial strategy and the budgetary process should have one major purpose— to provide an effective mechanism for allocating resources to achieve the university's mission. To do so requires a transparent set of rules, differential pricing (tuition), and market-disciplined prices for central services.

III POLICY AND ANALYSIS

7   Subsidies to Public Higher Education

The demand for subsidy in the 'public interest' must be regarded as special pleading pure and simple.
—Milton Friedman

Controversy over Subsidies

There is a wide range of opinion concerning the efficacy of subsidizing higher education. Students and public universities express broad support for subsidies, but taxpayers sometimes balk. Economists rarely find subsidies beneficial unless there is convincing evidence that markets fail to support sufficient enrollment to meet society's needs. This chapter considers arguments both for and against subsidies to higher education and examines whether society is better or worse off when taxpayers support public universities.

Prominent critics of subsidies include Nobel laureates and former university presidents. According to economist Robert Solow, "You feed people poison and they will die. But feed them a subsidy and there is no telling what will happen. Some will use it wisely, others perversely, and some a mix of both."[1] Milton Friedman's condemnation focuses on a political explanation for the existence of subsidies, denying any economic justification. James Garland (2009, 191–92), for ten years president of the University of Miami (Ohio), argues that public appropriations are the source of a number of problems for the following reasons:

- They are not contingent on institutional performance.
- They shield institutions from the efficiency-enhancing forces of competition.
- They benefit the wealthy at the expense of the poor.

- They raise costs and protect inefficient programs.
- They are episodic.
- They create a culture of defensiveness and lobbying.
- They are set inefficiently outside the control of universities and support an inefficient form of price fixing.
- They create a regulatory burden that increases the level of bureaucracy and stifles initiatives.
- They discourage innovation and entrepreneurial activities.

Finally, it appears that some legislators who award subsidies do not seem to know why they do so, as Michigan state senator Tom George makes clear:

> We look at what (Michigan universities) got last year and then we increase or decrease it by the same percent. I'm not necessarily saying that's good or fair, but that's what happens. It goes back over decades . . . it would reflect their research status, it may reflect political pull at varying times in history—it's not a specific formula.[2]

Moreover, subsidies are significant, amounting to nearly $80 billion in 2010 (*Grapevine* [2011])[3] and allow tuition to be set considerably below the full cost of education. Gordon Winston (1999, 17) says that "this sustainable excess of production costs over price . . . is a defining characteristic of higher education, both public and private."

Is it beneficial to charge a price that is below the full cost of the product? Not everyone thinks so. From an economic point of view, subsidies can be beneficial when a market system fails to produce the social optimum. In higher education, some of the most frequently expressed arguments in their support include (1) that public higher education provides social benefits in excess of private benefits; (2) that higher education provides a high rate of return to regional and national economies; (3) that access to higher education should not be limited by ability to pay, so there are distributional (fairness) reasons for taxing one segment of society to subsidize another; and (4) that economies of scale without subsidies cause inefficient market outcomes. We discuss each of these arguments in the following sections.

Subsidies and Social Welfare

Is social welfare enhanced by providing a subsidy that lowers tuition paid by students? This seemingly straightforward question is actually quite complex.

Some of the complexity derives from confusion about the several definitions of tuition, the true cost of education, and the actual price that students pay. The media focus on published tuition rates, often called "sticker prices," but these are not what students pay. Financial aid from state governments, federal grants, and universities provide support that lowers effective tuition, especially for low-income students. Loans, often with low-interest-rate options, allow deferred payment. All of these factors influence net tuition, which is the price students pay and, as such, is the price that influences initial enrollment decisions and the subsequent annual rate at which students participate.

To assess the impact of a subsidy on social welfare it is important to understand the relation between published tuition, loans, the subsidy, net tuition, and the cost of education. In Chapter 8, we provide a complete analysis of the determination of tuition rates. Here it is useful to extend the break-even formulation described in Chapters 4 and 6. As a baseline, we start with the no-subsidy case. Tuition T is set by universities to cover full-time-equivalent (FTE) cost c. With no subsidy, all students pay the same tuition $T = c$ and bear the full cost of their education. The issue is whether society is better off if some portion of that cost is borne by taxpayers. If the state offers a per-student FTE subsidy to residents equal to s, resident tuition falls below the unit cost of education and the published rate for tuition becomes $T = c - s$. Students also receive a variety of grants and subsidized loans from universities and federal and state governments, and these reduce tuition by the amount g. Now, setting tuition to allow the university to break even, with $T = c - s - g$, implies that every dollar increase in the level of either state support or the federal grant leads to a one-dollar decrease in the net tuition the student pays.[4] The university simply passes the subsidies and grants along to students to lower net tuition. In a later section, we consider the implications of allowing universities to use pricing power to adjust tuition as support from the subsidy changes.

Published tuition rates have increased recently at rates that substantially exceed the rate of increase of the Consumer Price Index (CPI). These increases have led to concern expressed by parents, students, and legislators about the rising price of public higher education. While published prices, as measured by $T = c - s$, have risen sharply, net prices, $T = c - s - g$, have not. Average published prices at public universities increased by about 24 percent from 2005–06 to 2010–11, but average net prices in real terms fell over this period because of increases in financial aid and cost containment.[5] The College Board Advocacy and Policy Center (2010a) reported that average published tuition, $T = c - s$, for residents at all four-year public universities was $7,605 and for nonresidents was $19,595. For private four-year universities, the average published tuition was $27,793. The average tuition at the very-high-research public universities was $8,798, and the average full cost of education was $17,445, implying that the average subsidy at these schools was $8,646.[6] Average cost at comparable private universities was $63,339.[7]

Contrarian Welfare Arithmetic

Net social welfare rises if the return to society associated with an increase in enrollment is greater than the subsidy that society pays. Is this the case for higher education? If students receive support in the form of subsidies, financial aid, and loans, the issue becomes whether the private benefits a student receives (ignoring distributional questions) more than cover the taxpayer's cost of providing them. Since some students receiving the subsidy would have attended without it, one immediate question is whether it makes sense to subsidize them. Other students enroll because of the subsidy and because the cost of providing their education is greater than their willingness to pay.

We use a numerical example, with tuition and cost figures based loosely on the data presented previously, to illustrate these issues. A derivation is provided in the chapter appendix. We start with a situation where there is no subsidy and enrollment is 19,500 students. The average per-student tuition of $17,000 covers full cost. Student welfare is measured by net consumer surplus, and social welfare is measured by net consumer surplus minus total subsidy. As the first row of Table 7.1 indicates, without a subsidy students bear the full cost and student welfare and social welfare are identical, equaling $126.5 million. Next we introduce a subsidy of $7,000 per student that reduces net tuition to $10,000. To compute the effect on enrollment, we assume that a decrease in tuition by 1 percent will lead to an increase in enrollment of 0.50 percent. This implies that the tuition elasticity of demand is −0.50, which

TABLE 7.1 Welfare associated with subsidized higher education

Subsidy	Enrollment	Tuition revenue ($M)	Unit cost ($/FTE)	Subsidy per student ($/FTE)	Net tuition per student ($/FTE)	Total subsidy ($M)	Student welfare ($M)	Social welfare ($M)
No	19,500	331.5	17,000	0	17,000	0	126.5	126.5
Yes	30,000	300	17,000	7,000	10,000	210	300	90

is a reasonable and fairly widely reported estimate and one we use throughout our examples.[8] As shown in the second row of the table, enrollment increases to 30,000 students and the total subsidy is $210 million.

What are the welfare implications of the subsidy? Without it, students pay the full cost of education, and there is no distortion in the allocation of resources; tuition equals cost. With it, tuition falls below the cost of education for all students and enrollment increases. Reducing tuition below cost attracts students who would not have attended without the subsidy because the cost exceeds their private return from higher education. For each of these students, there is a loss in social welfare because the benefit to the marginal student is below the marginal cost of providing the product. Specifically, social welfare declines under the subsidy because the gain in student welfare of $173.5 million ($300M–$126.5M) is more than offset by the taxpayer cost of the subsidy, which is $210 million. Overall, the *net social welfare loss* associated with adding the subsidy is $36. 5 million ($126.6M–$90M). Therefore, while a subsidy allows additional students to enjoy the private benefits of higher education, the cost to society of providing it exceeds those private benefits.

Many argue that enhanced access is important, and they use this as a major argument for lower resident tuition. But for students who will attend college anyway, the subsidy does not increase enrollment or expand their future opportunities. It is difficult to argue that social welfare is enhanced by transferring income from working taxpayers to students who will attend college and then earn more over their careers than those who partially paid their way.[9] As an alternative, the subsidy could be targeted only to students with a low willingness to pay. We can examine this alternative using the numerical example.

We begin again with no subsidy and enrollment equaling 19,500 students. These students possess a high willingness to pay, and they are charged the full unit cost of $17,000. We now ask how large a subsidy is needed if it is given only to entice new students in order to attain the same 30,000 in enrollment achieved earlier with a subsidy in place. Based on our formulation, a public subsidy of $73.5 million will attract 10,500 "low-willingness-to-pay" students who pay a net tuition equal to $10,000. This total subsidy is less than the $210 million that results when all students are subsidized. The loss of social welfare, $36.5 million, is exactly the same in both cases. The difference introduced by the targeted subsidy is that students who are willing to pay full cost do not enjoy the subsidy's distributional benefits but are made no worse off.

The targeted subsidy transfers income from high- to low-willingness-to-pay students and reduces the taxpayer burden. One can appreciate why proposing a shift from a common to a targeted subsidy will be resisted since the latter redistributes income away from some students. The main point is that any wedge driven between revenues and costs distorts resource allocation. Subsidies, targeted or general, reduce social welfare if they cost society more than the value of any benefits created.

Public Goods and Externalities

It is widely claimed that there are social benefits associated with higher education that are greater than the benefits that flow to, and are captured by, individuals. If social benefits exist and are significant, they have the potential to offset the negative impact of the subsidy on economic efficiency. Proponents of this claim assert that education creates broad societal benefits well beyond the private benefits that graduates receive from a substantial earnings return on their investment, including better health and an enriched life. As economist Howard Bowen (1977) argues, "The total returns (private and public) from higher education in all its aspects exceed the cost by several times." To Bowen, the returns to society include higher productivity (presumably to others besides those acquiring the education), higher tax contributions, enhanced participation as citizens, and greater tolerance of diversity.[10] The benefits of these social products are captured by everyone, whether they pay for them or not.[11] If such positive spillovers exist, private demand for higher education is not large enough to offer universities sufficient incentives to provide enough capacity to support both private and public interests. Why should anyone pay for the social benefits of higher education if they get them anyway? One way to resolve this nonexclusivity dilemma is to provide a public subsidy.

The Carnegie Foundation (1973) asserted that if external benefits do develop, they are concentrated mostly in the first two years of higher education, For this reason it suggested concentrating public support in those years. Leading educators often agree with the public-good claim, and some argue "that higher education, like elementary and secondary schooling, should be provided by society at little or no cost to all who want it or who are qualified" (Breneman and Finn, 1978). Duderstadt and Womack (2003) argue that "The historical rationale for public higher education, its raison d'être, is that, since education benefits all society, it deserves to be supported by public tax dollars." Undoubtedly, there is merit to this claim, and an active debate about the extent of the social benefits of higher education has continued for over a century.

Problems with the social-benefit approach arise when there is fuzziness concerning what constitutes the private versus public returns of higher education. Goldin and Katz (1999, 51) see the original reason for a higher education subsidy as providing "private goods and services of value to citizens and local industrial interests." Indeed, most original public support was targeted at the training of teachers and providing educational and research programs in industries such as agriculture, mining, and manufacturing.[12] Goldin and Katz imply that subsidies are needed to help develop a highly educated and productive workforce that provides economic benefits to the (local) state economy, presumably because the market's supply of these services is insufficient. Indeed, when public universities were founded, there were few private alternatives for providing the education necessary to advance a state's agriculture and manufacturing base. It was assumed that students would stay in the state after graduation and "repay" their educational costs through taxes on the higher incomes they earned in the industries deemed critical to the state economy. This claim is still made today. According to Iowa regents David Miles and Jack Evans (2011), higher-education programs will "grow Iowa's population, create good-paying jobs, knowledge-economy jobs, increase family incomes and improve quality of life."

The confounding issue is that successful private investment in physical or human capital can also generate high income and profits to those who own the resources. Such returns lead to economic growth and productivity and to higher tax receipts from sales, property, income, and profit. Higher spending on education can be associated with enhanced economic growth in GDP without externalities. All of these desirable outcomes apply equally well to the private employment activities of companies. Public higher education may exhibit elements of a public good, but it is not a poster child for public support. Today, there are many accessible universities; many students come from other states or from the rest of the world, and they return to their homes and pay taxes there. Graduates with high-tech, scientific, and medical backgrounds often migrate to high-paying jobs elsewhere. Public higher education in many states has become a net exporter of instruction and research products, and the higher subsequent taxes paid by these exported graduates are not appropriable locally.

To Jane Shaw (2011), higher education is a bad example of a public good:

> Students at public universities pay less than the full cost of their education and therefore are less savvy consumers than they would be if they paid full fare. They are also less committed to becoming serious students and many never finish. Administrators get a lot of their funding from state and federal governments, rather than from students, and that affects their incentives: students' education becomes less important. Research often dominates teaching; inexperienced students teach undergraduates; special interests often hold sway.

Even so, students and their parents do not want to forgo their long-standing public subsidy. But, then, neither do taxpayers want to give up their income. We argue that key elements of the public-good argument are debatable and that many of the positive externalities attributable to higher education, while broadly claimed, are difficult to measure. What is the monetary value of improved citizenship? Most evidence suggests that, from the perspective of rate of return, subsidized public higher education offers a substantial private return and, most likely, a modest social return. Better educated societies do in fact display higher productivity than less educated societies, but higher productivity can also be the result of the private return from education and a host of other factors.

An appeal to externalities is not required to argue that investment in human capital enhances the wealth of a nation. We do not deny the existence of external social benefits, but we point to evidence that social spillovers are modest at the margin. It is also not clear that all of the social externalities to higher education are positive.[13] For example, producing vast numbers of college-educated people in economies with limited employment opportunities can produce political and social unrest.

It may make sense to subsidize higher-education programs where the social return clearly exceeds the private return. The best example is basic research that provides outcomes broadly beneficial to society but not captured easily by researchers. Agencies like NSF and NIH choose to subsidize certain research areas presumably because the benefit to society is greater than that to the individual. In the United Kingdom, where it has been decided to cut nearly 80 percent of the subsidy to instruction, the remaining 20 percent will be used to support STEM (science, technology, engineering, and mathematics) areas.

It is important to recognize that the *marginal* social benefit to higher-education determines the subsidy rate. One need only observe the continued fall in state subsidies per enrollment to conclude that state governments do perceive the marginal benefit as declining. The global trend outside of a few areas like China is similar, with several countries increasing tuition and reducing dependency on public funding. The primary effects of a loss of the public appropriation are higher tuition, lower enrollment, and a gain in economic efficiency. As disruptive as a cut in the subsidy might be to universities and students, these funds will likely be shifted to other valued public services, with a minimal impact on aggregate state income. An essential social choice question is this: What matters more, public higher education, K–12 education, job training programs, or health care for the poor?

Rates of Return from Higher Education

An additional argument often made to defend the subsidy is that "investing" public funds in higher education generates a high rate of return (ROR). Some claims about the return on additional allocations to higher education border on the spectacular. In Iowa, two regents assert that every state dollar invested in public higher education returns $14.50 in aggregate economic activity, which is a rate of return of 1,450 percent.[14] The president of the University of Iowa trumps this by claiming an annual rate of return to the public appropriation of 1,600 percent.[15] These ROR projections lead university leaders to conclude that the aggregate impact on the Iowa economy of $550 million in state support for higher education is worth $8 billion in state revenue. Are these claimed impacts reasonable? How do leaders in public higher education come up with these valuations?

Input-Output Studies

The value of public higher education is often measured by applying a mechanical input-output formulation using numbers like those in Table 7.2. These data are from a recently completed economic impact study for the University of Iowa (see University of Iowa and Tripp Umbach [2010]).

In this example, the university's total direct spending is $2.6 billion. As this spending enters the regional economy, it stimulates private spending by connected firms and organizations. This private spending works through

TABLE 7.2 Input-output structure for determining value of public higher education for the University of Iowa

Total direct revenue	$2.6B
Public appropriation	$379.4M
Spending multiplier	1.31
Total direct and indirect revenue	$6.0B
Rate of return to public appropriation	1,581%

a multiplier process to stimulate other spending. The additional indirect spending associated with the direct spending of $2.6 billion is estimated to be $3.41 billion. The implied multiplier, 1.31, attempts to measure how a dollar of direct spending eventually affects the indirect spending of the entire regional economy. The estimated total impact of direct and indirect spending in this example is $6 billion.[16] The ROR is computed by dividing that amount by the public appropriation of $379.4 million, and the result is an implied rate of return to that investment of an astounding 1,581 percent per annum. This widely used valuation method is the essence of the regents' claim for a rate of return to the entire state subsidy of 1,450 percent for the system, and it is the basis for the president of the University of Iowa's report of a rounded rate of return of 1,600 percent.

The input-output valuation process, in our opinion, leads to statements that are distortive at best and wrong at worst. For example, while some might accept the valuation just given, presumably few would accept the implications of applying the same methodology to estimate the effect of a substantial cut in the public appropriation. In 2011, for example, Iowa's governor proposed to cut the public appropriation by approximately $50 million for the next fiscal year. With a rate of return of 1,450 percent, this cut implies a loss of state income of $725 million.[17]

We argue that the mechanical application of the input-output formulation omits many materially significant effects and is grossly inaccurate. Some of the most apparent shortcomings include the following:

- There is no inherent logic in computing a percentage rate of return to the public appropriation based on the university's entire expenditure; this gives the impression that the existence of the university depends only on public subsidies. It would make equally little sense to use this method to compute the rate of return from nonresident tuition or from the return from federally funded research.

- There is no accounting for how the subsidy is funded. When the subsidy rises, taxpayers' income (and spending) goes down, and universities' income (and spending) goes up. While there is still some impact on total spending, presumably because taxpayers save a portion of their income while universities spend it all, the net impact is much smaller than that just described.

- The input-output method does not account for alternative uses of funds. If there were no public subsidy to higher education, either taxes would be reduced or tax revenues would be used elsewhere (on, say, Medicaid, highways, other public services, prisons, or pensions). These expenditures have a multiplier impact that may be as large as, or even larger than, that attributed to public higher education.

- No account is taken of capacity constraints in the economy; in the extreme case of full capacity, an increase in spending on public higher education would have no impact on total output. When the economy is capacity constrained, public spending crowds out private spending.

- The method of valuation ignores relative prices. When demand for anything changes, relative prices adjust to clear markets. Price increases mitigate demand, and price decreases stimulate it. In the case of inelastic supply (full capacity), an increase (decrease) in demand for public higher education simply raises (lowers) its relative price and has no impact whatsoever on output.

Why, then, are such multipliers and exorbitant rates of return so frequently cited? Consultants, that is, "neutral parties," develop these estimates, and higher-education leadership uses them to make enthusiastic appeals for public support. Unfortunately, by claiming rates of return on the public subsidy that are excessively high compared to those in other areas of the economy, the leadership loses credibility. Better arguments for higher education should focus primarily on long-term growth consequences—for example, estimating the return from training in engineering, science, math, and technology is more meaningful than computing dubious short-run multipliers.

We next discuss more rigorous estimates of returns as calculated by the Organization for Economic Co-Operation and Development (OECD).

OECD Present-Value Estimates

The OECD applies a systematic methodology using standard present-value analysis to assess the value of higher education.[18] A real rate of return, assumed to be 3 percent, is used to compute the present value of present and future benefits and costs associated with tertiary education for each OECD member country. Private and public present- value payoffs are computed separately for males and females. The sum of the public and private net present value is the value of public higher education.

The private benefits of higher education include future gross earnings net of income taxes, social contributions, transfers, and an unemployment effect. The primary private costs are the direct costs of education to the individual and foregone earnings. Using these definitions to compute the private net present value, the OECD estimate (in 2006 U.S. dollars) for a male is $145,859 and for a female is $91,532. The internal rates of return are 11.5 percent for a male and 10.7 percent for a female.[19] The public benefits include subsequent income taxes, social contributions, various transfers, and the unemployment effect. The costs to the public sector include the direct costs of the public subsidy and foregone taxes on earnings of those in school. The OECD average public net present value for a male (in 2006 U.S. dollars) is $86,404 and for a female is $52,436. The public internal rate of return for a male is 11 percent and for a female is 9.5 percent.[20]

The total net present value including both public and private valuations is calculated as

Total net present value = gross private earnings − (direct cost of education to the individual + direct cost of education to the public sector) − foregone private earnings − forgone tax receipts

In the OECD calculations, adding the private to the public net present value, apart from some timing issues, cancels out the tax contributions. What private individuals pay in income taxes, for example, becomes part of the subsequent revenue stream of the public sector. Under the current distribution of direct costs, for the OECD average the combined net present value for a male is estimated to be $232,263 in 2006 U.S. dollars.

These calculations, which are based on a sensible imputation of economic value, indicate that there is a substantial payoff to higher education from the perspective of both the individual receiving it and the government providing it in OECD countries. The OECD net present value calculations do not include social benefits of higher education that are not captured by individual earnings. There are no imputed benefits, for example, to better public health, enhanced citizenship, or greater trust, although the OECD does find that all of these social measures increase with the level of education.[21] While the return from higher education is clear, who pays for it remains a contentious issue.

Empirical studies also reveal the positive association between attainment of education and economic outcomes. Most of them presume that higher education causes earnings, income, and wealth to rise and that these increases reflect an effect above and beyond that associated with the fact that talented individuals acquire more education. Empirical studies that do account for the simultaneous nature of educational attainment, ability, and earnings find that the imputed rates of return from education are actually even higher (see Card [2001]). Table 7.3 provides some results from a 2007 survey conducted by the National Opinion Research Center at the University of Chicago for the Survey of Consumer Finance (see Díaz-Giménez, Glover, and Ríos-Rull [2011]). It shows that education and economic performance are clearly positively related. College graduates earn about 5.4 times more than high school dropouts and about 2.2 times more than those who do not finish college. The differences in wealth are even greater.

Finally, another valuation approach can be used to examine the belief that more education leads to higher economic growth. For example, does a strong positive empirical relationship exist between growth in real GDP and spending on public education? Actually, there is no general agreement that spending on higher education increases economic growth. Indeed, a recent study from a sample of 47 countries between 1960 and 2007 identified a significant

TABLE 7.3 Relationships among education, earnings, income, and wealth of U.S. households from 2007 survey of consumer finances

Education	Earnings ($K)	Income ($K)	Wealth ($K)
Dropouts	20.5	31.3	142.9
High school	39.1	50.8	251.6
Some college	51.0	67.8	366.3
Completed college	110.1	142.4	1,095.1
Average	63.8	83.6	555.4

SOURCE: Díaz-Giménez, Glover, and Ríos-Rull (2011, 16).

negative relationship between growth and educational spending, although this may actually be a non-linear U-shaped pattern.[22]

We have shown that subsidies may decrease social welfare; that positive social benefits probably exist but are modest, especially marginal social benefits; and that claims for external rates of return based on input-output analyses are questionable. We turn next to the fairness argument.

Fairness of Subsidies

Fairness, perhaps the most often expressed rationale for public subsidies to higher education, relates to who pays for and who receives the subsidy. One view of fairness is that taxpayers should provide subsidized access to students, who then become the next generation of taxpayers. When these perceived entitlements are removed, students claim that they are being unfairly treated by society. In the United Kingdom, students argue that it is unfair to require them to pay for higher education when previous generations were admitted at no charge. Middle-class parents who failed to save enough for their children's college education because they did not anticipate tuition increases claim that they, too, are being unfairly treated. Are these valid complaints? Milton Friedman (1968, 108) questions the belief that public universities do indeed provide access and support for low-income groups:

> The facts are clear. Consider the typical city or state or university. The average income of the parents of the students at such schools is much higher than the average income of taxpayers, as every study has shown. More important—because this is the truly relevant comparison—compare the incomes that the young men and women now in college will have over the rest of their lives with the incomes that their contemporaries who do not go to college will have. Is there any dispute that they will be far higher? Why then should the men and women who do not go to college pay any of the costs of those who do? Why should the families in Watts pay taxes to subsidize the families in Beverly Hills who send their children to UCLA?

In an influential paper, Hansen and Weisbrod (1969) use California data to argue that subsidizing public university tuition is inequitable because students from more affluent families are being subsidized by less affluent taxpayers. In contrast, Johnson (2006) shows that subsidies are slightly progressive.

Recent shifts in the burden of income tax and the widespread introduction of federal Pell programs to support the economically disadvantaged provide targeted subsidies to lower-income students.[23] Subsidization through such programs makes sense if impediments restrict capital markets from supporting human-capital investments in higher education. When fairness relates to who pays for access, society may choose to provide targeted subsidies to individuals whose willingness to pay is lower than the cost of their education. It should be clear, though, that admitting one subgroup of students such as residents or those with low incomes can limit the admission of others who are willing to pay full cost. While some may believe this is a fair thing to do, it can lead to inefficient outcomes.[24]

Fairness issues are framed and supported by existing tuition-setting practices. Because of the desire for enhanced access, average tuition revenue is set substantially below average cost, and the subsidy is used to meet the break-even requirement. Since the unit cost of academic programs differs markedly, the subsidy flows to those that are high cost. The usual pattern is that engineering, medicine, dentistry, and law receive substantial subsidy relative to liberal arts and business. The association between high cost and high subsidy can be seen in the data that were presented in Table 6.2 for the University of Iowa.

To maintain the existing pattern of cross-subsidy when the public appropriation declines requires that additional tuition revenue be reallocated from low- to high-cost programs. This scheme is sometimes defended on the basis of fairness, but is it fair for an undergraduate in English to provide tuition revenue to support a first-year medical student? Providing access to majors and programs based on student or faculty interest and not on differentials in price and cost is staunchly, even passionately, defended by academics and many administrators. In particular, those who benefit the most from them have developed arguments to justify the continuance of internal subsidies. For example, vast differences in the cost of teaching various subjects are justified as being appropriate to specific disciplines. It may well be that entrenched defenses of traditional instruction patterns are the major impediment to a more effective allocation of resources in public universities. Perceived fairness is a powerful force in higher education and will not yield easily to efforts to improve efficiency.

Economies of Scale and Efficiency

A credible argument, and possibly the most important one, supporting subsidies relates to the impact of economies of scale on efficiency in situations where universities can exert pricing power. We have pointed out several times that price setting, where tuition is set equal to marginal cost, does not allow universities to cover their large fixed costs. When fixed costs dominate, public universities must set tuition above marginal cost to break even, which reduces welfare. In this situation, subsidies, grants, and loans can help to mitigate economic inefficiencies that accompany tuition setting.

Fixed costs, which include libraries, museums, wellness centers, laboratory facilities, most research of tenured faculty, and various quality expenditures, are important features of research universities. It is significant that tenure also creates fixed costs. Awarding tenure to a new associate professor commits the university to paying salary and benefits for at least twenty-five years. Given a new associate professor's average salary, the capitalized value of this commitment is about $3.25 million, and it imposes a constraint on the number of tenured faculty that can be supported by the institution. If this constraint tightens, there will necessarily be fewer faculty tenured, not because there is less preference for tenure but, rather, because it is too expensive to maintain in its traditional form. As noted by Henry Rosovsky (1990, 189): "In a public institution, the ultimate guarantor of tenure is the state's taxing power." With declining public support, the increased use of more part-time and adjunct faculty, who represent variable costs, can be at least partially explained by the reluctance of public universities to accept the fixed-cost implications of tenure.

As a prelude to the tuition-setting issues to be discussed in Chapter 8, consider the implications of allowing universities to exert pricing power to adjust tuition. The extreme case would be to set tuition to maximize profits. When the university uses its pricing power, it no longer passes on to students one to one any increases in the subsidy or in financial aid. Instead, it absorbs some of any subsidy change. The social welfare implications of this are interesting and possibly counterintuitive. Increases in the subsidy reduce tuition toward marginal cost and increase access. As long as tuition remains above marginal cost, subsidy increases also increase social welfare. The gain to the marginal student of a reduction in tuition is greater than the cost to the taxpayer of a higher subsidy. These results are presented more formally in the chapter appendix.

Examples of Setting Subsidies and Tuition

The relationship between the public subsidy and the setting of tuition can be illustrated using several examples: the Carnegie Foundation in 1973, the Iowa

Board of Regents, the University of California system, and the Browne Report of 2010 (concerning this issue in the United Kingdom).

Carnegie Foundation, 1973

The best-known framework for developing tuition and subsidy policy is that presented by the Carnegie Foundation (1973) and reviewed by Jane Wellman (2001). Under the leadership of Clark Kerr, the foundation based its recommendations on two key assumptions:

- Higher education is both a private and public good with private returns reflecting higher future incomes and enhanced personal lifestyle benefits. The social benefits include lower crime rates, reduced social expenditures, higher voter participation, greater tolerance of others, and enhanced willingness to accept political change. The external benefits of higher education are more apparent at the entry levels and in community colleges than in the upper divisions.

- Tuition charges should reflect true costs, with tuition and fees linked closely to student aid. Financial aid should be made widely available to allow students to attend high-cost programs. A wide mix of private and public financial support is appropriate.

On the basis of these assumptions, the Carnegie Foundation recommended that undergraduate tuition should account for about one-third of the total cost of educating a student. It also recommended differential tuitions based on several factors. Lower tuition should be charged at the entry levels and then increased at the upper levels to reflect both rising costs and the declining importance of external benefits. Higher tuitions should be charged for professional programs based on higher expected earnings. The public responsibility for funding higher education should increase, especially at the federal level, with higher education's share of GDP also increasing.

The Carnegie report argued that social returns, if they exist, are most likely concentrated in the first two years of higher education and that they taper off in the last two years. There are modest societal returns to professional graduate education. This argument might lead to a subsidized tuition for students in their first two years of college, followed by tuition priced at full cost for the next two years, with possible exceptions made for identified areas like STEM. Professional graduate programs such as business, law, education, engineering, dentistry, medicine, and public health should charge tuition that

TABLE 7.4 Suggested Carnegie criteria for allocating public appropriations

Institution type	First two years	Second two years	Research
Doctoral-granting	Yes	Yes/selective	Yes/selective
Masters-granting	Yes	Yes/selective	Yes/very selective
Baccalaureate	Yes	Yes/selective	No
Associate college	Yes	Not applicable	No
Other	Yes	Not applicable	No

covers the full cost. If students in some of these areas face limited access to private capital markets, increased access requires subsidized government loan programs. Public support might extend to covering basic research activities when there are significant social returns that cannot be appropriated privately or when substantial fixed setup costs cannot reasonably be covered by an increase in tuition. The suggested pattern of subsidy might appear like that presented in Table 7.4.

Public Support per Student Among Iowa Universities
Total enrollment at the University of Iowa remained basically constant for the years 2006 through 2010, even as real tuition rose. Thus, it appears possible to continue to attract qualified applicants in the face of falling public support and increased tuition revenue. However, Iowa's student mix shifted during those years to a larger percentage of high-tuition-paying nonresidents. In 2006, residents made up 63.05 percent of the student body; by 2010, they made up 57.10 percent. Over the five years under discussion, the real value of the state's appropriation to the university's General Fund declined by 20 percent, which prompted some education leaders in the state to call for major programmatic changes (see Cawelti and Lubker [2011]). To compensate, total real tuition revenue increased but only by 12 percent, mainly because of the infusion of nonresident tuition. The result of all of these adjustments was that the real purchasing power of the instructional General Fund at Iowa, which is the primary funding source for the core academic programs, declined by approximately 4 percent.[25]

These revenue and expenditure data reflect the reality of the break-even requirement. The General Education Fund balances each year, so it is not surprising that total expenditures on instruction equal total revenue received.

The University of Iowa reports that its overall cost per student in 2010 was $17,653 (Collegemeasures.org, 2010). When the current sum of the public appropriation and tuition revenue for this same year is divided by the number of students enrolled, the average revenue (public and private) per student equals $17,611.

Essentially, UI, as well as many other similarly positioned public research universities, operates as an "instruction business" that just manages to annually break even. As tuition revenue continues to replace public funding, the percentage increases in tuition per student needed to maintain the General Education Fund will decline. Today, each dollar decline in the state appropriation requires a seventy-cent increase in tuition revenue to sustain the General Fund level. Thus, to offset a 10 percent decline in the state appropriation requires an average increase in tuition of about 6 percent. The one technical caveat to this estimate is that tuition elasticity of demand does not increase rapidly at the higher tuition rates.[26]

There are three regent universities in Iowa, and their appropriation data are presented in the Table 7.5.[27] Given the differences in classification of the universities, both undergraduate tuitions and the public appropriations per FTE are set similarly for all three. At the University of Northern Iowa (UNI), the highest proportion of state support funds instruction broadly defined, and the standard faculty teaching load is higher. At Iowa State University (ISU) and the University of Iowa (UI), state appropriations fund both teaching and research missions. The similar per-student allocation of the public appropriation leads the differently positioned schools to employ their resources in quite different ways, with ISU and UI using a greater proportion of teaching assistants, part-time instructors, adjuncts, and increased class sizes as the only possible way to accommodate their research mission.

TABLE 7.5 State appropriations per FTE, fiscal year 2008, for Iowa state system

Institution	Appropriation per FTE ($/FTE)	Carnegie classification
University of Iowa	7,455	Very-high-research
Iowa State University	7,008	Very-high-research
University of Northern Iowa	5,827	Large four-year, residential

SOURCE: University of Iowa, Office of the Provost, personal communication, 2010.

Public Support Among Universities in the
University of California System

Figure 7.1 shows considerable variation in the levels of per-student funding across the various institutions in the University of California (UC) system. Allocations to specific institutions are affected by enrollment levels, program composition, historical precedence, and inertia. However, the simplest explanation for the variation is that these allocations, using CAM, were made at different points in history. Once the base allocation was established, subsequent ones were increased (decreased) across the board. This historical treatment for each institution is as difficult to explain for California as it is for Iowa.

Financing Public Higher Education in
England: The Browne Report

The most dramatic set of suggestions for revamping the financing of public higher education in response to declining government support is that

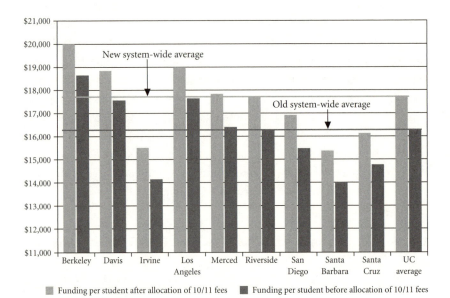

Funding per student after allocation of 10/11 fees ■   Funding per student before allocation of 10/11 fees

FIGURE 7.1 University of California System general campus funding per student after allocation of fee increases

SOURCE: UCSC Planning and Budget Office, personal communication with F. B. Moini, assistant director.

NOTE: Funding includes permanently budgeted general funds as of March 1, 2010, with adjustments for health sciences functions budgeted under General Campus. Also includes estimated revenue from summer educational fees net of financial aid.

developed in a recent and controversial report, *Securing a Sustainable Future for Higher Education* (Browne, 2010), produced for the English public higher education system by an independent committee chaired by Lord John Browne, former CEO of British Petroleum. The report argues that the traditional reliance on public support for what is basically a private good is no longer financially sustainable.[28] It recognizes that tuition revenue raised in recent years did little more than replace the decline in public support, and that some drastic changes need to be made to maintain and, hopefully, improve the quality of higher education.

The Browne report lays out a new framework in which qualified-student access is assisted by universities and enabled by government loans rather than direct grants. Students are provided low-interest loans that permit them to study anywhere they can gain admission. The new twist is that public universities compete with each other for student fees, with the hope that increased competition will both increase efficiency and improve quality. The government acts as the guarantor of university revenue by assuming the role of a funding bank for student loans.

Under the proposed scheme, students are guaranteed sufficient government loans to cover their tuition and living costs over the expected course of study for their selected degrees, with low-income applicants provided additional living support (maintenance). Public universities are granted, within a set of contingent rules, the ability to set their own levels of tuition, with a current upper limit of £9,000. The repayment of the loans, using the government rate of interest, commences when the graduate's income exceeds a prescribed base-income level, currently suggested as £21,000, and is linked to future inflation. If the prescribed base level of income is not surpassed, repayment is not required; also, the repayment obligation terminates completely after thirty years. Nobody is required to pay more than the cost of the course of study, which is a feature that distinguishes this plan from the previously suggested plan of a progressive graduate tax. Part-time enrollment programs are also supported.

The thrust of the Browne report is to refocus financial responsibility for higher education from the general taxpayer to the benefiting student, with limited continuing public support for instruction. The plan also emphasizes and relies heavily on competition among public universities, arguing that the quality of education programs, even though admittedly difficult to measure, is best enhanced, if not guaranteed, by the mounting competitive pressures that fee-paying students place on public universities to deliver valued products. There is unquestioned acceptance in the report that competitive market forces are better than government mandate and formal quality assurance programs at delivering the quality that consumers demand. Those universities and courses of study that fail to provide value will be disciplined with lower revenues; some may fail altogether. In essence, the idea is to replace the "dead hand" of the state with active forces of market competition. This is the same argument that James Garland (2009) makes, but he prefers redirecting public support to students in the form of direct grants rather than replacing it with student loans. There remains a role for continued state support of instruction in the Browne report. Public funds under the plan will be targeted at (highly utilitarian) STEM areas that are deemed essential to national productivity. The report does not discuss the implications for academic research, which leaves an open question, especially when the cross-subsidy of research comes through reductions in faculty teaching loads. This subsidy is harder to justify when tuition is paying nearly all instruction expenses.

The financing model presented in the Browne report is a dramatic alternative in the European context, where public higher education is often provided free to all qualified applicants. Even in England, the charging of tuition did not commence until 2006, and universities in Wales and Scotland continue to restrict tuition or impose no tuition charge. The implications are profound. As pointed out on the editorial page of the *Financial Times* (2010),

> To remove the limit on university fees will demand real bravery. This is a once-in-a-government's lifetime opportunity to tackle university funding. The coalition [current government] will never again have the chance to transform higher education so profoundly. It is time for the government to teach the future a lesson.

In response to the Browne report, hundreds of academics published a white paper, or reply, entitled "In defense of Public Education".[29] It remains to be seen how this about-face on the funding of public higher education will be received politically (violent student protests broke out in London in November, 2010). And it is not yet clear what lessons will be taught or learned. It is clear that students of all ages are not pleased that future payment for public higher education will fall not on the general taxpayer but rather on those who receive, and benefit from, it.

Summary and Conclusions

Subsidies for higher education are and will remain controversial. Most proponents base their support on fairness (access) arguments that are increasingly difficult to support financially. While we do not deny the external social benefits of higher education, the evidence leads us to conclude that higher education is primarily a private good, with most of its returns flowing to the recipients. From this perspective it cannot be argued that higher education should receive a significant subsidy. Still, there is a significant private return from higher education, and this return can support productive economies without any significant externalities. At the margin, the external benefits are weighed against alternative uses of scarce resources, including, for example, health and primary education.

Evidence from declining subsidies by state governments in the United States and from fading government support for higher education in a number of other countries suggests that the public-good argument is losing favor. There is a role for targeted subsidies in supporting specific academic areas such as STEM, where the social return through research may be difficult to capture privately. A subsidy can also enhance social welfare by helping to offset the inefficiencies associated with tuitions that exceed the marginal costs that can result when universities attempt to cover large fixed costs. This effect is examined in the next chapter.

Appendix: Tuition-Setting Approaches and Social Welfare

The goal in this appendix is to develop the enrollment and social welfare implications of establishing a common tuition that will support a break-even budget for a public university.

Break-Even Tuition
We specify a willingness to pay function that links enrollment to tuition and measures the value that students attach to higher education. That function is $T = a - bE$, where E is total enrollment and the positive parameters a and b represent, respectively, the maximum willingness to pay for education and the substitution parameter. This expression indicates that enrollment increases when a lower net tuition is offered to students who possess a lower

willingness to pay. If net tuition is set to break even, $T = c - s - g$, the resulting enrollment determined from the demand function is

$$E^* = \frac{a+s+g-c}{b}$$

This expression indicates that subsidies and grants stimulate additional enrollment by lowering the student's net tuition and, effectively, augmenting the maximum willingness to pay. The larger the substitution parameter b, the higher the unit cost c, and the lower is the total enrollment.

The direct benefit from the subsidy, which is called "consumer surplus," flows to each student who has a (subsidized) willingness to pay that exceeds the full cost of education. The sum of these net benefits across all such students is their total benefit. For the case of the linear demand specification we chose here, the total consumer net benefit B is[30]

$$CB = \frac{(a+s+g-c)^2}{2b}$$

Net student benefit is increasing in the state subsidy and federal grants and is decreasing in unit cost. Both the benefits and *total* costs C should be taken into consideration to formulate an expression for social welfare W:

$$W = CB - C$$

To examine the impact of the subsidy on society, the student benefit is measured against the cost to taxpayers of providing the subsidy and financial aid. Total cost is obtained by multiplying the per-student subsidy and government support by the resulting level of enrollment E^*:

$$C = (s+g)E^* = (s+g)\frac{(a+s+g-c)}{b}$$

After subtracting C from CB, we find that social welfare is *decreasing* in both subsidies and grants.[31] Social welfare is actually maximized when there are neither state subsidies nor federal grants. To encourage students to enroll, subsidies and grants are provided. The social problem is that the benefit that each student receives privately for her education is less than the cost to provide that education, and this condition holds true for all students who need a subsidy to enroll. The discrepancy between the value that taxpayers place on education, expressed by the taxes they pay to cover its cost, and the value of

the benefit received by the subsidized student results in an inefficient allocation of society's scare resources.

Monopoly Tuition
Rather than setting T to equal cost net of subsidy and grant rates, we can assume that the university selects the value of T to maximize net revenue. The
resulting net tuition is

$$T^* = \frac{a+c-s-g}{2}$$

The profit-maximizing price exceeds the full unit cost of education net of
the state subsidy and the federal grant. With monopoly pricing, a university
that faces a linear demand curve reduces its tuition by one-half for every unit
increase in the grant aid per student. In effect, there is an equal sharing of an
increase in the grant between the student and the university. When the university exercises pricing power in the setting of tuition, it no longer passes on
to students, one to one, increases in the subsidy or financial aid. For example,
the long-standing assertion that universities raise tuition when there is an
increase in federal Pell grants has some conceptual support in this case.[32]

When there is an exercise of pricing power, an increase in the subsidy can
increase social welfare. This case occurs as long as the maximum willingness
to pay for higher education net of the unit cost of education exceeds the sum
of the state subsidy and federal loan per FTE. That is, social welfare increases
in the subsidy when

$$a - c > s + g$$

When the university exercises market power in setting tuition, enrollment
is restricted even for those students whose willingness to pay exceeds the full
cost of their education. Introducing a subsidy or grant aid in these circumstances decreases net tuition. This leads to the somewhat surprising result
that subsidizing a monopoly enhances social welfare. In particular, maximum
social welfare is achieved when $s + g = a - c$. Then tuition equals the full cost
of education, $T^* = c$. The subsidies and grants are employed to drive tuition
toward full cost. The result that there is a welfare-enhancing role for a subsidy
when tuition is set above the cost of education provides an economic rationale
for subsidizing public higher education that makes sense under certain cost
and market conditions.

8 An Efficiency-Based Subsidy and Tuition Policy

> The value of a man should be seen in what he gives and not in what he is able to receive.
> —*Albert Einstein*

Satisfying Students and Society While Keeping the University Solvent

Our prescriptive model for setting tuition is based on a framework suggested in the context of public utility pricing. For public higher education, as for utilities, each organization incurs large fixed costs to offer its services, and the existence of those costs relative to variable costs creates a problem. The efficient strategy of setting tuition equal to marginal cost does not generate sufficient revenue for a university to remain solvent. Specifically, if students are charged the marginal cost of their education, which covers the cost of adding one more student to the university, the sum of the subsequent revenue across all students is insufficient to cover the university's fixed costs. On the other hand, setting tuition at full unit cost leads to significantly diminished enrollment and inefficient provision of educational services.

Given the typical cost structure, if there is neither a subsidy nor regulation of tuition, public universities must increase tuition to levels that substantially exceed marginal cost. In the extreme case, they will act as monopolies, extracting maximum profit and generating welfare losses. The standard regulatory practice in these "monopoly" circumstances is for the state to restrict profitability. For universities, this typically means providing a subsidy to resident students in exchange for lower tuition. Thus, the existence of large fixed costs provides a plausible reason for subsidizing higher education.

With a break-even condition imposed, there are many tuition strategies that can be employed in conjunction with a subsidy. For example, all students can be charged a reduced tuition that reflects the per-student subsidy provided to the university, where the sum of the discounted tuition revenue and the subsidy is sufficient for the university to break even. This formulation is one interpretation of the approach adopted in the University of California system, where historically relatively few nonresident students have been admitted.[1] Alternatively, residents can be charged marginal cost and nonresidents charged full unit cost, with the public subsidy calculated to make up the difference. This latter strategy might characterize tuition policy at the University of Iowa, which admits a high percentage of nonresidents.[2] In fact, a variety of enrollment levels and sets of tuitions can be chosen, with each meeting the budget constraint. The challenge is to decide on an appropriate objective and then to set tuition to obtain an optimal solution.

We argue that the overall objective is a strategy that will satisfy the preferences both of students, who pay tuition, and of society, which provides the subsidy, while recognizing that public universities are constrained to break even. *Tuitions should be set to maximize consumer (student) welfare* under the condition that revenue from all sources (tuition, public appropriation, grants, and donations) will cover instructional cost.[3] In this economic model, student demand patterns and the subsidy then determine the allocation of staff and faculty resources.

To allow universities to cover their fixed costs, we develop a tuition-setting structure that provides "optimal departures from marginal cost pricing," following the well-known formulation summarized and extended by Baumol and Bradford (1970) and employed by Fethke (2011a) in the context of higher education. The main implication of this structure is that systematic deviations of tuition rates from the marginal cost of education are required to achieve a near-optimal allocation of resources. The basic idea is that the need to cover fixed costs requires a departure from marginal-cost pricing, but that departure should be constructed in a way that is minimally disruptive to achieving efficient outcomes. In the following sections, we use aspects of our formal analysis, as well as a set of articulated numerical examples, to develop the prescriptive implications.

Tuition Strategies

There are several ways to present the main proposition for quasi-optimal tuition rates.[4] The tuition-setting solution without consideration of fixed costs is to set tuition for each identified student grouping to equal the marginal cost of enrollment. If the marginal cost is the same for all students, setting a uniform tuition rate is the efficient outcome. However, when there are fixed costs, this efficiency rule leads to insolvency. Recognizing the presence of common fixed costs implies that tuition will be set proportionally above marginal cost. The factor of proportionality, called the markup of tuition above marginal cost, increases with the level of fixed costs and decreases with increases in the tuition elasticities of demand. The primary role of the subsidy in this setting is to provide a socially preferable alternative to higher tuition as a way of reducing the markup of tuition over marginal costs. In addition, the role of the subsidy is reinforced if there are societal benefits that do not accrue to individual students. Taxpayers incur the subsidy's social cost, and students (consumers) enjoy benefits in excess of the tuition they pay.

It may be possible for tuition to cover fixed costs if students are charged different tuitions based on what they each is willing to pay to attend the university This possibility, referred to as first-degree price (tuition) discrimination, can be examined by thinking of a large number of students, each associated with a reservation price that is determined based on their personal return from higher education, the opportunity cost of attending, and other factors. We can rank the students in decreasing order of their individual willingness to pay to obtain a negatively sloping curve. With this reservation-price schedule identified, a different tuition can be charged to each student, leading to a realized level of tuition revenue that absorbs all consumer welfare (surplus). If the tuition revenue captured in this manner covers all costs, then the balanced-budget solution can be achieved without introducing a public subsidy.

This discussion presents two extreme cases concerning who bears the burden of covering fixed costs: one where the burden falls on taxpayers and one where it is entirely on students. The likely situation lies between these two poles. For example, as state support declines, tuition increases place more of the burden of fixed costs on students. Here, quasi-optimality can be achieved in tuition setting but students bear a larger burden of financing their education.

One immediate implication of the proposed framework is that differential tuition rates for diverse groupings of students will augment revenue
when there are identifiable variations in preferences and program costs. These
variations can be identified for groups such as residents/nonresidents, lower/
upper divisions, academic majors, and the self-selection by applicants to
universities within a quality-differentiated state system. Rules can be established to prevent students from moving between classifications; for example, strict residency requirements can maintain separation of in-state and
out-of-state classifications. If differential tuitions are applied to majors (for
example, engineering, medicine, business, or art), enforceable restrictions or
additional charges will be necessary for moving between them; otherwise,
students would declare a low-tuition major as long as possible and elect the
high-tuition program late in their career. In all cases, tuition rates should be
set so that the highest tuition is applied to the groupings with the highest
willingness to pay (lowest elasticity of demand) and the highest program cost.
The rationale for differential tuitions is not tuition discrimination per se but
rather facilitating the largest reduction of the tuition markup above the marginal cost of a program. The motivation is the quest for greater economic
efficiency using the least distortive forms of revenue enhancement.[5]

A special case can illustrate the insights provided by the proposed pricing
structure. Take the familiar case where the subsidy applies only to resident
students. If marginal cost is constant and the tuition demand elasticities are
identical for residents and nonresidents, the proposed pricing plan implies
that the ratio of nonresident to resident tuition, T_2/T_1, should equal the ratio
of unit cost relative c to the unit cost net of the resident subsidy s:

$$\frac{T_2}{T_1} = \frac{c}{c-s}$$

The university will break even with resident tuition lower than nonresident
tuition by exactly the amount of the per-resident subsidy. This intuitive result
describes a relationship among observable parameters and variables. With no
subsidy for nonresidents, knowledge of marginal cost and the resident subsidy
provides a useful guide to the optimal ratio of nonresident to resident tuition,
assuming no differences in demand elasticities.[6] As the subsidy declines, according to this formula, nonresident and resident tuition should approach
equality.

While the proposed tuition rule leaves out much institutional richness, its implications are powerful. The higher fixed costs are, the more tuition increases above marginal cost. Students with low tuition elasticity (higher willingness to pay) and/or higher marginal costs should be charged higher tuition as a way to achieve greater efficiency. Cost differences among academic programs should lead to optimal tuition differences—for example, a medical education costs more than an English degree just as engineering costs more than business. Accommodation of international students may mean greater costs, such as recruitment, visas, and orientation. In practice there does appear to be wider acceptance of using cost differences to motivate tuition adjustments than there is of basing tuition on differences in willingness to pay.

When Are Differential Tuitions Optimal?

Students are different in both their ability and their willingness to pay for education, and these differences are reflected in varying price elasticities of demand. Marginal costs clearly differ among academic programs. The proposed tuition-setting structure implies that educational services that have low demand elasticity but high cost should be charged at a higher tuition than that of programs that feature large demand elasticities but lower costs. Using the principles just laid out for setting tuition and subsidizing higher education may provide sufficient revenue for the university to cover its cost, even when a common tuition does not do so. Each situation allows flexible admission decisions to be based on program quality and improved alignment of program interests.[7] There are many commonly suggested applications of differential tuition; some of the more familiar are briefly discussed here.

Resident and nonresident tuition. Resident and nonresident tuition, in the absence of a subsidy, should optimally be set at the same level unless there is a difference either in willingness to pay (price sensitivity) or, less likely, in the marginal cost of education. Nonresident tuition can exceed resident tuition if residents receive a subsidy.[8]

Differential tuition for different schools or majors. Differential tuition should be charged for majors in high demand or that are costly to offer. Students enrolled in majors with higher marginal cost should be charged a higher tuition. Majors that have greater potential returns generally are in high demand by students who are more willing to pay.[9]

International students and other groups who are more costly to educate. International students and those requiring special courses may have identifiable higher marginal cost associated with their recruitment, language vetting, orientation, testing, and support services. In such cases they can be charged a premium.

Differential rates across different universities within the same system. Differential tuitions should be charged across heterogeneous universities, even within the same state system. This will be the case if applicant pools reflect identifiable differences in willingness to pay or if universities are differentiated with respect to focus, quality, or other attributes that affect costs, preferences, and willingness to pay.

How Does a Subsidy Affect Welfare?

We have mentioned two possible ways that a public subsidy can be used to align tuition with marginal cost. The first is to attach the subsidy to enrollment and lower tuition for all students, or at least residents. This method is equivalent to a reduction in marginal cost. The second is to provide a lump-sum subsidy that acts as a direct offset of fixed costs. Under certain circumstances, these two forms of subsidy have equivalent impacts on efficiency. When there are high fixed costs, both subsidies reduce tuition toward marginal cost. The enrollment subsidy acts in a manner that is equivalent to a reduction in marginal cost, while the lump-sum subsidy reduces fixed cost. If marginal cost is constant, it makes no difference whether a given amount of public subsidy is used to reduce fixed cost or to reduce variable cost.

Is it possible that a public subsidy enhances social welfare measured as net consumer benefit minus its social cost? Yes. Under certain conditions, the presence of large fixed costs can provide a welfare-enhancing role for the subsidy even in the absence of a social return from higher education. The social benefit implications of either a lump-sum or an enrollment subsidy are illustrated by a series of numerical examples. Table 8.1 provides insight into the following issues: the total value (social welfare) created by different subsidy rationales, how that value is distributed, and who will cover fixed costs, with the options being the taxpayer, students, or, most likely, some combination.

We base our numerical examples on the fully articulated model developed by Fethke (2011a), which is presented in the chapter appendix. There are two groups of students, resident and nonresident, with demand curves that are

TABLE 8.1 Impacts of subsidy on benefits (welfare) for students and society

Constraint	Subsidy type	Student benefit rank[a]	Society benefit rank ($M)
Monopolist, no constraint	None	1	1 (82.9)
Break-even	None	2	2 (118)
Break-even	Lump sum	5	5 (151)
Break-even	Enrollment, residents and nonresidents	5	5 (151)
Break-even	Enrollment, residents	3	3 (144)

NOTES: The society benefit is measured in millions of dollars.

[a] Comparing down each column, 5 = highest benefit; 1 = lowest benefit.

identical and linear; marginal cost is constant; and there are both variable costs and significant fixed costs. The social benefits are approximated by the sum of consumer benefits and university profit, where consumer benefits are measured by the familiar consumer-surplus measure.[10] Each row of the table represents one scenario. A numerical example illustrates the subsidy's welfare-enhancing effects.

As an initial point of comparison, we consider two cases with no subsidy. Row 1 of Table 8.1 shows the outcomes when the university acts as an unrestricted monopolist. The numbers in parentheses reflects social welfare measured in real dollars. The remaining rows display cases where there is a break-even constraint imposed on university net revenue. Since the university is breaking even, the social benefit is now the benefit to students minus the costs of the subsidy. Row 2 shows the no-subsidy case under a break-even condition. Row 3 shows the effects of a lump-sum subsidy that offsets a portion of fixed costs. Row 4 captures the effects of an enrollment subsidy provided for all students. Row 5 shows the impacts of an enrollment subsidy to resident students only. In all, Table 8.1 reveals rankings of the subsidy's impact on the benefit to students (consumer surplus) and society (social welfare) ranging from the highest (5) to the lowest (1) across the different scenarios.

The first two rows of the table show that, when there is no subsidy, the imposition of the break-even constraint increases student welfare. The break-even constraint leads to lower tuition, and the resulting benefit to students exceeds the loss to the university. To help cover fixed costs and meet the constraint, tuition exceeds marginal cost and equals the higher unit cost of education. Residents and nonresidents have the same demand curves, so tuition rates and enrollments for each group are identical. Because there is no subsidy, net consumer surplus measures the welfare of both consumers and society.

The third row of Table 8.1 illustrates the impact of a lump-sum subsidy that partially offsets fixed costs. Effectively, such a subsidy reduces the common markup factor in both tuition rates and leads to a reduction in the common tuition. With tuition declining toward marginal cost, there is an associated increase in consumer welfare. Social welfare exceeds the no-subsidy case.

The fourth row shows the impact of an enrollment subsidy that is given to all students. When its total cost of is equivalent to that for the lump-sum case, the enrollment subsidy offered to all students has exactly the same effects as the lump-sum scenario. Both reduce the common tuition toward marginal cost. If the total subsidy equals fixed cost, tuition equals marginal cost and social welfare is maximized.

Fixed costs are common across all enrollments, but a lump-sum subsidy may be politically resisted because it is viewed as benefiting residents and non-residents alike. The common outcome is to subsidize only residents with the obvious result that the quantity demanded by residents increases.[11] Perhaps more surprisingly, a resident subsidy also lowers nonresident tuition because it increases enrollment and overall revenue and thereby relieves the pressure to mark up tuition above marginal cost. The result is lowered tuition for both groups compared to the case of no subsidy, with resident tuition below non-resident tuition.

This analysis provides clear strategies for setting tuition and determining enrollment in response to a permanent decline in the state subsidy. With tuition equalized for *identical* residents and nonresidents, states will not be exchanging students based on some form of resident-rationing scheme. The incoming student cohort will reflect admissions decisions made on the basis on quality and the best match with the institution on the dimensions that are consistent with the university's mission.[12] The next section considers issues relating to the adoption of high-tuition–high-aid programs and to the possible effects of increased competition on the future viability of major public research universities. The welfare-enhancing effects of the subsidy are illustrated in the chapter appendix with a more complete set of numerical examples.

Effects of Competition on the Viability
of Public Research Universities[13]

Is the high-tuition–high-aid model now being favored by major public and private universities a viable one in an increasingly competitive environment, where market forces are replace governing boards' determination of tuition? We know from direct observation that elite private universities can compete effectively in their oligopolistic market environments. Indeed, the top private universities in the United States are widely acclaimed to be among the best in the world. Private universities have the advantage over their public counterparts of being the recipients of long-standing and significant private donations, which have led to substantial endowment income growth, even to the point for some, where they no longer need to charge tuition. Harvard University, with an enrollment less than that the University of Iowa, has a 2010 endowment ($30 billion) that is more than thirty times larger than Iowa's. Even if the current public subsidy to the latter were capitalized in perpetuity, which is highly unlikely, Harvard's endowment would still be four times larger. The same would hold true for most top public research universities.

Apparently, private university governing boards find it in their best interest to avoid list-price competition. The elite privates have adopted "niche" strategies that exploit high degrees of academic program distinction, considerable brand image, and student selectivity that is based on a form of individual-student price competition, where they compete with one another using tuition discounts to attract the best students.[14] Private research universities feature high-cost delivery structures and distinctive faculty; as a result, they enjoy substantial barriers to entry. In fact, challenging the strategic groupings of elite private universities is all but impossible, with the exception of a very small number of flagship public institutions.

In contrast to the benign oligopoly that describes the competition among elite private universities, the challenging environment facing public research universities includes much lower public appropriations, new low-cost competitors, new products delivered through web-based channels, increasing international competition, and greater reliance on tuition revenue and private donations.[15] What can we say, when confronting this environment, about the continued competitive viability of public universities that provide a bundled offering of instruction and research as the distinguishing characteristic of their positioning strategy?

One feature of the competitive market is the relentless pressure on organizations and firms to innovate: to provide efficient products and services or, if they cannot, to be replaced by those who can. Competition tends to drive prices toward the lowest unit costs of providing a product of a given quality, with excessive profits drawing aggressive competitive response. The socially attractive feature of the competitive pricing structure is that prices, which reflect the marginal consumer's willingness to pay, are driven to equal the marginal cost of providing the product.

We have argued that the competitive market result of realizing the efficiency condition of setting tuition equal to the marginal cost is not feasible when there are fixed costs. Public appropriations that offset fixed costs can benefit society as long as the net benefit to students is greater than those fixed costs. With permanent reductions in state support, the practical difficulties of covering the legitimate costs of public higher education are becoming formidable. Some alternative must be found.

When governing boards determine tuition, our formulation suggests seeking maximum consumer welfare, while imposing a break-even constraint on their profitability. As public support wanes, tuition may increase above marginal cost to provide revenue that offsets fixed costs. The other option is to allow universities some tuition discretion to maximize profits, under the assertion that market competition from existing and new rivals will be intense enough to force efficiency and also eliminate excess profitability. This option relies on market forces to ensure that universities are forced to provide their products as efficiently as possible. In both cases, the tuition charged to students will exceed the marginal cost of instruction by enough to allow the institution to break even.[16]

If they embrace the market solution, what are the implications for the major research-oriented public universities? The answer seems to depend significantly on the drivers of demand and cost that both define and distinguish public research universities from their rivals. It can be argued that the very-high-research public universities feature fixed costs that exceed those of their non-research-oriented rivals. It also appears that the demand schedules for the products of individual public research universities are less responsive (less elastic) to tuition changes than are those faced by many of their rivals, possibly because their educational programs appeal to a profile of students with varied preferences.

How will research universities fare in an increasingly market-directed economy? Will a move to greater emphasis on market solutions tend to favor educational products that feature relatively inelastic consumer demand schedules and high fixed costs? Or will markets tend to favor rival products that feature lower costs and more demand elasticity? The answer does not appear to be particularly promising.

A recurrent theme in the literature of business strategy is the effectiveness of low-cost positioning strategies. Thus, in industries where there are economies of scale and demand is relatively elastic, it makes sense to pursue a *share strategy* where a company attempts to maximize market share. This is the strategy of Wal-Mart, Vanguard Index Funds, and many others. Its primacy, specifically as it has been applied to Wal-Mart, is widely noted.

The share strategy appears to be the strategy of low-fixed cost entrants into higher education, particularly the for-profit entrants. From this perspective, the providers of low-cost higher education can take market share and thus impact the viability of major research public universities as these universities are forced to rely on tuition revenues and less on public support. With new entry into a market, existing enrollment is spread over an increased number of institutions and the enrollment demand an individual university faces declines. The demand schedule for research-intense universities may become less tuition sensitive as well. A reduction in tuition elasticity of demand will occur if new providers of higher education set tuition options that are attractive to a significant number of low-willingness-to-pay students. Thus, new competition may reduce both the level of demand for instruction and tuition sensitivity because the more price-sensitive students are attracted to the lower-cost options. These students are not interested in paying tuitions that exceed those of the low-cost provider. With a loss of revenue from low-willingness-to-pay students, the bundled product of teaching and research offered by major public universities may not have the potential for earning revenues sufficient to cover fixed costs.

The desertion of low-willingness-to-pay students that occurs when tuition increases and financial aid becomes inadequate raises the fundamental issue of whether research universities can capture enough tuition revenue to continue to cover their fixed costs in the face of intense market competition. If two providers of educational services have the same costs but face different demand schedules, the long-run market solution will accommodate the producer whose demand schedule is the most tuition elastic, and may not accommodate any university whose demand schedule is tuition inelastic. Similarly, even if the demand schedules are identical, the market will tend to favor universities with low fixed costs over those with high fixed costs. Thus it appears that intensive market competition favors providers of higher education that feature low fixed costs and elastic demand schedules. The conceptual insights regarding the outcomes of market competition do not bode well for very-high-research public universities, nor do they predict a bright future for the academic medical centers that characterize major public universities, both of which display relatively inelastic demand and high fixed costs.[17]

Summary and Recommendations

Permanent declines in public support make tuition revenue more important, and students who are paying more will likely become better informed about their options. Market discipline and increased competition mean that tuition rates need to be set in a way that provides program efficiency. This claim does not mean that fairness in the allocation of scare educational resources is unimportant but only that it becomes more difficult to sustain "fair" outcomes as funding sources change and competitive pressures increase. Providing efficient programs requires that tuition be established as close as possible to the marginal cost of education and still allow the break-even requirement to be met, with revenues from tuition and public subsidy covering instructional costs.

A public subsidy that acts to offset a portion of fixed costs can increase social welfare. With enhanced economic efficiency as a goal, tuition policy should consider differences both in student willingness to pay and in various cost conditions confronted by public universities. Distinctions in student groupings that are often considered for the setting of differentiated tuition include resident and nonresident status, lower- and upper-division classifications, high-cost majors and programs, international students and others for whom cost can be higher, qualified students with low ability to pay, and quality-differentiation within a state university system. The costs and productivity conditions for each grouping and identifiable differences in willingness to pay are the factors that should drive tuition policy.

We recommend that universities do the following:

- Set tuition rates as close to possible to program marginal costs, with a proportional deviation above marginal cost used to cover common overhead costs.
- Set differential tuition rates for programs/students that depend on reflected differences in willingness to pay and/or on differences in educational costs.
- Avoid using cross-subsidies to respond to unfunded mandates and become selective in subsidizing low-enrollment–high-cost programs.

Increases in tuition will encourage competition from alternative providers, both existing and potential. Higher tuition increases the demand for substitutes and facilitates entry from both existing and new competitors. Alternative providers may offer desirable product features like location and convenience that are aided by the Internet and other information technologies. Disruptive *technologies* may well be lurking with the potential to overwhelm the current competitive advantages of public research universities. Bypass competition that connects product providers directly with customers has unalterably changed the structure of major industries (book stores, retail video outlets, airlines, newspapers, certain types of insurance, travel bookings, retailing, etc.) and can change public higher education. These competitive threats are a call for action; they are not an excuse for denial.

More needs to be done to ensure continued consumer interest and willingness to pay. Public research universities can be positioned to leverage their brand images and distributional capabilities to compete effectively. Branding and the certification of credentials are powerful differentiation drivers of competitive advantage, and can be leveraged using the same technologies and processes that are now used by the prominent, successful for-profit programs. If there are hybrid models for delivering instruction lurking behind the scenes, it would be an excellent idea to start benchmarking them with an eye to implementation. It is difficult, given the disruption of other once prominent, overly confident industries, to believe that methods of classroom instruction that are centuries old will continue to withstand the imminent threats presented by Internet-based instruction delivery, especially if it is combined with a recognized brand and traditional methods. Thus, we consider it important that major public universities analyze competitive threats on a regular basis and, where appropriate, adopt new instructional technologies that complement existing competitive advantages, even if this requires major changes in faculty and staff activities. To do so will become critical in a market environment.

Appendix: Optimal Tuition Setting and the Welfare of a Public Subsidy

To frame the social-welfare decisions associated with a public subsidy, we will describe a two-stage decision process involving the legislature and the university's governing board. At the first stage, the legislature determines the subsidy to maximize social welfare. At the second stage, tuition is set by the governing board. As with all problems of this kind, the decision process is carried out starting with the second stage and working back to the first. Intuitively, the board acts in the interest of the university and its students, setting tuition with the subsidy taken as predetermined. Since the university is constrained to break even, social welfare is the aggregate private benefit to students (net consumer surplus) minus the cost of the subsidy to taxpayers. The purpose of the subsidy is to mediate increases in tuition above the marginal cost of higher education in order to cover fixed costs. The subsidy is introduced as a welfare-enhancing way of accommodating the well-known problems of economies of scale associated with fixed costs.

The governing board selects tuitions to maximize the weighted sum of university net revenue and net consumer surplus, taking as given the subsidy set by the legislature. For the case of linear demand curve and constant marginal cost, the objective function of the governing board is

$$\max_{T_1,T_2} G(T_1,T_2;s) = \sum_{i=1}^{2}\{(1+\lambda)[(T_i-c+s_i)(a_i-b_iT_i)-K]+(1/2b_i)(a_i-b_iT_i)^2\} \quad (1)$$

The first expression in Eq. (1) is university net revenue; the second is net consumer surplus.[18] Here λ is the "shadow price" associated with the university's fixed costs, T_i is tuition, c is marginal cost, s_i is the enrollment subsidy, F is fixed cost, and a_i and b_i are the parameters of the linear demand, $a_i - b_iT_i$. We limit our analysis to two groupings of students: residents and nonresidents.

In setting tuition, the board seeks the largest possible benefit to students but is limited by the requirement that the university receive sufficient tuition revenue and subsidy support to break even. The value assumed by λ determines the relative weighting of net revenue and net consumer surplus—the larger that value, the more weight is applied to university net revenue. The solutions can be represented most conveniently as functions of the price of fixed cost:[19]

$$\frac{(T_i^* + s_i - c)}{T_i^*} = \frac{\lambda^*}{(1+\lambda^*)\varepsilon_i^*} \tag{2}$$

$$q_i^* = \frac{1+\lambda^*}{1+2\lambda^*}[a_i - b_i(c-s_i)] \tag{3}$$

$$\lambda^* = -\frac{1}{2} + \frac{1}{2}\sqrt{1/(1-\kappa)}, \text{ where}$$

$$\kappa \equiv \frac{K}{(r_1^2/4b_1)+(r_2^2/4b_2)} \leq 1 \tag{4}$$

with $r_i \equiv a_i - b_i(c-s_i)$ and $\varepsilon_i^* = (T_i^*/q_i^*)b_i$ for $i = 1, 2$. Equation (2) indicates that the optimal deviation of tuition from net marginal cost for each consumer group equals a common markup factor times the inverse of the tuition elasticity of demand.[20] The lower the markup and the larger the demand elasticity, the closer is the tuition to marginal cost.

Optimal enrollments are given by Eq. (3). The solution for the price of fixed costs is given by Eq. (4), where the denominator of κ is the maximum net revenue obtainable under full profit maximization. This expression implies that a feasible solution requires fixed costs not to exceed maximum obtainable net revenue. If fixed costs exceed the maximum revenue that the university can earn, the break-even requirement is infeasible. It can be observed from Eq. (4) that the tuition markup is increasing in fixed cost and decreasing in the per-enrollment subsidy.

While the solutions may appear formidable, special cases illustrate the insights. If demand elasticities are constant and identical, Eq. (2) implies that

$$\frac{T_1^*}{T_2^*} = \frac{c-s_1}{c-s_2}.$$

Here the ratio of resident to nonresident tuition equals the ratio of net marginal program costs. If there is no nonresident subsidy, $s_2 = 0$, then, knowledge of average variable cost and the resident subsidy provide a guide to the optimal resident/nonresident tuition ratio. Resident tuition declines relative to that for nonresidents as the resident subsidy increases. More generally, if there are differences in demand elasticities, then, given the resident subsidy, a higher tuition should be charged to the student grouping with the least elastic demand.

Equations (2) through (4) provide the solutions determined by the board once the enrollment subsidies are established by the legislature. The legislature can affect eventual tuitions by anticipating these enrollment responses and altering the subsidy accordingly. We assume that the subsidy determination is guided by its effect on social welfare, which is defined as the net welfare benefit of students minus the subsidy's total cost. We consider the case where residents and nonresidents exhibit identical demand curves and the legislature selects a subsidy applied to all students. Other alternatives are illustrated using numerical examples.

At the first stage, the social welfare function faced by the legislature is

$$W^*(s) = q^*(s)^2 / 2b - sq^*(s) \tag{5}$$

Social welfare becomes net consumer surplus minus total subsidy cost. Enrollment, which is determined by Eq. (3), is an increasing (concave) function of the subsidy. Since the legislature, in choosing the subsidy, takes into consideration its implications for enrollment, social welfare depends on the subsidy entirely.[21] It will increase in the subsidy as long as the increase in net consumer surplus, $(q^* / b)(dq^* / ds)$, exceeds the increase in total subsidy cost, $dq^* / ds + q^*$. Using Eqs. (3) and (4) to evaluate these marginal conditions implies that social welfare is nondecreasing in the subsidy when the following inequalities hold:

$$1 \le \frac{q^*}{q^* - bs} \le \frac{1 + \sqrt{1 - \kappa}}{2\sqrt{1 - \kappa}} \tag{6}$$

If there are no fixed costs, $\kappa = 0$ and the second condition fails to hold. An enrollment subsidy in which there are no fixed costs decreases social welfare, and in this case tuition is optimally set at marginal cost. With positive fixed costs, $\kappa > 0$, social welfare increases in the enrollment subsidy and is maximized when tuition equals marginal cost, enrollment is determined at the efficient level, and the total subsidy equals fixed costs $T^* = c$, $q^* = a - bc$, and $s^* q^* = K$.

An enrollment subsidy is equivalent to a reduction in marginal cost, and an increase in it will lead to a reduction in tuition and to an increase in social welfare, with social welfare improving until tuition equals marginal cost and the total subsidy offsets fixed costs. The equivalent solution is obtained by providing a direct grant to the university equal to fixed cost. Specifically, when the direct subsidy offsets all fixed costs, social welfare is maximized, with $T^* = c$, $q = a - bc$, $S^* = K$, where S^* is the optimal total subsidy. The equivalency between an enrollment subsidy and a direct offset to fixed cost occurs when the subsidy is applied uniformly to all students. It will not hold, as demonstrated next, when only residents receive subsidized support.

The welfare-enhancing effects of the subsidy can be illustrated using a numerical example. Two linear demand curves are $q_1 = 15,000 - .5T_1$ and $q_2 = 15,000 - .5T_2$. Here q_1 and q_2 are enrollments and T_1 and T_2 are the associated tuitions. Marginal cost is $c = \$6,500$ and fixed cost is $F = \$125M$. It is convenient to use identical demand curves as a way to isolate the effects of subsidizing one group and not another. The welfare of each grouping is measured by (indirect) net consumer surplus (NCS), which is given for each by $NSC = q_i^{*2} / 2b_i$.

Two interrelated issues are now confronted. First, what is the total value (social welfare) created? Second, how is that value distributed? The interesting specific issue is who will cover fixed costs, with the options being the students, taxpayers, or, most likely, some combination. Resolution of this issue affects tuitions, enrollment levels, and total social welfare.

Case 1: Profit Maximization
The profit-maximization solutions are

$$T_1^* = T_2^* = \$18,250, q_1^* = q_2^* = 5,875,$$

and

$$NCS_1^* = NCS_2^* = \$34M$$

Monopoly profits are $13 million. Social welfare is the sum of the net consumer surpluses and profit,

$$SW = \$13M + \$68M = \$81M.$$

By allowing the university to maximize profit, the monopoly solution requires no public subsidy, but it leads to tuitions that exceed the marginal cost of education and thereby to a loss of social welfare.

Case 2: Social Welfare Maximization

The solutions are

$$T_1^* = T_2^* = \$6,500, \, q_1^* = q_2^* = 11,750, \, s^* = \$5,319,$$

and

$$NCS_1 = NCS_2 = \$138M.$$

Since university net revenue is constrained to equal zero, social welfare is the aggregate net consumer surplus minus the total cost of the subsidy,

$$SW = \$276M - \$125M = \$151M.$$

Social welfare is maximized if the public subsidy is used to offset all fixed costs, which leads to an improvement in efficiency over the monopoly case. If the subsidy is applied to all students, it does not matter whether it takes the form of an enrollment subsidy that costs $125 million or of an equivalent direct grant to cover fixed cost.

These first two cases illustrate the efficiency implications of monopoly pricing versus social welfare maximization. Monopoly pricing drives a wedge between willingness to pay and cost, thereby leading to a loss in both consumer benefit and resource allocation. Ignoring distribution issues between (relatively few) student beneficiaries and (relatively many) taxpayers, the offsetting of fixed costs with a public subsidy reduces the wedge between tuition and marginal cost, increases enrollment, and, most important, increases social welfare.

It should also be noted that, since the total net consumer surplus in case 2 is $276 million, there can be a sufficient degree of student-specific tuition discrimination to allow enough tuition revenue to be captured to cover all fixed costs without affecting total enrollment. With price discrimination students with a high willingness to pay (high income) are charged higher tuitions than students with a low willingness to pay (low income), which is a popular mechanism for transferring tuition revenue from students to the university. Thus, the use of price discrimination adds other participants to the issue of who pays, where we can now classify high-income students, low-income students, and the general taxpayer as sharing to one degree or another the cost of supporting higher education.

Case 3: Break-Even Constraint with No Subsidy
When the break-even constraint is imposed and no subsidy is provided, the solutions are

$$T_1^* = T_2^* = \$14,635, \; q_1^* = q_2^* = 7,682, \; NCS_1^* = NCS_2^* = \$59M.$$

The break-even constraint lowers tuition below the monopoly solution, increases enrollments, and increases consumer surplus. To permit the university to cover all costs, tuition must exceed marginal cost and just equal the (higher) unit cost of education. A net consumer surplus of $118 million reflects the welfare of both consumers and society, and is higher than that for the monopoly case. With the break-even constraint, which moves away from monopoly, consumer surplus increases by more than profit decreases because of efficiency enhancement.

Interestingly, as demonstrated by Dixit and Stiglitz (1977), the constrained case also can be used to characterize the standard monopolistically competitive case where market competition drives tuition to equal average cost.

Case 4: Enrollment Subsidy to Residents Only
A lump-sum subsidy may be politically resisted because it benefits residents and nonresidents alike. A resident-only subsidy reduces the relative price of resident to nonresident enrollment and increases the enrollment of residents. More surprising, a resident subsidy reduces nonresident tuition because it reduces the common markup factor. Increasing the resident subsidy adds to social welfare to the point where $s_1^* q_1^* = \$88M$. Under the resident subsidy,

$$s_1^* = \$7,250, \; T_1^* = \$5,761, \; q_1^* = 12,119, \; T_2^* = \$11,476, \; q_2^* = 9262, \text{ and}$$
$$NCS^* = \$118$$

As an extension of this last case, consider an Iowa resident choosing between the University of Iowa and the University of Illinois. She faces resident tuition in one and nonresident tuition in the other because both schools subsidize residents but do not directly subsidize nonresidents.[22] We can see the result by expanding the numerical example in case 4. If both Iowa and Illinois have the same fixed and marginal costs, a resident-only subsidy of $88 million duplicates this case. However, if each state provides a subsidy to all students at a total cost to it of $88 million, the resulting net welfare gain is $150 million, or a $32 million increase over the resident-only case.

9 The Quality of Education

> Quality is never an accident; it is always the result of intelligent effort.
> —*John Ruskin*

Defining Educational Quality

The quality of higher educational products and services is both an important and an elusive concept. Two useful ways to think about educational quality have been developed in an extensive literature in economics and related fields. The first is based on the observation that consumer preferences for products and services are varied, which leads to a diversity of offerings. This is often called "horizontal" product differentiation: students prefer a variety of educational programs: some business, some chemistry, some computer science, and so on. The second definition pertains to a situation where students can rank programs from high to low based on their objective assessment of quality. Referred to as "vertical" product differentiation, this occurs whenever more of the identified characteristic is systematically preferred. Under this second definition, if two different educational products are offered at exactly the same price, students can agree about their quality ranking.

The processing speed of a computer is an example of vertical quality differentiation; seat materials in an automobile are an example of horizontal product diversity. If two computers are identically priced, everyone will prefer the one with greater processing speed, but not everyone will prefer a car with leather over cloth seats, even at the same price. In a public university context, we might think about the quality of instruction, measured by average class size, as reflecting vertical differentiation, while the number of majors and academic programs reflects horizontal differentiation. Everyone might prefer smaller average class sizes, but not everyone benefits from an increase in the number of majors.

The distinction between vertical and horizontal product differentiation is important for both social welfare and strategic design. Does the current higher-education industry offer too much or too little variety? Are public universities providing students with too many or too few choices? David Collis (2004) weighs in on this issue:

> The ideal structure for higher education in the future is not homogenization of offerings but rather the differentiation and specialization of those offerings by institutions that distinguishes their strategies and satisfies only some subset of customers' needs. In the future, consumers would be offered real choice, and institutions would face less overt competition as each targeted different segments. The current tiering of higher education reflects vertical differentiation around the quality of the educational experience provided. What is lacking is horizontal differentiation in which, as an extreme example, Yale specializes in history, Princeton in economics, and Harvard in French.

The strategic choices regarding quality are apparent. Quality can be associated with making distinctive program choices that differentiate one set of universities from another. Alternatively, expenditures can be made to affect the perceived overall quality of the university as reflected by relative reputation and media ranking. These two ways to differentiate a university, horizontal and vertical, are not mutually exclusive, but they do require strategic choices.

Cost of Quality

Quality is not free. The quality of education (vertical differentiation) is a choice variable of each public university. The quality choice is constrained by the cost of producing quality and also by the willingness of society (students and taxpayers) to pay for it. A university varies the quality of instruction and research by adjusting its expenditures, particularly on faculty and on attracting students, with higher-quality faculty and students being associated with higher costs and higher quality. Faculty talent, which is a primary input into providing quality, is scarce; talent is in high demand and costs more to acquire.

Another critical measure of quality is the native ability and the preparedness of entering students. Highly intelligent and better prepared students are easier to teach; in fact, some teach themselves. They also provide external benefits to their peers. Talented students are an input into producing high-quality education. For this reason, many rankings focus on admissions standards and many universities offer substantial merit-based awards to students with high standardized test scores and high grade-point averages. The "best" colleges and universities feature high instructional costs and low faculty-to-student ratios, are selective in admissions, and demonstrate higher graduation rates and effective placements.

Variation in product quality can also derive from redesigning and improving products and programs or adopting new processing technologies. The implication is that expenditures on quality in higher education are chosen strategically, in much the same way that expenditures on research and development or advertising are selected in other contexts. The decisions regarding what to spend on recruiting students and faculty, and how to facilitate instruction and research, involve making purposeful choices.

The marginal cost of quality (MC), represented in Figure 9.1, plots the efficient relationship between real expenditure per unit of quality and a one-dimensional quality measure. We can think of quality, Q, which is plotted on the horizontal axis, as being measured by the educational attainment of the faculty engaged in instruction, where Ph.D. instruction is of higher quality

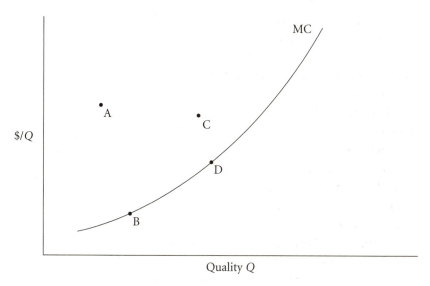

FIGURE 9.1 Schedule for marginal cost of quality

than MA instruction, or by the amount of individualized attention paid to each student or by the average ability of student peers. We assume that consumers prefer more quality to less, but higher-quality education costs more to provide. The marginal cost of quality is increasing at an increasing rate.

For an efficient quality offering, a university will operate on the marginal cost curve. There are four types of public universities represented in Figure 9.1. Universities A and C, while expressing different degrees of quality, are inefficient quality providers. For these two, any movement in a south and east direction toward the MC curve reduces cost and increases quality. More specifically, any purposeful steps made by A and C to improve their processes and eliminate wasteful spending can be undertaken without having to make strategic choices between quality and cost. For A and C, quality is free because they are inefficient.[1] Many think that the main strategic problem facing public higher education is the elimination of waste, and they would define A and C as typical cases. An argument based on elimination of wasteful spending implies that the responsibility for improving quality rests entirely with public universities.

Universities B and D, in contrast, are located on the MC curve. For these two, no resources are being wasted. D offers a higher-quality, higher-cost product than does B. An analogy in private business is to identify B as Wal-Mart and D as Nordstrom; both are effective corporations, but Nordstrom offers a higher-quality shopping experience at higher prices. For efficient universities, the trade-off decision involves whether to allocate more resources to increase quality. Figure 9.1 reveals the fundamental need to make strategic trade-off decisions that are consistent with the university's vision. It helps to explain strategic issues involving vertical product differentiation. For example, D may be a major public research university and B a two-year community college. D selects a quality offering consistent with its vision, which requires different resources from those chosen by B. Each university makes strategic decisions regarding the quality of education to offer, and these decisions depend on consumer demand as well as on similar choices being made by competitors. There is nothing intrinsically better about either of these strategies; they both involve strategic positioning and trade-offs.

Interaction between universities can also be illustrated by the MC curve. If educational products are search goods about which there is ample information, potential students will be aware of the quality dimensions associated

with particular offerings. If two universities locate at the same point on the
MC curve, they offer the same quality, and an informed student will not pay
more for one than for the other. In a competitive market, universities that
offer the same quality charge the same tuition, in which case the only way to
compete is through operating efficiency and cost reductions.[2] The tuition any
university is able to charge depends on the quality offered by its immediate
rivals. In this one-dimensional setting, there exists a good strategic reason for
a university to differentiate its quality from a rival's. The more a university
can do so, the more tuition discretion it will have (see Ronnen [1991] for a
technical treatment of these issues).

One implication of this discussion is that the decisions of immediate
rivals will affect a university's choices regarding both tuition and quality of
education. Suppose that two-year colleges decide to provide a higher-quality
education, perhaps by hiring additional academically credentialed faculty.
These attempts to increase quality are strategic responses to changing student preferences.[3] As their quality increases, community colleges can attract
some students from research universities. A likely strategic response by public
research universities is to increase their quality, which permits them to charge
a tuition premium, but only at higher cost. The result is that the decision by
community colleges to increase quality leads to a strategic increase in quality by major research public universities. This example illustrates a concept
known as "strategic complements," where the quality choices of different
universities reinforce one another. While it may pay community colleges to
increase quality as they seek to attract students looking to complete their first
two years of college close to home, tuition competition becomes more intense
as their quality approaches that of four-year institutions.

The lessons for strategic planning are apparent. Almost every research
university's strategic plan includes increases in quality as a major goal and
usually provides a series of metrics by which to measure success. Regarding instructional quality, these metrics can include number of "student-
centered" educational opportunities, six-year graduation rate, percentage of
classes taught by tenure-track faculty, and hiring of distinguished research
faculty. If these activities are to enhance product quality, we argue, they have
to be paid for, which leads, naturally, to higher unit cost of instruction and
thereby to higher tuition. On the demand side, it is important to recognize
that a critical relationship exists between students' willingness to pay for

quality enhancements and changes in tuition and fees that are required to support quality improvements.[4] Because not all students may be willing to pay for higher quality, a critical question must be asked: Are enough students willing to pay?

Quality Perceptions Are in the "Eye" of the Beholders

The fact that a higher-quality education requires more costly investments by students, the state, and the university is illustrated by a consistent pattern of increases in instructional costs, net operating subsidies, and tuitions as quality increases. In the Carnegie Foundation classification (2010), beginning with the very-high-research universities and moving through high-research, doctoral, master's, bachelor's, and two-year institutions, one observes declining list-price tuitions, declining instructional costs, and declining operating subsidies, with comparable private institutions showing the same pattern but with uniformly higher list prices and instructional costs.[5] In Figure 9.1, we could replace the horizontal axis quality measure with the Carnegie classification of public universities. As one moves to higher classifications, expenditures per full-time student increase.[6]

State appropriations per student are also positively associated with the Carnegie classification. For example, in Iowa, for 2010 the level of public support per student at state universities was $11,585 per pupil as compared to $2,053 at community colleges, a difference of nearly six to one.[7] The basic resident tuition at the state universities was $6,824 and at community colleges $3,842. These differences in supporting revenues are associated with the universities' higher costs of instruction and, using expenditures as one plausible measure, a higher level of educational quality. Presumably, consumers are willing to pay higher tuitions and taxpayers are willing to support higher subsidies because they feel that they are receiving a higher-quality product at the state research universities.

Tuitions and fees charged by colleges and universities in the United States present a wide variety of choices for students. The available offerings differ in price, cost, and quality. Using the vertical concept of quality, if the same tuition were charged by every institution, students would flock to the highest-quality offering, but this characterization is not realistic. We see in Table 9.1 that over 70 percent of students are enrolled in public universities, with the majority in public two-year schools that charge the lowest tuition. Private not-for-profit colleges that present the highest tuition enroll about 20 percent

TABLE 9.1 Gross tuition rates and enrollment shares for U.S. colleges and universities

Institution type	Gross tuition rate ($/FTE)	Enrollment share (%)
Private four-year	27,293	20
Public four-year (resident)	7,605	46
Public four-year (nonresident)	19,595	Included with resident share
Public two-year	2,713	25
For-profit	13,925	10

SOURCE: College Board Advocacy and Policy Center (2010a).

of students. There is a distribution of both tuitions and enrollments in U.S. higher education. Students appear to be making choices based on tuition.

The private not-for-profit institutions in the United States are some of the most distinguished and highly recognized in the world. Certainly, a perception exists that the quality of private education exceeds that of comparable public institutions.[8] All of the top twenty universities in the *US News & World Report* ranking (2010) were private universities, with four major public universities (UC Berkeley (22), USC (23), Virginia (25), and UCLA (25)) barely cracking the top twenty-five. As we will argue, while similar rankings of universities and their major programs, including business, engineering, and hospitals, remain controversial, focusing on input rather than output measures, the *US News & World Report* rankings do reflect a number of factors that relate to product quality, including first-year student retention, graduation rate, faculty resources, incoming students' ACT/SAT scores, acceptance rate, and alumni giving. So, from these patterns of tuition and expenditures, there appears to be a positive trade-off between the instructional cost of education and consumer perception of quality.

The implication of the data is that students with higher willingness to pay enjoy high-cost educations and receive higher public subsidies. Students care about education quality just as they care about the tuition they pay. There are many examples of students willing to pay a relatively high tuition for the increased (perceived) value they associate with a higher-quality product. There is nothing unusual about this situation, which is exactly what we expect to see in private markets for goods and services where, with enough competition, "you get what you pay for."

Choices for Students Facing Increasing Tuition Rates

As a way to motivate the discussion of vertical quality differentiation in higher education, suppose that all students have the same preferences for quality but that, because of income variation, there are differences in their ability to pay for it. Income is broadly defined to include family income, grants, loans, and various federal and state tax benefits. The tuition schedule students face depends on the university's cost structure; higher-quality programs cost more to provide and thus charge more. The above market characteristics result in a considerable array of quality and tuition options, from two-year community colleges, to four-year public and private undergraduate programs, to major public and private research universities. From the student's perspective, the value of attending college is compared with the alternative of not attending. What are the options in the labor markets if a college education is not chosen? The no-college options are changing in modern societies. The choice facing students thus includes consideration of the price of quality, as reflected by tuition schedules and students' ability to pay, which depends on income.[9] Changes in income, the cost of education, and the available no-education alternatives lead to changes in a student's decision to select a particular university, to defer attending, or even not to attend at all.

The level of income above which a student attends a high-quality university and below which a student attends a lower-quality university defines which program to attend. High-income students are able to pay the high tuition required to cover the costs of an enhanced-quality education at elite private and public institutions; middle-income consumers select subsidized-tuition major public universities; and low-income consumers select low-tuition community colleges. Because of low income or ready alternatives, some do not attend. Others choose to stay in the workforce and enroll in conveniently offered, but relatively high-tuition, for-profit programs, perhaps financing their study through student loans. Students and their parents try to make informed choices that depend on their particular circumstances. Universities must be aware of how these choices might change when circumstances change. For example, if the total income available to the low-income group falls, some students who previously might have been able to attend a lower-cost program will not. Depending on the distribution of students, there can be a significant decline in demand, especially for universities that have a low-cost positioning strategy. This raises an obvious strategic issue. Should the providing university reduce costs and quality and lower its tuition by enough to retain the now lower-income population? Or should it be prepared to maintain quality and tuition and face a decline in enrollment?

The response to changes in student incomes and the cost of quality is of significant importance to universities. Part of the key to choosing an appropriate one lies in understanding whether quality is a substitute for or a complement to tuition from the student's perspective. If quality is a complement to tuition, offering more of it will increase the (marginal) return of increasing tuition. In this case, students will be willing to pay for higher quality. But if quality and tuition are substitutes, offering higher quality will decrease the return associated with increasing tuition. If the costs of providing enhanced quality are increasing, as in Figure 9.1, it may be possible, when quality and tuition are complementary, to pass higher costs on to students. If the targeted student population's ability to pay declines or the cost of providing quality increases, it may be necessary for the university to lower both quality and tuition.[10]

Rankings

The quality of both instruction and research in higher education is difficult to encapsulate in a single measure, or "ranking," but there is some agreement on how to quantify higher-quality outcomes. On the research side, quality can be recognized by publication in peer-reviewed journals, by the quantity and distinctiveness of citations to faculty research, and by distinguished faculty awards and recognition. On the instructional side, an important dimension of quality is student placement. Tracked over time, do graduates of an institution succeed in getting educationally—relevant jobs? Are graduates admitted to selective graduate schools? Do Ph.D. graduates obtain jobs in peer or better institutions? Do artists, poets, and writers produce works that are published and appreciated by critics? These are quantifiable measures of academic quality, and there are more. These measures do not conflict with the assertion that a deeper purpose of higher education is to help students develop logical processes of thinking that allow them to relate more effectively to a broad range of life challenges.

Students and parents often seek guidance to sort through the advertised characteristics of the several thousand institutions of higher education in the United States. There is good reason to want better information because finding the right match between an individual student and a university is complex. There are many differentiating factors to consider: location, cost, quality and reputation, size, and campus life. Caroline Hoxby (2011, 3), refers to literature in behavioral economics that shows that small differences in the context or framing of information may have a large impact on decisions made. She indicates that focusing on readily available information is inexpensive relative to the cost of "resource-type" activities, and that there are also positive spillovers as individuals spread useful information to others.

Recognizing a revenue opportunity, in the 1980s the media began to rank business schools, then entire universities; currently, law, medical, and engineering schools are ranked as well. The basic idea was to capture many complex concepts with a single number, "the ranking." The *Chronicle of Higher Education* (2010) lists thirty, mostly input, measures used by the media rankings to assess the quality of institutions of higher education (see Richards and Coddington [2010]). These indicators reflect identifiable categories: admissions selectivity and student demographics; subjective evaluations; finances; diversity; financial aid; student, faculty, and alumni achievement; and teaching. The rankings are a way of capturing in a single measure the notion of vertical quality differentiation.

Not surprisingly, views on the impact of such rankings are mixed. The positive aspects include forcing university leadership to become more sensitive to both student needs and competitive external forces. The negative aspects include overemphasis on imperfect measures; too much weight being placed on rankings by students; and schools unwilling to take risks with applicants who do not score well on the rankings' heavily weighted variables. Possibly, the most insidious aspect of rankings is their alleged support of a kind of academic "arms race" in the recruiting of students who exhibit a particularly narrow profile of attributes, namely those receiving the highest weights in the *US News* ranking of colleges.[11]

A point of contention between the media and academia is whether it is possible to capture the differences between programs by assigning a number "to each school, and whether this adversely affects the decisions of both students and schools. The rankings can aid the perspective student's discovery process by helping her to sort through and thin the list of available options."[12] But once the list has been trimmed to a reasonable size, how effective is the ranking in helping the student decide? An unfortunate effect has been to influence applicants to place more emphasis on the rankings than on other critical factors, such as personal fit, the research capability of faculty, the amount of instructional resources and advising services, and the overall ability of the instructional environment to meet the student's learning style. All of these aspects of the decision process and others cannot be captured by an ordinal ranking.

The media drive differences among schools by assigning arbitrary weights to the selected measures, with different weights creating a different rank order (see Policano [2005, 2007]). These weights can drive decisions. Those given to high-school GPA and standardized test scores like GMAT cause schools to accept fewer individuals who have potential but do not fit the "quality" standards. The ranking effect is significant, not because of differences in real outcomes but because there is little variation in the GPA and standardized test scores of students applying to peer-category schools. Thus, any small relative variation can lead to a large change in a program's ranking. It is not uncommon for MBA programs ranked between twenty-five and fifty to rise or fall twenty slots in one year because of a minor change in one of the underlying variables.

In the absence of rankings, universities could afford to take greater admissions risk, but it is too costly for any to have a class that does not have a high GPA and high test scores. For the business-school ranking, a key variable is average GMAT scores, where the range across the top twenty programs is 690 to 726. The Graduate Management Admissions Council,[13] which oversees GMAT, recommends caution in comparing GMAT scores across applicants, and its evaluation indicates that GMAT score differences among the top programs are not statistically relevant.

Is there an alternative that provides useful information to students and avoids the standard pitfalls? Since 1988, seventeen of the top twenty MBA programs have remained in the top twenty, with limited variability in the measures that underlie their relative positions. Perhaps a more accurate way to provide information is to *rate*, not rank, schools. The top twenty, for example, might be given "five stars," the next, thirty rated "four stars," and so on. The star system would allow a perspective student to identify schools within the cohort that closely match his academic capability and potential against program cost. The key is to identify the set of schools within each rating. One method would be to group schools with the break points computed so that there is a statistically significant gap between the means of the variables used in the rankings between cohorts.

Why do the media rank, rather than rate, universities? The answer is that a stable rating of schools provides little new information from one year to the next. If there is no information, then the need to purchase a rankings issue falls. As the editor of one of the major media rankings outlets once said, "Do not expect me to adopt any change that will lower circulation."

Access and Quality

Public universities have increased tuition revenue to offset the decline in public support, and adjustments have been made to maintain the real unit cost of instruction. We argue that permanent reductions in the public subsidy will lead not only to increases in tuition but also to decreases in the quality of education. Greater use of part-time faculty and elimination of small-enrollment options do have some effects on quality.[14] The quality of public universities is a source of pride and identification, a basis for establishing and defending market position. Negative effects on product quality, which are often publicly denied by university administrators, might in the long run be the most insidious consequences of the changing pattern of financial support for public higher education. The potential erosion of quality that may be caused by a decline in public support is a matter of national concern.

In extending the discussion to include quality, we are relying on the same guiding principle used in defining optimal tuition. After accounting for quality, setting tuition equal to marginal cost will achieve an efficient allocation of resources. With quality thus taken into account, the same basic question extends to the welfare implications of providing the public subsidy. Is social welfare, defined as net student benefits minus public subsidy, enhanced by using a public subsidy to cover a portion of university expenditures to protect quality?

It is useful to focus attention again on a single quality dimension that is preferred by all consumers: vertical product differentiation. The cost of quality will increase, plausibly at an increasing rate. In particular, there are enrollment-independent expenditures that enhance quality, including an excellent library, a research-productive faculty, and an attractive campus. These fixed costs of a higher-quality education may be more important than variable costs. Naturally, if students have a higher willingness to pay for quality and the costs of providing it are low, we should see a high-quality product. To study many of these issues, we can adopt a framework developed by Fethke (2011b) in which the following assumptions are employed:

1. Students display a distribution of willingness to pay for a high-quality education, with some being willing to pay more for a higher-quality product.

2. Students either purchase one unit of the education product or none; that is, they either enroll or do not enroll. Those whose willingness to pay exceeds some critical level will enroll, while those whose willingness to pay is below this level will not.

3. The marginal cost of instruction is increasing in the quality of education, and there are enrollment-independent ("fixed") costs associated with providing a higher-quality education.

4. The university's total revenue consists of tuition revenue and a public subsidy.

5. The governing board, given the public subsidy, determines access and quality to achieve maximum student benefit (consumer surplus) subject to a break-even constraint on university net revenue.

6. The governing board seeks to deploy the public subsidy to maximize the welfare of students while maintaining the university's financial solvency.

In Fethke's framework, changes in the level of public support can affect both optimal tuition level and education quality; the actual impact depends on student willingness to pay for education, the cost structure, and the nature of the subsidy. Subsidies can offset fixed costs or subsidize access. When a subsidy for access declines, the governing board will respond to ensure that the university breaks even. Typically, a lower subsidy for access leads to an increase in quality-adjusted tuition. Thus, reducing the subsidy leads to a reduction in access and, surprisingly, to an increase in quality. Why does this happen? When access is reduced, universities can increase tuition revenue only by attracting more higher-willingness-to-pay students. But to do so requires offering them a higher-quality product. While there is an understanding of the fact that reductions in state support reduce access for low-income student populations, there is less appreciation for the fact that the remaining students are attracted by the offering of a higher-quality product.

An alternative to subsidizing access is to use state support to achieve a higher-quality product by investing in the fixed costs of quality. Under this approach, a reduction in subsidy that decreases fixed costs will lower quality

TABLE 9.2 Access and product quality responses to public subsidy type

Subsidy type	Access	Product quality
Support of access	Positive	Negative
Support of quality	Negative	Positive

but increase access. If, for example, the subsidy to higher education takes the form of hiring more Ph.D. research faculty, its reduction will prompt the university to reduce quality and simultaneously increase access to attract additional tuition. In Table 9.2, the subsidy types and their effects on access and quality are presented. The strategic intent of public support depends on whether that support promotes access or promotes product quality.

For a given product quality, the criteria for evaluating the social welfare of the public subsidy are the same as for tuition setting. A public subsidy benefits students by permitting greater access to education. It is paid by state taxes, which reflect its social cost. Social welfare increases in the public subsidy as long as tuition exceeds the marginal cost of education. Maximum social welfare occurs when students are charged their marginal cost, which depends on quality. In all cases, tuition rates that are set either above or below marginal cost will lead to an inefficient allocation of resources. A subsidy that allows tuition to approach the quality-adjusted marginal cost of education will increase social welfare.

Summary and Conclusions

The quality of public higher education is much discussed, but difficult to define. A public university's instructional quality is reflected in student readiness and in program costs, and every university makes spending decisions concerning the quality of its research and teaching programs. Funded research is viewed as the "gold standard" of university prestige and image, and, thus, its quality. Standards for both instruction and research should be defined and articulated at the highest level, and leaders must be prepared to make difficult trade-off choices to sustain and support quality at that level.

From a conceptual perspective, there are two useful ways to think about providing differentiated products. There is *horizontal product differentiation*, where some product features are preferred by some students, such as a major in French versus a major in accounting. When making program scope decisions, universities are deciding what horizontally defined products and services to offer and what not to offer. In the second definition, *vertical product differentiation*, all consumers possess the same ranking of quality. Some observers, like David Collis (2004), argue that there is too much emphasis on vertical differentiation and not enough on horizontal differentiation in public higher education, and we tend to agree. A theme of this book is the need to embrace sharper program choices, to narrow program scope, and to make decisions that distinguish public universities in their horizontal program offerings. Major research public universities often look the same horizontally, with similar academic programs and related services, and then aggressively direct their spending on quality competition. The problem of accommodating high-cost programs with cross-subsidies is one implication of having a program scope that is too broad.

Another useful way to describe education products is from the student's perspective, which involves classifying them as either *search* goods or *experience* goods. This distinction is important when thinking about how a university positions itself in the marketplace for students. A search good is one for which the student knows, or thinks she knows, before purchasing what product features she will receive. In this case, the student is presumed to be reasonably informed and selects the academic program that best suits her preferences. University rankings are intended to help students and parents decide on a program by positioning it on an index of quality. Alternatively, an experience good is sampled before the student can appreciate its benefits. This is one reason for campus visits and for permitting students to change majors. It is also why universities resist charging different tuitions for programs that have vastly different costs.

An important issue for search goods is that if students understand the product characteristics being offered by a particular university, so do competitors. Positioning among universities in the same strategic group, that is, offering the same search goods, involves adopting a quality position that is not too near that of immediate rivals; otherwise, there is no tuition discretion. For vertical product differentiation, where students display a distribution of willingness to pay for a search good, it makes a difference how a subsidy is directed. If ease of access is the objective, reducing the subsidy will prompt an increase in (quality-adjusted) tuition, which will reduce access.

However, accompanying the reduction in access is increased quality, which is required to attract students with a higher willingness to pay. This pattern is consistent with the observation that permanent declines in state support lead to reduced access for low-income students and increased spending on emoluments that attract those with high incomes. A decline in a direct subsidy of quality prompts a decrease in quality and an increase in access.

IV CULTURE AND GOVERNANCE

10 Cultural Impediments to Change

In the battle between culture and strategy, culture usually wins.
—*Stefan Stern*

Overview

The governance structure and culture of selective public universities are resilient and resistant to change. The seemingly top-down framework displayed in organization charts is an illusion, primarily because there is considerable bottom-up faculty governance. The degree of faculty influence confounds external constituents, especially members of oversight boards, whose suggestions for strategic initiatives are often met with resistance, if not outright hostility.

In this chapter, we argue that a formidable obstacle facing public universities as they adapt to a more competitive environment is a weak central administration that faces conservative faculty from below and micromanaging governing boards and legislators from above. In multi-university systems, this power structure limits the ability of individual leaders to react differentially. We conclude that public universities will require a more responsive governance structure, one that elevates the appropriate leadership role of central administrators.

Shared Governance

Many public universities operate within a multi-campus system that is nominally overseen by a single governing board.[1] A division of labor (shared governance) is a defining feature and is thought by many to be responsible for ensuring quality and enhancing the distinction of the top public universities in the United States. This sentiment is embodied in statements like that issued by the Office of the President at the University of California: "For more than a century, shared governance between the Board of Regents, the system-wide president and the faculty has ensured the highest standards of excellence in fulfilling the University of California's mission of teaching, research and public service."[2]

The governance structure can accurately be described as an "hourglass" with powerful governing boards at the top, a culture of faculty governance at the bottom, and between them a relatively weak central administration. At the "top," a governing board sets the educational mission and plays a primary role as the interface between the legislature (taxpayers) and the university system. It is responsible for fiduciary oversight of multiple campuses and makes critical decisions including admission criteria, tuition rates, and allocation of the subsidy among system universities. At the next level, the chancellor oversees and coordinates system-wide activities and presents the case for public higher education to the board; together, the board and the chancellor apply to the legislature for increases in the public appropriation. On each campus, a central administration, which includes the president, the provost, and deans, oversees all activities within a culture of faculty governance.[3] The primary activities of teaching and research are implemented by departments and institutes with significant faculty involvement.

Research public universities can be characterized as federations of departments run by faculty who make key academic decisions with important financial implications.[4] Recruiting, review, promotion of faculty, curriculum development, and course scheduling occur at the department level. Faculty leadership is a source of strength and vitality for such critical university activities as fostering stimulating open and free inquiry and exchanging ideas, especially *within* academic disciplines. The priority for each department in a major research university is to enhance its prestige through the development of a high-quality research-oriented faculty. In this environment, the size and quality of its faculty is a department's "currency." The most prestigious programs in major public universities are often identified with a few dedicated, entrepreneurial faculty members who discover opportunities and then see them to fruition. The great creative strengths of public universities reside with their faculties, and the predominance of public universities in the United States is due largely to faculty accomplishments.

Within research universities, recruiting and retaining a recognized faculty require that the reward, support, and incentive structure focus on research. In disciplines where external support for research is available, faculty are accustomed to being responsible for generating some portion of their own resources. In other disciplines, the faculty depends for support on internal subsidies. A faculty member's value and reward is established through discipline-based research in an environment that is externally driven and internally isolated from other activities. Highly compensated faculty members are those whose research is distinctive. Generations of assistant professors are advised not to allocate significant time to either pedagogy or service, as these divert from valuable research time. As a result, many faculty members display higher loyalty to their discipline than to their department or college.

Tenure can be an important contributing element to faculty vitality, with a positive function being the assurance of high-quality researchers.[5] However, there is also the potential for conflicts of interest to develop under the tenure system, where divergence between individual interest and organizational value can arise. Tenure combined with elimination of mandatory retirement leaves universities with few ways to replace unproductive faculty.[6] It can also be a significant barrier to an effort to reduce program scope. What do you do with specialized faculty in emergent nonstrategic teaching and research areas?

Department chairpersons are elected or appointed for each academic unit, with a term than can vary considerably from a few years to decades. While the degree of responsibility of chairs differs across units, in many situations they work primarily to shield other faculty members from routine administrative tasks. In some programs, the administrative operation of academic departments is borne by professional staff who possess the knowledge base for policies and procedures. The chair delegates responsibilities that the faculty prioritizes to faculty committees including recruiting, course development, and graduate program oversight.

One problem discussed earlier is the separation of department and college decisions from budgetary information or control over revenues and costs. Departmental activities are overseen by college administrators having various degrees of budgetary responsibility and decision-making authority. College deans may be able to say "no" to faculty-initiated proposals, but have limited ability to say "yes" to an action within the faculty's domain. It is unusual for a dean to initiate a specific faculty hire or promote anyone who does not receive a positive vote of confidence. A dean, or any administrator, typically has little say in course content. On balance, these practices ensure quality, but they can also inhibit change. Like the reviews of the president and other administrators, the standard practice in many universities is to conduct a periodic review of the dean, using a faculty committee from the participating college. Peer reviews are a common feature of higher education that mystify outside constituents, who sometimes have a better understanding of the responsibilities of a dean than the faculty have.

One unit that espouses a central governance structure is the academic senate, a governing body whose members are selected by the faculty at large, often from a pool of the willing. The academic senate scrutinizes and defends the faculty's role by responding to innovations proposed by the administration. The scope of interest in governance questions is extensive and is centered increasingly on the university's budget and compensation system.[7]

Senates vary across universities in the power and influence they exercise; there are both strong and weak ones. Much depends upon the willingness of central administrations to share governance. There is no doubt that some central administrators see their personal and professional interests as more closely aligned with those of the faculty senate, even when these interests clash with the broader concerns of external constituents. The choice between conflict with a senate and conflict with a governing board is always present. Central leadership may choose the former over the latter, perhaps for personal reasons such as retaining the option of advancement to a more distinctive university because the de facto selection process for presidents and provosts is often conducted by faculty.

Because many productive individuals recognize that senate membership involves a significant time commitment with little or no professional recognition or financial reward, they will not serve. Johnson and Turner (2009) suggest that serving members of the academic senate are not among the most valued faculty in their academic departments and/or are those who have the most to gain from resisting change.[8] In the worst case, critical decisions are made from the perspective of protecting the vested interests of a group of individuals who are frequently not among the visionaries and, for political reasons, are most likely to oppose new strategies. Conflict of interest and agency problems can certainly develop if the shared-governance structure acts through the faculty senate to promote insider interests.[9]

Faculty unions have developed in some public universities to extend collective bargaining rights over wages and employment conditions, and, possibly, to slow the replacement of tenure-track faculty with part-time and adjunct instructors. Unions appear where the primary mission is teaching, with approximately seventy institutions and systems affiliated with the American Association of University Professors (AAUP) presently unionized.[10] Collective bargaining in higher education can be even more of an impediment to effective strategy than a faculty senate. Unions not only have all the powers attributable to a senate but they also can bargain for wages and working conditions. Unions seem to develop where there are limited opportunities for merit advancement.

Most research-oriented faculty resist unionization, possibly because they view their market opportunities as better and their mobility as higher, and they may view themselves to be at the center of governance. However, there are a number of graduate student unions in major public research universities, with support for graduate student unionization concentrated in academic areas with limited job opportunities.[11] Institutions with strong faculty senates, the protection provided by tenure, and the opportunities afforded by recognized merit compensation are unlikely to unionize. Why pay union dues for what is already in place?

Interest in faculty unionization may grow as public support for education declines and universities make increasing use of part-time instructors as a way to combat shrinking funding and to convert fixed costs to variable costs. Any erosion of tenure might accelerate this move. The countervailing force in the current environment is the resistance to public unions by governors and legislatures in budget-strapped states; this is happening in Wisconsin, Ohio, Indiana, New York, Florida, and elsewhere.[12] In 2011, a bill proposed in the Florida legislature threatened to dismantle university unions if fewer than half of the eligible employees were members; the result has been scrambling by unions to boost membership. Another controversial bill, also proposed in 2011, that would strip faculty collective bargaining rights was proposed in Ohio (see Balona [2011] and Schmidt [2011]). The AAUP has responded to these threats by claiming that some governors and legislators are using the recession to undermine unions, to shrink the issues on which they can bargain, and to increase the requirements unions must satisfy or face the threat of dissolution. While top very-high-research public universities traditionally have not seen organization of the research faculty, a move toward limiting or abolishing unions might induce faculty interest in unionization.

TABLE 10.1 Decision-making authority in public universities

Decision	Board of Regents	Central administration	Departments/faculty
Undergraduate tuition/fees	Primary	Secondary	None
Access criteria	Primary	Secondary	Secondary
Total budget allocation	Primary	Secondary	Secondary
Specific resource allocation	Secondary	Secondary	Primary
Cost per student	Secondary	Secondary	Primary

In this environment, provosts and presidents are constrained from both above and below by decisions that are not under their control. University leadership is left focusing on consensus building, persuasion, and consultation. This structure of decision making, which we describe as an hourglass configuration, is based on cultural and shared-governance imperatives that are unique to higher education. A summary of the primary decision authorities is presented in Table 10.1.

We have suggested in this section and previous chapters that many challenges would be overcome if the university system could develop a strategic plan with appropriate positioning and then set quality and tuition to achieve the desired access and sufficient revenue. Still, our description of the decision-making authority of public universities indicates why embedded cultural impediments can often hamper, if not stymie, effective strategic responses. The key decisions regarding tuition and entry criteria are made by governing boards. The costs of entrenched programs and associated instructional and research traditions determine the flow of internal subsidies. They are often unpublished in the academic community, making sound decisions difficult. University presidents, provosts, and deans effectively serve at the pleasure of the faculty, albeit a tenured faculty whose relative size and influence is diminishing in major public universities. The result is a cumbersome, disjointed structure for making overall strategic decisions.

Strategic Planning in a Culture of Faculty Governance

Effective strategic-planning structures view the setting of an organization's key objectives to be the major responsibility of top leadership. But top-down planning is not something that occurs regularly at public universities. As described in Chapter 3, the typical pattern is to develop lists of aspirational goals, with limited attempts made to establish distinctive value propositions or to develop a supporting financial framework. Omission of a viable financial plan is the most apparent deficiency. Why do universities avoid a process that has the potential for significant benefit?

A combination of interacting incentive mechanisms, the subsidy, and the governance structure provides much of the explanation. Fundamentally, there is little incentive for the leadership in public universities to undertake planning that requires difficult choices. The rewards of planning, which include a better use of resources and the identification of distinctive market positions, are diminished by the financial security of a subsidy. Why engage in a challenging, even contentious process that requires trade-offs? And why put academic units in a position of defending their resource allocation, quality, and performance relative to other units when the overall subsidy and internal cross-subsidies provide at least acceptable funding for every program? Even when an innovative path is proposed, leadership faces a faculty that, while often described as "advisory," views its role as leading.

Visionary central administration leaders do not receive the bonuses expected in corporate life; rather, they face strife, contentious and sometimes hostile meetings, and little hope of achieving real change. A sobering reality is that the most likely reward for anyone who proposes strategic, innovative change that involves trade-offs is a short tenure in office. Paradoxically, achievement of broad consensus may be most effective for sustaining leadership, even if everyone is marching in the wrong direction.

Governance in a Changing Environment
With little incentive to effect strategic change, how have public universities been able to achieve the high level of quality and distinction they enjoy today? Faculty governance, peer review, and the tenure system all serve to establish and ensure quality standards, and sometimes help to avoid wasteful program duplication through quality thresholds. This governance model performs reasonably well during periods when subsidies are plentiful and predictable. A faculty-centric system with deliberate approval processes can be beneficial when there is considerable time to grow infrastructure. These are all positive attributes of governance, but unfortunately they can become liabilities in a rapidly changing environment.

As academic specialties expand, traditional bottom-up development of new programs follows suit. Faculty members with specialized research interests create courses and sometimes develop full programs in narrowly defined areas, often using the rationale that doing so establishes links between their teaching and their research. These courses are electives that attract low enrollments, which is desirable to the faculty introducing them. Interdisciplinary initiatives are proposed that have broad faculty appeal but no accompanying funding model. Departments approve new courses in spite of low enrollments because, with the subsidy providing funds, cost is not a major priority and there is always the unmeasured promise of growing student interest. New programs continue to be added, but few are ever removed. The ultimate result is inordinate growth in horizontal program scope, much of which requires subsidy. The main reason that program expansion occurs is the separation of budgetary accountability and curriculum and program development.

Some large public universities offer hundreds of undergraduate majors and allow considerable flexibility for students, who, with little or no cost, can change majors and/or extend the length of their study.[13] Each major requires a costly infrastructure of advisors, clerical staff, and faculty oversight, and some have only a few students in highly specialized courses. The evolved program structure is almost impervious to criticism from nonexperts.

When the environment changes, the inertial faculty culture expects administrators to espouse a faculty-centric position, which often leads, conveniently, to administrators avoiding having to take an independent position. External governing and advisory boards cannot realistically be expected to engage in program selection, and occasional attempts to do so are blocked. The two most basic questions of strategy—What programs should we be offering? and, by implication, What programs should we *not* be offering?—are difficult to ask in a top-down fashion and are too rarely asked at any level. It is precisely this feature of shared governance that becomes an impediment to future success. At its worst, internal governance conflicts can bring the university itself to a standstill and invite both closer public scrutiny and increasing management and meddling from outsiders.

Can Universities React to Emerging Needs?

Imagine the difficulties faced by a president or provost who attempts to eliminate an academic department, let alone an entire college, even when that unit has few students and a faculty that does little research. No sensible administrator would dare to suggest program elimination—the entrenched governance structure stands in the way. The only response one can reasonably expect is the appointment of a faculty committee to study the issue and make recommendations, which are then usually ignored. While consultation is critical, leadership cannot be delegated to ad hoc faculty committees and various commissions. Perhaps the consultative process emboldens university administration, which is its likely intent, but it is rarely used in private business, where the "vision" of the organization is laid out by the CEO and supported (or not) by the external governing board. Steve Jobs at Apple was well known for this kind of visionary leadership.

In the event that a significant reallocation is proposed, one can expect faculty protests and even the possibility of legal action. In fact, when a planning process recommends that an academic area be eliminated, there is often such a revolt from faculty, students, and alumni that, rather than being eliminated, the area ends up with increased funding as administrators react to placate constituents. Perhaps because of these difficulties, the more common reaction by university systems to declines in public support is to increase tuition and, if necessary, to impose hiring freezes and across-the-board cuts to each campus. Campus central administrators react to these cuts by passing them along to each college, and the deans follow suit with across-the-board cuts to their departments. The departments do their best to accommodate the existing course schedules within the allocation they are given. Many believe that their discipline must be preserved and that others, preferably those remotely connected, can be eliminated. When they realize that substantial barriers exist to differential cuts, they support cutting all activities equally.

One can argue that across-the-board cuts are all that can be done given the limited authority held by administrators to control key variables like tuition, enrollment, and teaching loads. But it can also be claimed that these cuts are viewed internally as an inevitable, yet fair, way to accommodate changes imposed from the outside. Still, as declines in the subsidy become more significant, it becomes more difficult to avoid challenging choices. With necessary increases in tuition, students become quality sensitive and, quite appropriately, expect more services, higher-quality instruction, more individualized advising, and more resources devoted to the areas they wish to pursue. Clark Kerr, president emeritus of the University of California, commented (1996), "My reading of the history of higher education in the United States is that enrollments, both in general and profession by profession, mostly follow job opportunities, not intellectual and cultural interests, and that jobs requiring higher education will always fall far short of the total population."

As tuition revenue replaces the subsidy, if resources are not allocated to the areas of student interest, the university will face declining enrollment and a drop in revenue. This resource loss impacts both teaching and research funding. As financial incentives change, it is no longer in the best interest of some research-productive campus constituents to avoid becoming involved in discussions of strategic issues. As public higher education becomes less publicly supported and more market sensitive, faculty culture and governance will face strong pressure to change, possibly drastically.

Even when planning works well and identifies promising areas, the governance process can stymie good ideas. Just how difficult is the governance process in practice? How long does new program approval usually take? At least in one case in our experience, the answer is four to five years. In a later section, we describe an attempt to react to a market need by developing a new degree program at the University of California. The approval process is explained in a document that is over one hundred pages long and involves multiple approvals both on the originating campus and at the system level. Checks and balances are important—every organization needs a system to ensure quality standards—but such drawn-out procedures hardly qualify for meeting financial realities or facing the competition. Based on the sanctity of the process, participating groups are likely to justify any existing procedures, at any cost. The shared-governance structure, which is the pride of the University of California and many other public university systems, can hamper the ability to retain prominence in the changing financial environment.

What Should Governing Boards Do?

The "hourglass" governance structure, with specified authority at the top and bottom of the university system, is a formidable obstacle for central administrators. Here, we consider the role of the governing board and ask what it *should* do. James Freedman (Freedman, 2004), who was president of both the University of Iowa and Dartmouth College, argues that the main board responsibilities are (1) to select and support the president; (2) to help formulate and pursue the institution's missions and purposes; (3) to oversee all academic and other programs; (4) to protect financial assets; and (5) to protect intangible assets, especially academic freedom, the commitment to excellence, impartiality, and ethical standards. Clark Kerr (1996) suggests an overlapping list of "long-run" governance priorities: (1) access for qualified students; (2) core programs; (3) libraries; (4) faculty salaries; and (5) plant and equipment. Current priorities listed by the Iowa Board of Regents on its web site include (1) to provide state educational policy leadership; (2) to set the public agenda for higher education in the state; and (3) to connect higher education with the future of Iowa. These lists suggest that governing boards should be engaged in overseeing the permanent capabilities, values, and quality of universities to ensure their ongoing competitiveness and sustainability.

The Role of the Board in Establishing Strategy and Synergies
There is a large descriptive research literature on corporate boards, which has been reviewed by Adams, Hermalin, and Weisbach (2010). When asked, board members assert that their primary responsibility is to be directly engaged in the strategic decision-making processes of their companies. In our experience, governing boards of public universities make the same claim, perhaps with even greater credibility given their direct control over admissions criteria and tuition and fees. We think that the primary role of the governing board is to establish the principles and values that guide the establishment of distinctive missions. The reality in many states where multicampus systems exist is that the governing board does not act as the leader coordinating independent entities. Rather, it sets a nearly common undergraduate tuition schedule, establishes similar entry criteria for units within the system, and attempts to guarantee a combination of tuition revenue and state appropriation to cover university costs.

Entry standards for public universities are governed by articulated rules and are widely discussed, usually well thought out, clearly communicated, and infrequently changed. There exist well-developed processes for engaging students, and others, in discussion regarding tuition changes. Tuition policy, traditionally guided by indexes of family income and consumer prices, is increasingly being set in reaction to changes in the appropriation. This structure of rules for admissions and discretion for tuition does facilitate some better decision making for the legislatures, the governed institutions, and students and their parents. It also imposes restrictions on the ability of individual institutions to develop unique positions.

Many states and their university governing boards exhibit a preference for equality of treatment across institutions. One interpretation of this is that there is a kind of symbiotic relationship between the espoused ideology of the state and the behavior of its governing boards. These governance structures promote equity, fairness, and equal opportunity over distinctiveness, merit, and competition. The effect of this "one size fits all" culture is to eliminate elements of distinctiveness and to impede the ability of universities within the system to compete for students and resources by adopting different positioning models.

In overseeing multiple institutions and maintaining a level playing field, duplication of programs, processes, and activities can easily develop, making efficiency of academic offerings hard to achieve. One purpose of a public university system is to develop synergies across the campuses and to create a collective value that exceeds the sum of the individual values. These synergies may include sharing of resources, creating economies of scale, transferring competencies across programs, jointly using information technologies, and easing student transfer between courses and programs. However, if synergies can create value, excessive duplication can destroy it, especially by eliminating the potential for economies of scale. How many public business schools can be supported to serve the needs of the state population? How many colleges of engineering? How many juris doctor programs are enough? Should the colleges of education be consolidated? How many departments offering the same subject can exist? The conflicts caused by academic program duplication extend to administrative functions, including purchasing, benefit management, accounting, and information technology.

Questions of synergy and duplication are properly within the purview of the governing board and the system. There is also in some states growing interest in the specific conduct and orientation of teaching and research activities. States like Texas, with the endorsement of politicians, are developing controversial proposals to guide public university assessments of teaching and research productivity, and then connect measured outcomes to resource allocations (see Texas Public Policy Foundation [2008]).[14]

Governing Board Qualifications

In most states, regents come from all walks of life. They are usually well-intentioned and socially oriented individuals, but they are not often experts in academic research or instruction. Some have enormous capacity for leadership and for leading change; others do not. The selection of a regent president who has a deep understanding of public higher education, a clear vision, the ear of the governor, access to the legislature, and powers of persuasion can lead to remarkable outcomes. A public university is a complex organization, and ample background and experience are necessary to grasp all of its parts. This much-needed understanding sometimes seems to escape well-meaning regents, who are either technically unprepared for the job or are unwilling to spend countless hours in developing a working knowledge of basic financial, operational, and strategic issues facing public higher education. Indeed, there seems only a modest, or at least uneven, attempt by governors to nominate regents who have a deep understanding of these key aspects or by the system to provide adequate training or background on issues. For example, rarely does any regent possess a knowledgeable perspective on basic academic research. Another, possibly more insidious, problem is the appointment of regents who possess personal agendas and are somehow able to convince a sitting governor to nominate them to push those agendas through.

Corporate boards, especially in light of recent SEC requirements, select members based on the skill set they bring. Public companies are required to have at least one member who is a financial expert, and most boards fill seats with individuals who bring one or more skills of a diverse set identified by the board and the CEO. Among these skills are industry expertise, global strategy and marketing, expertise in compensation and pension plan strategies, and academic experience. It is rare that any board of regents strategically identifies the skill set of its members; many appointments are politically motivated. The result can be a group of sincere, accomplished individuals who collectively lack both background in and experience with higher education. Where Sarbanes-Oxley Act of 2002 pointed out similar issues with respect to corporate boards, it is now time for states to do the same for boards of regents.

A competency misalignment can easily develop between governing boards and university leadership. The former usually include people with significant business experience who are attuned to issues that develop in competitive environments. They are used to making decisions and accommodating change. University leaders are usually the product of an internal selection process that insulates them from important aspects of external economic reality. Indeed, the selection process for presidents and provosts can reflect the natural bias of a predominantly academic committee against anyone whose experience draws largely from private business. Ideally, each group benefits and gains insight from the points of view of the other; diverse opinions and approaches to problems often lead to improved outcomes. However, sometimes points of view are so divergent that a common ground for com-munication is lacking. Differences in vision about what a public university provides can lead, at worst, to dysfunctional relationships, misunderstanding, frequent departures of university leaders, and a general strategic drifting.

Example: The Iowa Board of Regents
The Iowa Board of Regents (BOR) oversees three public universities, the Uni-versity of Iowa (UI), Iowa State University (ISU), and the University of North-ern Iowa (UNI), and two special schools. It is composed of nine members appointed by the governor (subject to confirmation by the state legislature) to serve staggered six-year terms. In 2010, board members came from a variety of backgrounds and included three active business executives, the presidents of a major non-profit foundation and the Farm Bureau of Iowa, a retired business executive, and two attorneys. One regent is always a student from one of the three governed universities. Six have law degrees; one has an MBA. A one-person majority on the board is maintained to align with the current political affiliation of the governor, although there are few votes that proceed along party lines. The board meets nine times a year in open sessions, including two telephonic meetings. Board members are not compensated financially apart from a modest expense reimbursement.

One of the most significant functions of the Iowa BOR is to determine all tuition and fees. A long-standing tradition is that most of the costs of pub-lic higher education are borne by Iowa taxpayers, with a commitment made to provide low-cost access for residents. In addition to setting tuition and fees, the board defines common policies across public universities, lobbies the legislature, and establishes resident entry criteria. This latter responsibil-ity means that critical decisions regarding resident students' access and the price of education are affected directly, if not determined, by board policy. The board also sets the compensation of university presidents and approves general compensation policy; it is also the official grantor of tenure. Finally, the board approves requests for major capital expenditures, which are then forwarded to the legislature for funding approval. These responsibilities and others place the board squarely between the interests of taxpayers and univer-sity students and parents, and they try to represent both fairly.

While admirably developing guiding principles to govern entry criteria and tuition, the Iowa BOR's positioning strategy can best be described as low tuition–low subsidy. Every Iowa resident who meets the common entry requirement has equal, low-cost access to the three public universities, paying nearly the same tuition. The problem is that the three universities have very different research missions and face different competitive challenges, with two of them defined by the Carnegie Foundation as being very high research.

How has the strategy of maintaining a uniform tuition and uniform entry standards played out? The University of Iowa (UI) is a Big Ten institution and assesses its performance relative to Big Ten and other top-tier public universities. Yet its tuition and selectivity policies are unlike those of its competitors. Resident tuition, $7,417 for 2010–11, was the lowest in the Big Ten by nearly $1,500, and the first-year acceptance rate of undergraduates of 83 percent was the highest. In addition, the relatively low tuition was not offset by a relatively high level of public support. The appropriation of tax funds for operating expenses of higher education in Iowa increased by 19.1 percent from 1999 to 2009; in comparison, the national average increase was 48.5 percent. Only Michigan in the Big Ten, at 9.5 percent, stands below Iowa, but both the University of Michigan and Michigan State compensate for their low public support by setting relatively high tuition. In 2010–11, resident tuition at the University of Michigan was $12,400 and at Michigan State was $11,434.[15]

Clearly the Iowa BOR is less concerned about tuitions for nonresidents and those seeking professional graduate degrees, and there is a willingness to accept market rates. Since Iowa's public universities face different markets and offer quite dissimilar graduate programs, they are permitted to set different tuitions for professional graduate programs and for nonresidents. The nonresident tuition rates for 2010–11 varied considerably: $23,713, $18,563, and $15,348 for UI, ISU, and UNI, respectively. The ability of a particular institution to differentially influence its overall revenue stream depends upon whether it can attract and charge nonresidents a tuition that substantially exceeds the total unit cost of instruction.[16] The different nonresident tuitions provide a degree of market-based evidence that resident tuitions can be differentiated across the system.

Principal–Agent Conflicts

The shared governance structure presents challenges in many instances, but becomes particularly cumbersome in the selection of campus and system leaders and the setting of financial strategies, both of which have long-lasting effects on the university. Disagreements over who is actually responsible for making key decisions are often referred to as principal–agent conflicts; they develop between the principal (the individual or group that makes the decision) and the agent (the individuals charged with carrying it out). There are two interrelated types of agency problem. In one, conflicts can arise when the objectives and interests of the principal differ from those of the agent. This is common in nearly all organizations and can become acute if the principal empowers an agent but then cannot verify the agent's actions.

In the other type of agency problem, which relates more directly to public higher education, there is disagreement and tension over exactly who is the principal. In the university environment, Henry Rosovsky (1990, 261) asserts, governance concerns power; it is about "who is in charge; who makes decisions; who has a voice; and how loud is that voice." James Freedman (2004, 10) notes that presidents and trustees are likely to abut at the epicenter of power in higher education. This agency problem most likely occurs because faculty express strong commitment to merit and academic achievement, particularly in the context of a distinctive research mission. Thus, they seek leadership that supports the research mission, the ability to attract similarly disposed faculty, and the ability to compete with international rivals across defined academic disciplines. Passion for the academic mission can be blind to cost and efficiency issues. In contrast, citizen-based governing boards are committed to providing student access, promoting instructional programs, and, more recently, eliminating "wasteful" expenditures. Specifically, they are often more interested in the teaching mission than in the research mission, quite possibly because they are more familiar with the former.

Example: Selecting a President at the University of Iowa

Even considering our academic background, which includes several deanships and an interim university presidency, it was an eye-opening experience for us to observe a recent faculty-led committee in its search for a senior administrator. We were confronted with the obvious fact that the talented people who do the screening for senior leadership have, themselves, a limited notion of what the job they are seeking to fill requires. Search committees at major research institutions often have as many as two dozen members, selected for their diversity and inclusiveness, with a predominance of eminent (research-active) tenure-track faculty members.

Too often, items on a resume that imply that the applicant may possess needed administrative competencies are discounted as reflective of nonacademic activities. The refereed research papers, associated output, and related activities of candidates are scrutinized with great care and by practiced eyes. Numerous teaching accomplishments and successes are sometimes viewed with suspicion because they might portend a proclivity to prioritize the teaching mission at the expense of research. In the end, the screened candidates are naturally chosen to represent the people who select them, albeit with a few years of administrative experience as a department chair or dean, usually of a nonprofessional college. The basic intent of the internal search process is to provide a leader who is "comfortable" in the academic environment.

To some members of a board of regents who possess different world views, the internal process that proffers an "acceptable" candidate pool often ignores too many desired leadership and management capabilities, as well as the requisite experience needed to lead a major public university. In particular, regents realize that the academic members of the search prioritize scholarship and a fundamental appreciation of the academic environment above experience in strategic thinking, financial management and non-university leadership.

The basic agency conflict that develops in this situation concerns who is the principal, that is, who holds the power to appoint the university president. The governing boards of public universities often claim to have this responsibility. It even appears by statute that the "principal" in determining the leadership of a public university is the board of regents, with the internal university governance structure, including the faculty senate, being the "agents."

Intense conflict over who has the power to select university leadership developed at the University of Iowa during the 2006 presidential search. Prior to 2006–07, the not so long-standing procedure at Iowa was for a faculty-dominated search committee to identify a list of acceptable candidates, and make its ranked recommendations; the regents were then expected to select the president from this screened list. In 2006, the president of the Iowa BOR, who had a strong personality, a business background, and a significant public presence, sought direct board involvement in the screening process, presumably based on his perception that choosing a university president should not, de facto, be left in the hands of the governed. This adjustment of the process, coupled with the board's belief that it had the primary responsibility to select the president, caused sufficient disruption to terminate one presidential search and nearly finish off a second. Prominent members of the UI Faculty Senate, threatened by the perceived change in process, felt disenfranchised;

in turn, the governing board was astounded by the widely asserted claim that faculty should play the major role in the selection of their own top leadership. The agency problem became apparent, with each side insisting that it was the principal and the other the agent.

In 2006, the Iowa BOR was presented with a slate of potential candidates whom it viewed as untested, inexperienced, and narrowly focused on traditional academic objectives. It rejected the slate and called for a new committee. The faculty was incensed at the rebuff of its nominees, accusations broke out in the press, and the governor was called in to adjudicate. The experience was most unpleasant and unsettling for everyone. Eventually, a second committee selected a new slate, from which the BOR selected a new president.

*Example: A New Badger Partnership at the
University of Wisconsin-Madison*
The University of Wisconsin system includes thirteen four-year universities, thirteen freshman/sophomore colleges, and the statewide University of Wisconsin Extension. With 180,000 students, the system is one of the largest in the nation. The University of Wisconsin-Madison (UW-Madison) and the Wisconsin State Universities had merged into one system in 1971. In 2010, Carolyn "Biddy" Martin, chancellor of UW-Madison, proposed a New Badger Partnership, which would change the relationship between the state and the university.[17] The thrust of the proposal was to identify ways to sustain excellence in the face of impending budget cuts, and its key elements were the following:

- To develop an independent governing body separate from the UW system's Board of Regents, which would be appointed jointly by both the Governor and UW-Madison.
- To oversee the processes of tuition setting, procurement, and personnel matters.
- To maintain the existing level of state taxpayer support.
- To be the legal employer of all campus employees, although these employees would have the right to continue participating in state health care and retirement plans.
- To retain its unique UW-Madison shared-governance structure.

The proposal sought independence for the flagship campus and reflected the theme that each campus within the system would establish a distinct vision and be allowed degrees of strategic independence, particularly over the setting of tuition. What was most interesting was the process by which the chancellor chose to initiate the proposal. Her original version included seeking additional flexibility but did not ask to convert UW-Madison to a public authority. Seeking support, she met with newly elected governor, Scott Walker, who suggested the independence route without vetting the concept through the regents and the head of the Wisconsin system. When the plan was announced, it naturally was met with resistance by those not consulted. In a letter sent to the governor, the UW system president, the UW Board of Regents president, and board vice president expressed concern about the restructuring proposal, especially given its lack of widespread consultation and analysis. Eventually, a conflict ensued and the legislators, many of whom have UW system colleges in their districts, chose not to support the governor, and the proposal was defeated.[18] The legislature did, however, approve additional UW-Madison flexibility for construction, personnel systems, procurement, and accountability.

While Chancellor Martin's plan was not approved, the steps she took did lead to a set of changes that were referred to as the most significant since the creation of the system. The process surrounding this proposal was contentious. Here, an administrator attempted to exert direct leadership and was supported by the governor, but the power embodied in the system president's office and in the regents eventually defeated her initiative. Subsequently, Chancellor Martin left the University of Wisconsin for the presidency at Amherst College.

Example: Restructuring the University of California Pension Plan
The University of California system's pension plan provides an example of decision making where the principal (the head of the system) allowed the agent (the academic senate) to play a key role in deciding financial strategy, with the outcome causing potentially permanent financial problems. In March 2009, the president of the system appointed a Task Force on Post-Employment Benefits[19] to examine options in the face of a $12.4 billion funding shortfall in the defined-benefit pension plan. The task force deliberated for sixteen months, employed expert consultants, and issued a report in July 2010. The report's recommendations were shared broadly with the university community. Three alternatives were submitted for public comment. During the deliberations (see page 30 of their full report), members of the task force representing the

academic senate reacted negatively to the proposed recommendations, arguing that the employer (university) contribution was set too low and the employee (faculty and staff) contributions were set too high. The task force called in its own consultants, who agreed that some of the levels were not competitive. In the end, the task force proceeded with plans to implement higher employer contributions, with the academic senate reaffirming its preference for a higher university contribution. The UC system president sided with the faculty and presented this option to the Board of Regents, indicating that he thought this plan was the fairest to the faculty and staff and expressed a consensus. At one point in the deliberations, UCLA's chancellor explained the significant cost implications and informed the regents that by 2017, with the selected option, his campus would need to contribute an amount equivalent to the annual salaries of 700 full professors. Yet the regents approved the system president's senate-backed recommendation and adopted the consensus position.

Example: A New Master's Degree at the University of California-Irvine

This final example illustrates the way shared governance and associated processes can derail, or at least stall, an innovative concept. We initially describe the approval process for a degree at the University of California, Irvine, then we illustrate with the case of a new joint-degree masters program.

There are two process components: the first entails the identification of need and the details of the program, which is the responsibility of the proposing faculty and staff; the second is the approval process, which involves input from campus and higher levels of the university and system. The overall process is explained in a document that is over one hundred pages long, involving nine decision points at the university level and five at the system level. There are five voting points at the college and university levels, and two at the system level. The specific required steps are described next.

Step 1: Identification of Need
The academic unit analyzes how well its programs address current and future perceived needs, and identifies unmet needs. This analysis is followed by research to identify the quality and success of similar programs at other institutions, potential student demand, and employer needs and perspectives. If data support development, a financial model is created that estimates costs and revenues.

Step 2: Approval

The proposal is submitted to a school-wide faculty advisory committee and then to the dean and the executive vice chancellor and provost. If all reaction is positive, it is placed before the entire faculty for a vote to approve, seek modification, or reject. If passed, the proposal is submitted sequentially to the university-wide Graduate Council, the Council on Planning and Budget, the University of California, Irvine, Senate Cabinet, the Divisional Senate Assembly, and the executive vice chancellor or provost. The provost's office then notifies the University of California Office of the President that a proposal is in process. Once the proposal is received by the provost and senior vice president at the president's office, the coordinator of public relations requests comments from each of the other UC schools and vice provosts. Next, a coordinating committee requests reviews from external reviewers and holds a vote, which is followed a vote by the California Post Secondary Education Commission. Finally, the president of the University of California decides whether or not to recommend implementation.

The need for a joint degree between the School of Engineering and the School of Business at the University of California, Irvine, was expressed by recruiters, students, and faculty in early 2007. Leadership agreed that the program matched its strategies and that it would be financially successful. The first steps of the approval process, the need assessment, worked well, and development of the program began immediately afterward. Some five years later, the program was finally approved.

In reviewing the development process, we find that the two schools took about two years to do the background analysis, develop the curriculum, and move the proposal through the formal steps. During this time, the Business School spent about $200,000 in personnel time and other costs. Over 100 faculty members from the two schools reviewed the proposal to establish the degree, and the program received approval from four faculty subcommittees as well as the two full faculties from the Business School and the School of Engineering. The proposal was discussed with over seventy members of external advisory boards, several companies, and many current and perspective students and employers. The Graduate Council reviewed it and had three nonmaterial questions, which due to scheduling issues took both schools several months to answer. The remaining steps yet to be taken involve the University of California system, where review will take a minimum of one year.

The vast majority of programs that reach the UC system level are eventually approved. However, approval comes after substantial delay, mostly bureaucratic, sometimes political, with little value added. A fascinating aspect of the current approval process is that most of the decision units are acting appropriately. Each unit promises to complete its analysis with little delay, but most committees meet only monthly and only during the academic year. A wait of several months simply to be put on the agenda can easily develop; if we then add the time it takes to respond to usually minor issues the committee raises, months can pass. Not all curriculum innovation approvals take as long as the one described here. Changes in existing degree programs move much more rapidly through the system—even new degrees that fit certain standard profiles. There are better ways to conduct this process.

What might be done? The real issue is the cost and benefit associated with having so many decision points. Is the cost of each step greater than its potential benefit? Are there duplicative steps in the process? Rarely are these questions posed, and even more rarely are they analyzed with actions for improvement. Rather than having each academic unit conduct market research, identify new programs, monitor enrollment trends and track recruiter needs, these activities could be done by specialists and the approval process could be shortened using a cost-benefit analysis that measures how long each step might take in terms of faculty and staff time and the costs and lost revenue due to the delay in enrolling students. In Chapter 11 we analyze two successful program approvals, one where an existing degree was updated and one where a joint degree received the enthusiastic endorsement of the governing board and withstood limited faculty opposition.

Summary and Conclusions

The "hourglass" decision structure that we describe is a prescription for competitive failure in an environment where universities need to become more entrepreneurial. The current governance structure requires drastic change and—forces are at work to bring it about. As state subsidies decline and tuitions rise, students will naturally become more interested in both program availability and quality. The student who is paying low tuition is likely to more readily understand when options are limited than is a student who is paying market rates. Universities that fail to respond to students' demands and rivals' actions will find themselves with fewer students and smaller revenues, with adverse effects on both research and teaching.

Governance processes that continue to emphasize equity over merit will be increasingly difficult to sustain in competitive research and teaching environments. In such environments, leadership, rather than focusing entirely on consensus building and stewardship of traditional values, must form distinctive missions and value propositions, if possible with the backing of faculty.

The key factor in the development of every program and initiative is a supporting financial model. What are the sustaining sources of revenue, both public and private, and what are the continuing expenditures? The discipline required to perform an effective cost-benefit analysis of prospective programs will eliminate appeals to the importance of activities for which there are no sustaining sources of willingness to pay.

11 Templates for Change and Lost Opportunities

> The markets will come. They will be swift and they will be severe and this country will never be the same.
>
> —*Erskine Bowles*

An Owner's Manual for Strategic Planning

While an entrenched culture impedes adaptation to a changing environment, public universities do have programs that react to competitive threats and sustain financial viability. Many examples are found among university enterprises, but there are also examples among academic programs and research centers. Since we are familiar with public business schools, we will emphasize them as examples of the many academic programs that have been forced by changes in their external environment to become more self-reliant, to adopt comprehensive governance and planning processes, and to makes changes in programs and organizational structures.

This chapter can serve as an "owner's manual" for academic units that wish to develop and implement a viable strategic planning process. It applies the concepts developed in the previous chapters to illustrate planning initiatives, the creation of value, and difficult trade-offs. We first provide a template for any academic unit that wants to make strategic program decisions, offering several examples of how it can be implemented. This discussion applies to all units, whether self-sufficient or subsidized, instructional or research, student- or faculty-centric. The intent is to stimulate the idea that these responses to external factors have wide applicability. We then discuss the responses made by public business schools as their environment has become increasingly competitive and contested. We offer some cautionary notes derived from our business school experience that relate to all enterprises and programs that face imitation and increasing market competition. Success in strategic positioning requires being different from others and investing in capabilities that are hard to imitate. This lesson can easily be lost when cross-subsidies inhibit incentives and competitive forces capture market share.

Competitive Analysis, Needs, Priorities, and Implementation

The steps required for implementing a teaching or research program are presented in Figure 11.1 and are discussed next.

Competitor and Constituent Analysis

Environmental factors are essential in developing plans because many of them are beyond direct control. The planning process begins with an analysis of data for peer schools, aspirational schools, and major constituents. For example, the major constituents of a public university business school include prospective students, alumni, recruiters, internal advisory boards, the local community, external governing boards, and the state legislature. Internal constituents are students, faculty, staff, other academic units, and central administration. Information concerning the external environment is available from AACSB International, the Graduate Management Admissions

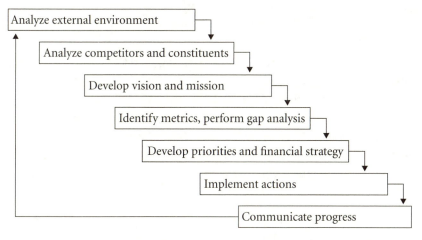

FIGURE 11.1 Key steps in strategic planning

Council, and numerous media outlets.[1] These sources also contain information on budgets, faculty salaries, faculty size, degrees, enrollments, tuitions, placement, and admission results. Rankings, which are based in part on admissions and placement data, require paying attention to external image and relative tuition.

Prioritizing constituent demands is a challenging task because the demands of different groups rarely coincide. Students seek a well-taught, relevant curriculum, with courses, extracurricular services, and programs oriented toward their subsequent employment. Research faculties prefer a convenient teaching schedule requiring only a few preparations in their areas of specific interest. The administration wants programs to produce tuition revenue that can be used to subsidize other programs. Students and alumni believe that faculty research is too theoretical and want more attention devoted to high-quality instruction, career enhancement and alumni services. The result is that, as much as any academic unit wants to see preference alignment among constituents, there are preference conflicts. Focused strategic planning provides a consistent way to respond to diverse preferences by prioritizing programs according to the value they add to achieving the school's vision. A competitive environment makes it hard to avoid choices that involve trade-offs between instruction, research, and service to external communities.

Vision and Mission

A vision provides a powerful message about purpose and distinction. Developing one involves making statements about program differentiation, student quality, research productivity, and scope. What level of quality does the school want to achieve? What are the school's strengths relative to those of peer schools? What is the profile of the desired student base? How can the school differentiate and distinguish itself? What parts of the value chain will the school feature and invest in, and how are these activities integrated and their quality controlled? What are the capabilities of faculty and staff that align with the vision? A visions can emerge, or even evolve, but there must be one to start with: "Where there is no vision, the people perish . . ." (Proverbs 29:18).

Metrics

While a vision statement is an inspirational message about emphasis, its accompanying metrics need to be measurable, consistent, and communicated. For example, a program might feasibly aspire to be positioned among the top twenty-five public universities in its discipline in the United States. Once that vision is proposed, the next step is to develop metrics that define the ranking profile used to delineate "top twenty-five." If the vision is centered on research, the strategic plan needs to define measures of research quality: examples include the number of publications per faculty member in top journals, citations per publication, quality of entering graduate students (test scores, undergraduate GPA, etc.), placement of students (time to completion, level of university), success of doctoral students (percent receiving tenure, level of university), and number of journal editors among faculty or number of faculty who serve on editorial boards. Similarly, instructional quality measures include quality of entering students, student placement, alumni financial success, assurance of learning measures, pass rates on professional examinations, teaching evaluations, and media rankings. Academic units that face high demand may decide to admit undergraduates selectively to improve entry quality and to better align graduates with employment opportunities. This might be accomplished by raising entry standards and capping enrollment.

It is relatively straightforward to compare all of the previous metrics across peer and aspirational groupings. Where there are gaps, either a strategic rationale is provided for the differences or actions are identified to close them. These actions are then prioritized based on their impact relative to implementation cost. Feasibility considerations can often impose a sense of reality. Not every program in the "top fifty" can achieve "top twenty-five" status.

A Financial Reality Check

The financial plan and strategy correspond to the priorities identified by the vision statement and are reviewed and may have to be adjusted. An axiom of any planning process is the following: *If you do not have a financial plan, you do not have a strategic plan.* The financial health of every program, existing or proposed, can be examined routinely, acknowledging both the limitations of the university budgeting process and the extent of entrenched vested interests. How much will the plan cost? What are the expected revenue flows? When private funds are identified as the main source of financial support, is there a realistic assessment of donor interest or financial capacity? Of particular financial importance are decisions to create new programs or to grant tenure, both of which can require resources equivalent to a large and perpetual subsidy. Finally, decisions need to be informed about how incremental revenues will be treated (taxed) by the central administration.

TABLE 11.1 Financial plan: Ten-year horizon

		Potential revenue sources		
Action	Additional annual expenditure ($M)	University ($M)	Self-funded ($M)	Donor-funded (development) ($M)
Increase faculty	2.0	1.0	0.75	0.25
Faculty chairs	1.0	0	0	1.0
Fellowships	0.5	0	0.25	0.25
Marketing/brand	0.5	0	0.25	0.25
Centers	1.0	0	0	1.0
Student services	1.0	0.75	0.25	0
Other	0.5	0.25	0	0.25
Totals	6.5	2.0	1.5	3.0

Financial planning works best if financial goals and potential revenues are examined over several years: five- or even ten- year intervals are common. Table 11.1 provides a hypothetical ten-year planning horizon. As shown, the projected new costs derive from strategic decisions and a well-communicated plan. Each element represents an incremental, annual expenditure flow. The plan proposes an increase in the size of the tenure-track faculty, which requires additional annual expenditures on faculty equal to $2 million per year. Potential funding sources include a subsidy from the university, new or expanded programs that generate additional revenue, and development efforts that provide additional donor funding.

If a financial plan is constructed as described, the link between priorities and finances is clear; the strategic plan prioritizes actions and the financial plan provides an assessment of revenues sources. Gaps between the funds required and identified sources become the goals for fundraising. The amount identified as donor funded can provide a reality check. In this example, donors must provide a permanent increase in annual income of $3 million. One way to generate this increase is to increase the permanent endowment by $75 million, which, with a 4 percent payout, will generate the $3 million annually. Leadership can evaluate whether the goal of an additional endowment of $75 million (received gifts, not just pledges) in a ten-year time period is feasible. Alternatively, if $500,000 of the additional annual revenue is obtained through continuing annual gifts, then the required endowment is reduced to $62.5 million. It is important that such statements be based on a realistic assessment of feasibility based on the alumni and donor base.

Implementation and Resource Allocation

Changes in position, priorities, and funding methods require execution. What steps are taken by whom, when, and why are important matters. Organization and integration of activities can be understood by referencing value-chain activities. Effective implementation of a new instructional program includes advising, career and academic counseling, instruction, placement, public relations, corporate relations, alumni relations, development, and fund-raising. In business schools, the organizing structure has expanded to include the leadership and oversight required for self-funded programs and the building of a staff that works with external constituents. Programs are often overseen by a program director who is responsible for the financial goals of the program and for the recruiting of students who meet quality and quantity criteria.[2] Resource allocations reflect realistic plans for improving quality.

Decisions concerning resource allocation reflect trade-offs among alternative uses of funds. Table 11.2 provides a framework that helps to illustrate these choices. Programs with satisfactory quality but negative net revenue may still be subsidized, depending on agreed on criteria. Programs with positive net revenues but unsatisfactory quality are considered for quality enhancement. Areas that are neither satisfactory in quality nor financially viable are examined for downsizing or elimination.

During 2011, the University of California, Irvine, adopted a modified version of Table 11.2 to evaluate and rank the quality of every academic unit in one of three categories: lowest and highest 20th percentiles and middle 60th percentile. The metrics used for measuring quality were those described earlier. Productivity, rather than net revenue, was measured in various ways. Facing a cut in the state allocation, programs in the middle would receive an average cut; those in the lowest portion would receive an above-average cut,

TABLE 11.2 Program quality and net revenue

	Quality	
Net revenue	*Satisfactory*	*Unsatisfactory*
Positive contribution	Add new resources	Enhance quality
Negative contribution	Subsidize	Downsize/eliminate

and those in the upper region would receive the smallest cut. The exercise was implemented, and differential cuts were made with little controversy.

Examples of Effective Implementation

One mistake in developing a new initiative is to create a program and then go searching for an agreeable customer. Decisions about entering new markets or not eliminating failed programs often suffer from this problem. In the following sections, we provide examples of four programs that do began with an expression of external demand and then developed sustaining financial models. The MBA Program at the University of California, Irvine, is one example of an on-book academic program that is administered under a college CAM. The Joint MBA Program at the University of Iowa is an off-book program that features many of the characteristics of an effective RCM. Iowa's undergraduate Hawkinson Institute is run as an independent RCM. A final example is an emerging program, the River Landing Ambulatory Clinic at the University of Iowa, which is a vision-driven RCM that will require significant adjustment in faculty culture.

MBA Program for the University of California, Irvine

Can a vision be translated into a distinctive program that attracts students whose interests match its offerings? How does understanding the value chain create value and quality? We consider the repositioning of the Full-Time MBA program at the Paul Merage School of Business at the University of California, Irvine, which took place from 2004 to 2010. The Merage MBA program quality measures consistently place the program in the top five to ten percent of accredited MBA programs. Its peer group comprises the schools in this tier and its aspirational group comprises those positioned as the top twenty-five (top 5 percent).

The Merage faculty and staff specified measures of quality and focused their strategy on the previous metrics rather than on those used by the media rankings. While media rankings have an important influence on perspective students and, arguably, on the actual investment behavior of colleges, as indicated in Chapter 9, current ranking methods do not provide a completely satisfactory measure of quality. Still, a focus on the intersection between the school's quality measures and those used in the rankings is useful because, in addition to measuring quality, these metrics can be easily tracked.

Some indicators of success for a full-time MBA program include admissions data, including the average GMAT score (the standardized test for entry into graduate programs in business), average undergraduate GPA of entering students, placement success, and the overall acceptance ratio of the program. As Table 11.3 shows, separating the data into averages for the peer group and the aspirational group allows for a useful comparison.

When the data were analyzed in 2004, the overall quality of admissions and placement at Merage was deemed to be close to the average of the aspirational group; the average GMAT, at 658, the average GPA, at 3.37, and placement, at 82.1 percent, were above the those of the peer group. There were two areas where gaps existed: program size was smaller than the average for the aspirational group, and the student acceptance rate was considerably higher than that for both the peer and aspirational groups. Before reacting, the faculty reviewed whether the gaps reflected a true difference in quality. While it was felt that the quality of the program was satisfactory, an increase in student quality could be achieved relative to both peer and aspirant groups by increasing the size of the applicant pool and by adopting a more selective admissions process. In this way, the average GMAT and GPA of the entering class could be increased and the placement of graduates made more effective. The costs of enacting this plan were evaluated, and it was recognized that it would be expensive if initially enrollment fell. Donors were identified to fund scholarships and other program activities, and it was decided that these funds could support the new program.

To increase the size of the applicant pool, it was decided to adopt a distinctive vision and make changes to achieve it. Ideas were discussed with the faculty and staff and with the Dean's Advisory Board. Based on the location in Irvine, California, which is a center of entrepreneurship in areas such as medical devices, information technology, and renewable energy sources, the school adopted a vision focused on enhancing sustainable growth through innovation. It was determined that this vision could provide an element of distinctiveness, since at that time the vision of most business schools centered on specializations such as finance, marketing, and consulting. Although some business schools did focus on innovation, few had adopted an approach combining innovation with sustainable growth. This approach promised a theme that could be incorporated throughout a program, and it was approved by the faculty. A committee was formed to develop ways to build the vision into the MBA programs and courses. Although novel at the time, it is now more common to discuss sustainability as a competitive advantage.[3]

TABLE 11.3 Comparison of peer and aspirational group data for full-time MBA programs

Program rank	Enrollment		Average GMAT		Average GPA		Percentage employed at 90 days		Acceptance rate		Ranking	
	(2003)	(2009)	(2003)	(2009)	(2003)	(2009)	(2004)	(2010)	(2004)	(2010)	(2003)	(2009)
Top 25	700	741	686	700	3.40	3.46	81.6	79.3	23.9	23.4	—	—
Top 26–50	290	219	655	664	3.32	3.35	81.0	80.5	38.0	32.7	—	—
Paul Merage School	200	194	658	675	3.37	3.42	82.1	91.7	44.5	27.2	50	36

SOURCE: *US News & World Report: America's Best Graduate Schools 2004 and 2010.*

It was decided that a smaller program would be an advantage in that it would allow each student to receive individual attention to assess and develop his or her specific strengths. The measurable goal adopted by the Admissions Committee was to admit an academically qualified class (average GMAT >660; average GPA >3.3) who were also sufficiently professionally qualified so that the school would have the potential to place 90 percent of the class within 90 days of graduation. Once this approach was established, a promotional campaign and a brand focus were adopted: the program's brand promise is that each student will be provided with *"innovation to shape the future and personalization to shape you."* Core faculty of the new program were asked to explain how their courses incorporated the thematic approach. To enhance the overall student experience, the size of the staff was increased and additional advising and career guidance were provided. Student satisfaction was monitored through student representatives in each cohort and via external rankings of satisfaction, including those used by *Business Week*.

By 2010, the average GPA and GMAT scores were higher and the admissions process had become more selective. Placement success improved. The plan is to continue to increase the size of the applicant pool and to create the momentum for increased quality of the student body and, ultimately, increased alumni success. The goal that the school identified was to increase quality as measured by entering student qualifications, integrated thematic programming, and subsequent placement results. The outcome is a better match between the school and its students. While it had not been the primary goal, the ranking of the program in *US News & World Report* rose from fifty in 2004 to thirty-six in 2010.

Joint MBA Program at the University of Iowa

In 1998, a major Iowa company approached the Tippie College of Business at the University of Iowa (TCOB) with a proposal to support development of a graduate program in engineering that featured significant business content. The company's vision was to provide general management education to engineers with the intent of keeping them involved in engineering fields. A long-time supporter of the standard Executive MBA Program and a consistent supporter of the MBA-PM Program, this company proposed that Iowa State's Engineering College provide the engineering content and that the TCOB provide the business content, with program administration directed by the TCOB.

The novelty of the proposal was the involvement of two Iowa regent institutions in a cooperative graduate program—a distinctive and hard-to-copy initiative. It took less than one year to develop the template for a five-semester program containing an equal distribution of course material from the two contributing areas; all applicants were required to hold an undergraduate degree in engineering. Student recruitment began in late 1999 even before the program was approved by the Iowa State Board of Regents in May, 2000. The first class began in October 2000. Since then, three student cohorts have graduated, and the next class is scheduled to begin in January 2012.

What distinguishes this program's initiation? The most important factor is that the combination of two existing degrees gained almost immediate external governance approval. The two degrees, an MS in systems engineering and the Executive MBA, had long been offered. The strong support from two large employers (Rockwell Collins and John Deere) facilitated the process. The Board of Regents was pleased with the cooperative nature of the program and, indeed, asked others in the system to seek out similar cooperative arrangements. Finally, the program was developed independently of the state subsidy and was offered in convenient off-site facilities "owned" by the TCOB. The critical success factors were the two existing graduate degrees, financial sustainability, employer sponsorship, and off-campus delivery.

There are many other examples where a streamlined approval process has worked smoothly and quickly. Examining these successes gives credence to this approach. While it would take years, if it were even possible, to develop a new undergraduate degree program for on-campus delivery, it appears relatively easy to extend the geographical scope of existing professional graduate programs. Indeed, doing so will likely receive the enthusiastic endorsement of a governing board and, in our experience, meet with limited faculty opposition. Apparently, geographic program expansion is viewed as being complementary to existing practices and not as a direct substitute. Any new program that is viewed as a threat to the continuing subsidy of existing academic programs is resisted; familiar programs that do not threaten the continued subsidy are not.

The Hawkinson Institute Undergraduate Program in Investment Banking

It is often the case that a vision emerges gradually and deliberately. The Hawkinson Institute began as a tribute to the renowned investment banker and University of Iowa graduate, John Hawkinson. After an initial set of private donations from his friends of nearly $1 million, Hawkinson provided the funding for a $1.5 million named chair. The institute director, a retired Morgan Stanley managing director, argued that teaching investment banking was not the critical strategic issue. For him, the challenge was to place graduates in an industry located outside the Midwest. The subsequent director, who had significant investment banking experience at Goldman Sachs, developed the implementable vision that led to success.

The Hawkinson Institute became an independently functioning center (RCM) for training and placing some of the best Iowa undergraduates in starting analyst positions in investment banking. Its unique features are a total dependence on private financing; administration by highly specialized staff with significant investment banking experience; a sharp focus on student career development, internships, and placement; a close and complementary working relationship with the Department of Finance; and a direct-reporting relationship to the dean and to college fund-raising resources. The ability of the director to react quickly and decisively within the boundaries of agreed on priorities is an important key to success. The Institute was able to move quickly from providing scholarships to supporting internships when it became apparent that internships were the appropriate path to subsequent employment. The Hawkinson Institute has thrived with an effective value proposition backed up by an accommodating private stream of revenue. No time was spent by any of its directors in trying to influence university administrators because they realized that they were a resource-centered unit.

Iowa River Landing Clinic for UI Health Care: A Bold Outreach Vision

How does a public institution integrate an outward customer focus, the teaching mission, the Value Net, rivalry, complementors, and financial independence? A good example is the Iowa River Landing Clinic. University of Iowa Health Care, which includes one the larger academic medical programs in the United States, is developing a large off-campus ambulatory care facility that will be completed in 2012. The facility will feature several prominent clinics with the latest diagnostic and treatment technologies, and it will complement off-campus quick-care clinics and a UI Sports Medicine Clinic that opened successfully in 2009. The 150,000-square-foot building and related furnishings and equipment are projected to cost $73 million, and will be staffed by the permanent faculty and staff of the UI Medical School. An executive medical director, with related experience at the Cleveland Clinic, was hired to oversee leadership and management functions. The facility is located about two miles from the main campus in a joint-use development that features a major hotel, restaurants, various shops, a large micro brewery, and, importantly, accessible parking. Many of these services are Value Net complementors of ambulatory care. For example, immediate access to a new Marriott Hotel is a distinct advantage. The site is strategically, and attractively, located along the Iowa River quite near the intersection of I-80 and I-380, which is one of the most important transportation intersections in the Midwest.

The interesting aspect of this project is its focus on customer service. Supporting physicians and staff will bring their services to the site and provide access at times that are most convenient to patients, many of whom will be private-pay and those with premier insurance coverage. Currently, too many on-campus clinics offer a weekly pattern of service that accommodates physicians but does not make effective use of clinical equipment and clinic capacities or accommodate patients. The River Landing Clinic will require a change in the cultural orientation of some providers, from their own preferences for clinical hours to customer preferences. The intended benefits of the relocation are to free up much needed inpatient space on campus, to increase clinical revenues, and to grow market share in a contested environment for medical care. The vision for the program is clearly articulated, but the issue is whether providers who are quite used to the culture of an academic medical center will adjust their behavior to the delivery requirements of a financially self-sustaining ambulatory clinic that must function efficiently.

The traditional function of clinical care units in academic medical centers has been to complement the teaching mission, with many of the specialty clinics required for medical school accreditation, as they still are. The teaching mission of medical schools and compensation of physicians were subsidized by taxpayers, and the budget allocations proceeded through a centrally managed General Education Fund. In recent years, this traditional model has been turned on its head. Clinical revenues are increasingly required to support both the teaching and the research missions of academic health centers. The new financial model is based on resource-responsibility management principles. The bold vision directing the River Landing project reflects the new reality of higher fees and lower subsidy that confronts all of public higher education.

Academic Enterprises: Distinguishing Features of Public Business Schools

In Chapter 5, we examined the features of enterprises, which are doing well in the public university environment. While many successful enterprises are outside the academic core, there are examples of academic programs that can achieve enterprise status, particularly as the public subsidy diminishes. In this section, we describe public business schools as emergent enterprises. There are certainly other good examples, including medicine and a variety of liberal arts concentrations that feature strong student demand, increasing tuition revenue, low-cost delivery, promising access for graduates to job markets and graduate programs, and supportive alumni.[4] We select business schools because we know them best. For major public business schools, competitive markets have come. Reactions to changes in the environment have led to the emergence of a set of defining characteristics of modern business schools that distinguish them from many other programs: reliance on tuition revenue and private donations; closer working relationships with external constituents, including recruiters and alumni; significant attention to student needs; a focus on cross-disciplinary instructional programs; and the necessity to subsidize research activities from tuition and private support.

External Focus

Many business programs derive as much as 75 percent of their revenue from tuition, up to 20 percent from private donations, and as little as 5 percent from state support and funded research.[5] The move toward financial self-reliance is the result of environmental factors and competitive forces, including rivalry with well-funded private university business schools, intense media exposure from rankings, rising student expectations, greater connection to the business community, economies of scope in instruction, and a solid donor base. The opportunity for business programs to become independent of state subsidies arises because student demand responds to the external focus of program content and to the changing needs of job markets. Systematic attention is paid to the development of effective processes, in part because accreditation standards focus on process evaluations as precursors to effective outcomes.[6] Most prominent business schools adopt a structured planning process that is based on time-bound, measurable goals and includes a sustaining financial strategy.

The ability to create and capture value will diminish if the competitive challenges are unmet. Graduate MBA programs, which receive the most media attention, require investment in and considerable attention to developing a program image. Reliance on tuition and fees requires promotion of programs, provision of selective grants and scholarships, and effective recruitment and placement strategies. Investments are made in outside-the-classroom activities, including speaking and writing programs and community engagement. The changing requirements of labor markets, which are viewed as influencing student interests, dictate modifications in programs and activities.

The most successful modern MBA programs have evolved into "pull" delivery systems with emphasis on employer preferences. The adoption of lockstep programs, in which students proceed as a cohort through at least the core of the program, provides a mechanism for coordination of emergent themes and attainment of prerequisite skills for each course. Alumni play a meaningful role by providing mentoring and placement opportunities. Business schools also react regionally to create convenient off-campus programs for full-time employees and globally to allow creative international interactions. Some schools have launched graduate programs in international markets, including China, India, and the Middle East. These not only provide new opportunities; they also require assessment about whether they meet student expectations and provide acceptable quality.[7]

The nature of MBA programs has changed dramatically. Offering integrated programs has implications for their organization, often requiring a matrix decision structure with reporting responsibilities to both department chairpersons and program directors. Business schools have expanded their part-time and executive programs, which are scheduled during evenings and weekends for students who are working full-time. The challenge is to provide relevant content to working (nontraditional) students and to recognize that the programs must be offered when and where students want to attend. The adjustment of faculty culture required to accommodate off-campus programs has been significant.[8] MBA programs have modified the academic calendar, altered the traditional frequency of weekly class meetings, and adjusted course length from the standard semester schedule.[9] These programs are student-centric. The financial success of these programs underwrites faculty research.

Unfunded Research and Its Dependence on Instruction
For major business schools, tuition revenue and private donations are the key drivers of success. In contrast to science-based disciplines, there is little

external research funding; successful business research programs are linked to the success of tuition-supported instruction. As in all areas, goals can conflict. Since one of the purposes of instruction is to provide students with subsequent employment opportunities, the discipline-based skills required to build distinctive research programs (applied mathematics, computer science, economics, psychology, sociology, and statistics) do not always complement instructional needs. Moreover, the academic training required to become an excellent economist or applied statistician may not connect culturally to the contextual teaching mission.[10]

Misalignment between teaching and discipline-based research interests can produce both financial difficulties and cultural challenges. For the financial model to work, research-oriented faculty need help to understand the benefits of a focus on teaching. They can also be encouraged to motivate their research-related material with contextual examples. Business schools have come to recognize these benefits and reward faculty members who teach successfully in high-demand areas, even when these areas contribute little to research.[11]

The quality of research has not suffered from the stronger customer focus in instructional programs. Research in accounting, finance, marketing, and operations has improved in quantity and quality as business schools have learned how to develop and present attractive instructional programs at the undergraduate and, especially, the graduate level. The main reasons that research has flourished are the infusion of tuition revenues and the increase in private fund-raising that develops when donors are willing to support enhanced programmatic orientations.

Advisory Board

Every top business school has an external board whose members are leaders in the business, not-for-profit, and academic communities.[12] These boards have limited fiduciary responsibility and usually serve in an advisory capacity. While bylaws and operation differ among schools, typically board members are nominated and selected by a board committee in consultation with the dean for a specified, usually renewable, term. Meetings are held at least twice and as many as four times per year.[13] Ideal advisory board members include both alumni interests and recruiter perspectives, and provide guidance on initiatives and strategic decisions. Their specific contributions include (1) encouraging college leadership to develop an outside-in view of customer needs (students, business, government, employers); (2) providing personal and corporate financial support, often in the millions of dollars; (3) facilitating academic-program extensions; (4) assisting in the development of new programs; (5) encouraging and supporting entrepreneurship and similar programs and (6) supporting public/private partnerships.

An important contribution of the board is to provide political support for business education and to express this support to university leadership.[14] One area where boards may insert themselves into faculty governance is the appointment of the dean. In our experience, their participation enriches and expedites the search process, and can often can bring board and faculty members together in positive ways.

Challenges and Threats to the Business School Model

Public business schools evolved because they were forced to adjust to a changing competitive landscape, market forces, and media scrutiny. Even so, they still have their critics. Certainly, not all activities and outcomes are laudable. In particular, there is too much program imitation and not enough distinctive investment. There is considerable criticism regarding the values and ethics expressed in business education, much coming from within. Some see business education as being "too vocational."[15] At the graduate level, questions are raised about points of emphasis, including profit maximization, the use of rational choice models, teaching ingrained beliefs in efficient markets, and the failure to address major global problems of poverty, inequality, or environmental degradation (see Podolny [2009]). These are legitimate concerns, as they are directed both at the fundamental purpose of higher education and at its ideology. Within universities, which are rarely governed by people sympathetic to business, there has always been an underlying tension about the appropriateness of professional education. Indeed, such arguments are used to justify extensive cross-subsidy from business programs to traditional areas in the arts, engineering, humanities, and basic sciences, which are viewed as being closer to the true mission of higher education.

Once one leaves the example of major public graduate business programs, new issues arise. Demand for business education over the past thirty years has risen dramatically. Undergraduate degrees in business dominate those in all other areas and have for decades. In 2009, over 20 percent of U.S. bachelor's degrees and 25 percent of master's degrees were awarded in business, a percentage with considerable staying power.[16] High demand is accompanied by an expanded willingness to enroll large numbers in established programs and to add new programs. Still, even with supply increasing, U.S. employment forecasts by Carnevele, Strohl and Melton (2011) suggest a gap of 2 million college graduates in 2020, with business degrees still in high demand. Programs in business are also expanding on a global basis. As reported by AACSB (2011)), there are over 13,000 business programs worldwide, and the pace of growth is continuing.

The global expansion of business education presents both challenges and threats to long-term viability, particularly with respect to quality and distinctiveness. The lack of barriers to entry for both not-for-profit and for-profit programs and limited quality control have led to growth in new programs that are not accredited.[17] It is not clear that this program expansion is always accompanied by sound strategic planning; instead, many programs appear to have been started simply to generate net revenue. If prospective students cannot differentiate on quality, the only available option is to compete on tuition, which is the hard lesson learned from countless examples in competitive markets.

The premier public business schools have developed defensible positions in these competitive markets. Their chosen positions, which are predicated on distinctive quality, are less threatened than those programs that develop low-cost strategies and depend on politically sensitive funding sources. Even more vulnerable are programs that uncomfortably straddle high- and low-cost positions. Colleges and universities that use the tuition revenue captured from low-cost business students to subsidize high-cost programs may be threatening the attractiveness and quality of business programs.

Summary and Recommendations

Success in competitive environments requires developing defensible positioning strategies and focused programs that provide sustainable value to prospective students. As stated by Porter and Kramer (2011), *"The essence of strategy is choosing a unique positioning and a distinctive value chain to deliver on it."* Universities can usefully adopt some aspects of the described template for enhancing value. The process we have outlined leads to key strategic discussions. What areas will expand? What areas will contract? What areas merit continued subsidy? The suggested criterion for measuring value is private and public willingness to pay net of the opportunity cost of resources, and it is possible to place monetary valuations on these constructs. With growth in tuition revenue, the planning framework and financial modeling that incorporate RCM principles appear to have wider applicability, especially for programs that lack opportunities for externally funded research but offer attractive instructional options. Overall, major business schools have become much more responsive primarily because they are *not* subsidized. They have reacted to external change and have exhibited an entrepreneurial focus that is primed to take on the challenges of deteriorating public support.

The environmental factors that have affected business for years now appear to be the key external drivers for public universities as a whole. Competition implies that public universities can achieve greater financial independence as they become more precise in their aspirations, actions, and implementation plans. Being able to identify and target students who benefit from the distinctive identity of a school, and delivering value by investing in the appropriate elements of the value chain, are key. Focused actions can lead to improved program coherency, better administration of internal systems, and greater control of resources that are guided by transparent metrics and accountability. We believe that those academic areas that are now financially self-reliant provide one useful template for others to adopt.

12   Public No More

Our remedies oft in ourselves do lie.

—*William Shakespeare*

A Trajectory Toward Privatization

Beginning in the mid-1800s with the inauguration of the first land-grant institutions in the United States, taxpayers viewed public universities as fulfilling broad societal needs, and accordingly, were willing to underwrite most of
the costs. The idea of low-cost access to a quality education was a powerful
motivating influence, especially when there were few private-sector alternatives. State governments, in particular, recognized the need to develop critical
local skills, an educated workforce, and centers for applied research. The initial impetus for establishing many of these institutions was a mission like that
articulated in the *Wisconsin Idea,*[1] in which the boundaries of the university
encompassed the boundaries of the state and research was applied to solve
problems that would improve the health, quality of life, and environment for
all Wisconsin citizens. The students who benefited were expected to remain
in the state, to contribute to state income, and to pay future taxes to support
ongoing investment in public higher education. In effect, there was support
for a repeatable intergenerational contract linking current students to taxpayers. The resulting high-subsidy–low-tuition model of support for public
higher education remained in place for over a century.

Where taxpayer support of public universities was once rationalized as a
way to provide local instruction and research benefits, the major public university of today is a global entity, attracting faculty and students from all over

the world and conducting broadly accessible research. In this environment, rapid growth in the supply of higher education and the inability of states to identify and capture returns has diminished both interest in and capacity for state funding. Specifically, the permanent decline in state support per student over the last twenty-five years reflects several underlying tensions: (1) the incremental financial needs of alternative societal programs, especially Medicaid, corrections, K–12, and underfunded public pensions; (2) reluctance to impose higher taxes on the struggling middle class; (3) skepticism concerning the marginal benefits accruing to the state associated with the funding of large, nonexclusive research and teaching enterprises; (4) recognition that students will capture the private returns to education through higher lifetime incomes; (5) reluctance to underwrite the education of out-of-state and foreign students; and (6) the notion that privatization of higher education, with its focus on competition, efficiency, and entrepreneurial initiative may offer improved educational outcomes at lower cost.

As state support for public higher education has declined, the federal government has not picked up the funding shortfall. Rather, federal support has been directed to loan programs, which have the effect of shifting the responsibility for financing higher education from parents and taxpayers to students, who are required to repay in the future what they borrow today. The rationale for these loan programs is that it makes sense that those who receive the primary education benefit should eventually pay for it.[2] A reduction in state support decreases the supply of educational services, while an increase in federal loan support raises demand. It is not surprising, therefore, that there is upward pressure on tuition. With state and federal actions causing taxpayer support of universities to be replaced with tuition revenue, higher education is becoming by default a private good.

Mission Conflicts and Intransient Cultures

The decline in state support and the rise in tuition portend a move by universities to become more self-reliant. But replacing lost state revenue with tuition introduces a host of challenges. A resistant internal culture presents substantial obstacles, including entrenched ideologies that can thwart efficient allocation of resources. Public universities offer both a vast array of self-supported and subsidized activities and programs. What might be perceived of as being "fair" under a system of state support becomes "unfair" when revenue is derived from students and private donors, whose preferences do not align with traditional offerings. In a colorful characterization, Gordon Winston (1999, 31) observes, "The donative-commercial firm [the terms used to describe a public university] is essentially part church and part car dealer— devoted partly to charity and partly to commerce, to 'ideology' and 'rationality.' The result is a tension between doing good and doing well."

Many lament the loss of "doing good," but what can justify the continuation of academic programs that lack both student and societal demand, are expensive to offer, and have no sources of revenue once public support declines? If no one is willing to support a program financially, there is no willingness to pay and therefore no expressed value. When pushed, many advocates of the societal benefits of high-cost programs simply expect somebody else to pay for them. Across-the-board cuts in college budgets in response to a decline in state support have acted to sustain such programs, but this cannot be the ultimate answer. It is the subsidized academic core that will have to adjust to the new reality of "public no more." Where entrenched culture is an impediment, independence from subsidies for academic enterprises will not come quickly. Accounting and budgeting systems have to track revenues and costs accurately; incentives have to be aligned.

Inefficient internal cross subsidies, facilitated by public support, have developed because there is little ability to vary tuition across programs as a way to confront significant variation in the unit costs of programs. Expenditures on programs are a matter of choice, and academic programs are delivered the way they are *because* they are subsidized, not because it is the most efficient way to do so. Increasing base tuition in order to accommodate chaotic, cross-subsidized budgets is a non-sustainable exercise. For one thing, higher base tuition not only closes the pricing gap with elite private universities, it also invites rivalry from for-profit colleges.

Adopting a system of self-reliance threatens areas that have traditionally been subsidized. Most threatened are the high-cost arts and science-based areas, along with highly subsidized basic research and Ph.D. programs. The challenge is to determine which areas to subsidize based on their value added to the university's mission and to society. This issue is particularly critical in the STEM areas, where the external social benefits of research and instruction arguably exceed the benefits that universities and the producing faculty can capture. Loss of state support also threatens the quality of teaching, especially if there is limited flexibility to increase instruction while still protecting research. These factors expose public research universities to a declining market share, especially when competitors exist that do not feature research missions and can more easily expand their instructional capabilities. The permanent loss of state funding and the currently misaligned financial model of public universities are forcing the transition toward self-reliance.

The competitive positioning of research public universities will require subsidy if it is to prosper. Conversion to a market-directed environment, with its emphasis on private returns, will threaten these valued areas, especially in basic research. In general, there is social value (high consumer surplus) associated with subsidizing areas where fixed costs are high and demand elasticities are low. These are the areas where competitive markets will work against the positioning of public research universities; this is one reason why university symphonies require public support and undergraduate business programs do not.

Some of the basic conditions for self-reliance are already in place. Many traditional areas in liberal arts and business are less threatened by declining public support because there is a willingness to pay commensurate with their low-cost delivery structures. Paradoxically, while a high-tuition–low-subsidy model actually favors these programs, their governance structures and traditional cultures, particularly in the liberal arts, are a source of resistance to any accommodation that emphasizes greater self-reliance.

The Way Forward: The Public-No-More University

The traditional contract between universities and taxpayers provided financial support to universities in return for their giving up the decision making regarding access criteria and tuition rates. As support wanes, restrictions on access and tuition hamper universities' ability to adapt to threatening external forces. The most critical of these forces are rising competition from local and international competitors, shifting technologies for delivering instruction, greater understanding and appreciation of what tuition and fees actually purchase, and an altered willingness to pay by students, parents, and taxpayer. As market pressures increase, the basis of external discretion over tuition and access will weaken.

The social-planning objective of providing enhanced access for residents is evolving toward a greater focus on private returns to education and market competition. This evolution exposes the fragilities of extensive internal cross-subsidies. With too little tuition variation designed to support access and significant variation in program unit costs, internal cross-subsidies are inefficient. If subsidies that support research, low-demand, and high-cost programs can no longer be relied upon, then public universities cannot easily protect the inefficiencies associated with them. In particular, it will become impossible to offer low tuitions for all high-cost programs. This means that some programs will narrow their scope or disappear altogether. The demands for financial self-sufficiency, the success of "enterprises," and increasing market competition will force scope-related choices and create the need to develop distinctive positioning strategies. With regard to vertical scope, the enhanced freedom to outsource activities to market specialists will provide another necessary measure of financial flexibility.

Critical to a new approach will be top-down strategic planning that is sensitive to issues of financial sustainability, efficient operation, and quality. Aspirational values and goals will no longer suffice for strategic planning. Clearly defined and communicated plans, measureable time-bound goals, progress monitoring, effective communication, and a financial roadmap to achieve goals will be needed to implement change. None of these changes can occur without a reorganization of governance and financial information. The possible replacement of CAM with RCM, with its emphasis on incentive alignment, entrepreneurial ventures, transparency, and operational efficiencies, is a likely first step. But building into an incentive-motivated RCM budgeting process those unit costs that prevailed under a subsidized CAM will perpetuate inefficient patterns of cross subsidy and inhibit incentives for needed change.

The hourglass power structure of public higher education that places most decisions in the hands of regents and legislatures at one end and in faculty at the other will have to change to permit central administrators more discretion. Public universities require flexibility to set differential tuitions to cover educational costs and to respect differences in willingness to pay. Flexibility is required in setting enrollment criteria, reducing operating costs, and modifying strategies. The power to obstruct change needs to be replaced by incentives to support it.

The new normal in public-no-more higher education will involve lower levels of government support, greater attention to competitive tuitions, purposefully determined quality, and willingness to succeed (or fail) in a broader range of entrepreneurial activities. Public-no-more universities can simultaneously invest in and cut academic programs. They can invest in identified areas of strength and communicate those investments, and they can cut and downsize areas that are neither critical to their strategic vision nor able to generate self-sustaining resources.

Significantly, the models and templates to carry out these measures already exist; they are being used by some professional schools and various university enterprises. Some academic programs are succeeding without subsidies. In Chapter 11, we focused on public business schools as an important case, but there are others within the traditional academic core that have the potential for greater independence, particularly among professional graduate programs. These programs will succeed if they face the competitive threats in their markets and respond by cutting costs, innovating, and developing self-sufficient, fee-based systems. The tuition derived from this customer-focused approach is often supplemented by the growing contributions of a successful donor base of graduates and supporters. Other academic programs are essentially succeeding by default, because their tuition revenue is rising and their expenditures are constant or even declining.

One challenge is for university leadership to recognize and accept that the diminished role of state government funding is permanent. Strategic recognition includes understanding the behavior of new and existing rivals, selecting a defensible positioning strategy, and focusing on the capabilities that are required to operate effectively. A vision that differentiates a university is important. Imitating others or continuing with an excessively broad program scope leads to ineffective straddling positions that are threatened by both low-cost providers and high-value niche players. The program scope of public universities can be aligned with permanent societal, donor, and student demand patterns. Under a defined vision and with a reduced scope, some areas will still have to be subsidized, but the critical issue is to determine which areas and by how much. Every university will make different choices; there is no "right" or "wrong" mix of programs but only consistency with the chosen strategic intent.

The defining characteristics for a public-no-more university include:

Creating a vision and value proposition that identifies
- Programs in which the university will excel
- Programs that the university will not provide
- A systematic process for identifying emerging areas of study and eliminating others
- Time-bound goals and metrics
- A reflective financial strategy

Adopting a high-tuition–high-financial aid model where

- Differential tuitions are established across programs
- In-state and out-of-state tuitions reflect delivery costs
- The government continues to provide support to offset the costs of basic research
- Student financial aid is based on ability to pay

Transforming the governance process with

- Vision-based leadership
- Diminished reliance on internal governance
- A reduced management role for the state and system-wide governing bodies

Encouraging entrepreneurial strategies that display

- Increased market sensitivity and accountability
- Incentive-based budgetary models

University systems in which each campus acts as previously described need to adopt a set of self-reliant strategies. The roles for multicampus systems include encouraging synergies whenever possible and, importantly, providing flexibility for each campus to develop a distinctive vision and accompanying revenue model. Differential tuitions can account for differences in targeted student populations and program costs. The services provided by system governance should be evaluated on the basis of cost relative to benefits; a decision should be made for each service to be provided centrally, moved to the campuses, outsourced, or discontinued.

A critical aspect of any plan for self-reliance involves how the tax rate is set for the underlying units. Attempts to encourage efficient behavior and entrepreneurial efforts can easily be undone by a nontransparent tax assessment. A credible, predictable tax-setting process based on well-articulated rules and measurable parameters is critical to an efficient system.

The Challenge to Acceptance

Some leaders in higher education are critical of the possible adoption of business-style budgeting and planning practices that are market driven and focused on treating students as consumers. Often, references are made to "corporate-style" governance structures as potentially replacing shared-governance traditions. One stated concern is that productivity in higher education will increasingly be measured by tuition and funded-research revenues, leading to less support for research in the humanities, arts, and social sciences. A related concern involves challenges to the liberal core curriculum, possibly by replacing or at least modifying it with courses that fulfill the employment, vocational, and technical needs of the economy. Many question moves to achieve efficiency at the expense of equity, and this questioning is legitimate, but, perhaps, moot. Our point is that achieving fairness that can only be sustained by cross subsidy is becoming an infeasible option as taxpayers support for higher education decreases.

The positive response to concerns over business-type approaches is to recognize that all programs and activities have to be supported by somebody, with the alternatives being students, enterprises, taxpayers, and donors. Appealing to donors provides little general support, since donors have strong specific preferences. Increasing tax rates on enterprises is self-defeating if it leads to efficient units subsidizing inefficient programs.

If governing boards and faculty governance structures are willing to relinquish control, will university leadership assume it? How quickly will leaders emerge? How many and how soon will others follow? Too many university leaders have been conditioned in their views by the low-tuition–high-subsidy environment. Indeed, it would have been impossible for them to become leaders without espousing traditional values of entitlement, inclusiveness, diversity, consensus building, and acquiescence to commonly expressed, but often underfunded, societal goals. All of these goals are laudable, indeed defining. Nonetheless, the goals of distinctiveness, financial independence, cost efficiency, and a sharply defined meritocracy have become the new keys to excellence for public universities.

The Future

With the transition to "public no more," will universities and society be better off? To date, the reshaping of public higher education has been too much by default and not enough by design. The major consideration in evaluating the social benefit of public no more is whether universities will be able to overcome the hindrances embodied in entrenched governing boards, university leadership, and traditional aspects of faculty governance. Tradeoffs that face resistance will need to be made by university leaders. Some of the most difficult involve identifying and subsidizing activities such as basic research, where returns extend beyond those captured by individuals. To do so, leadership can balance various entrepreneurial activities with the differently motivated activities of the academic core. Leaders can encourage a growing set of entrepreneurial activities that operate differently from traditional activities but whose financial success is critical to sustain both research and teaching in selected academic areas. Explaining the importance and impact of basic research will be especially important to justify funding from other sources as state support declines. A major consideration for evaluating the social benefit of the "public-no-more" university is whether it will be able to overcome some of the hindrances embodied in entrenched governance cultures. The best response is to make vision-directed program choices that are supported by sustainable financial models with aligned incentives. This does not rule out continuing some internal cross-subsidies, but it does require more explicit and transparent strategic choices about what areas to subsidize. The key ingredient is the parallel development of vision, strategic positioning, and credible financial models. The jettisoning of entitlement and the embracing of focused purpose and financial accountability express what we mean by "public no more."

Will the long-standing tradition of excellence in America's top public universities continue? Or will it erode as state support continues to diminish? The demise of the major research public university is neither immediate nor inevitable. There are abundant challenges ahead, but the fate of the distinctive public university lies not in the hands of the state or the taxpayer, but rather within the confines of the university itself. If the vast array of public university resources can be channeled into distinctive visions that create measurable value based on sound financial practices, there is indeed a bright future. The path ahead is not easy; there are many impediments and entrenched beliefs that must be overcome. Will public universities retain their distinction? In the end, one key question remains: Can strategy trump culture?

Notes

Chapter 2

1. The tuition–subsidy issue can challenge the viability of a government. For example, when the British government under Tony Blair first introduced tuition rates for all public universities in the early 2000s, the viability of the New Labour party was threatened. In 2010, the coalition of Conservatives and Liberal Democrats was ideologically divided on this important legislation. Conservatives preferred to increase resident tuition from £3,225 to £7,000, while Liberal Democrats preferred to eliminate tuition altogether, mimicking the approach taken by the governments of Wales and Scotland. Many compromise solutions, including the newly proposed "graduate tax," were offered up as a way to address this contentious political divide. Tuition issues in the United Kingdom are discussed in Grimston (2009).

2. Instructional quality depends on the initial preparedness of students and on spending on instruction; research quality depends on the type and selectivity of faculty and on the amount spent supporting research.

3. See U.S. Census Bureau (2009).

4. Ninety-six universities, public and private, are defined by the Carnegie classification as "very high research." There is considerable overlap with those listed by The Association of American Universities (AAU).

5. The pressing issues of sustaining research support are discussed by the Committee on Prospering in the Global Economy (2007, chap. 7). A recently established Congressional commission will examine the research funding issues associated with declining state subsidies (see *Chronicle of Higher Education* [2010]).

6. There is a literature documenting the effects of declining state support on public higher education with respect to both instructional and research missions. Papers by Kane, Orszag, and Gunter (2003) and Kane and Orszag (2004) provide empirical

documentation of these and related issues. McPherson, Gobstein, and Shulenburger (2010) examine the responses of public universities to the decline in state support and expose misconceptions regarding the behavior of higher education costs. Ehrenberg (2006) foretells the "privatization" of major public universities. Trends in college pricing are provided by the College Board Advocacy and Policy Center (2010a). The patterns of state subsidy, net tuition, and enrollment across the individual states are available from SHEEO (2010b).

7. See College Board Advocacy and Policy Center (2010a, table 6C) for averaged published tuition and fees state by state from 2004–05 to 2010–11.

8. According to Iowa senate minority leader Paul McKinley (Kinkade, 2011), "If they [students] are concerned about rising tuition, they need to go and talk to the universities and say, 'You need to run a leaner, more efficient, more productive university'—it isn't the state legislature that is causing them to raise tuition."

9. Duderstadt (2005) discusses these issues with reference to public universities in Michigan. He argues that the adage "Don't let the facts get in the way of a good story" applies to much of the discussion concerning the financing of public higher education.

10. NCES (2010) reports that tuition, including room and board, in constant dollars rose by 60 percent for public institutions between 1983–84 and 2003–04.

11. One way to understand directional changes in the quality of public higher education is to examine expenditure patterns, which show that real expenditure on instruction is declining (see Desrochers, Lenihan, and Wellman [2010]). The implications of these spending patterns are discussed by Ehrenberg (2011), and their contributions to declining six-year graduation rates are evaluated by Bound, Lovenheim, and Turner (2009). Evidence also suggests that high-school graduates are increasingly less prepared for postsecondary instruction (see ACT [2009]).

12. See the college ranking lists for 2008 through 2011 in *U.S. News & World Report*, http://colleges.usnews.rankingsandreviews.com/best-colleges/rankings/national-universities.

13. We will use the concept of "efficiency" to refer to the relationship between price (tuition) and the marginal cost of education. An efficient allocation of resources is one where price equals marginal cost. The common reference to efficiency often means the elimination of wasteful spending. These two notions can be confusing, and we will attempt to be clear in the way we use them.

14. Okun (1975) argues that the most important trade-off for many societal issues is between equality (equity) and efficiency; that is, subsidies that seem fair can lead to inefficient allocations of resources. While the issue of who pays for higher education is often framed as one of equity, we will argue that there are situations where increases in the public subsidy increase both efficiency and equity, but this requires ignoring certain distributional issues. For example, if the real monetary equivalent of the benefit received by some exceeds the cost incurred by others, it is possible to argue that equity has improved in the sense that the beneficiaries can reimburse the providers and still be better off.

15. The percent of part-time faculty is documented by IPEDS (2010). See also Ehrenberg (2011) for an expanded discussion of the consequences of substituting part-time for permanent faculty.

16. Fixing any price where demand exceeds supply results in the rationing of products and services. The question then becomes how to establish enrollment priority.

17. These trends, and others, are apparent in the data summaries provided by the College Board Advocacy and Policy Center (2010b). An insightful summary of the recent financial behavior of higher education costs is provided by McPherson and Shulenburger (2008), who argue that tuition revenue has replaced state support one to one.

18. The University of California, Irvine (2007) report and a similar report by the University of Illinois (2010) follow a familiar approach: committees are assigned specific areas to review, often including administrative service, and they develop separate, unlinked reports that list potential areas for cost saving and for increasing productivity. There is an implicit assumption that existing strategies and resource allocation processes will continue; the predictable outcomes are modest changes and little saving. Suggestions usually include, paradoxically, ways to *increase* instructional budgets by reducing faculty teaching loads, increasing faculty salaries, and reducing fringe benefits.

19. The data supporting the listed features come from the College Board Advocacy and Policy Center (2010a, 2010b); NCES (2010); McPherson and Shulenburger (2010), who draw extensively from the work of Wellman Desrochers, and Lenihan (2008); SHEEO (2010a); and the Digest of Education Statistics (2009).

Chapter 3

1. A Pew Research Center poll (Taylor et al., 2011) asked about the affordability of higher education and whether graduates were satisfied. Some 57 percent of parents of prospective students doubted that college was worth the cost, while 86 percent of graduates indicated that it was a good investment.

2. There are goods whose social benefits exceed their private benefits, but there are no market mechanisms for capturing them. National defense, basic scientific research, and pollution mitigation are often cited as examples of "public" goods. While a case is often made for the public benefits of higher education, governments are expressing a lowering of their willingness to pay.

3. The value of higher education decreases if graduates are unable to find acceptable places in the labor market(see Jacobs [2010]).

4. P&G (Proctor & Gamble) is seeking to gain a stronger market share in emerging markets by eliminating costly features that differentiate its products. This strategic decision involves trade-offs. The company has long sustained its strategic position (value proposition) by developing high-margin differentiated products to high-income markets in the United States and Europe. Similar choices face public universities if they are to succeed in the global market.

5. Enhanced airport security and its associated delays impose costs that adversely affect Southwest Airlines' value proposition, which features easy access and convenient low-cost service. Rapid increases in gasoline prices play havoc with the value proposition of Wal-Mart, given its lower-income customer base. Changes in the racial and demographic composition of the entering student body at the University of Texas pose special problems for the sustainability of the institution's value proposition, which has long focused on its appeal to middle-class students.

6. In November 2010, students across England engaged in the third of a series of active, sometimes violent, protests over a proposal by the new coalition government (Conservative and Liberal Democrat) to increase tuition to as much as £9,000 from the current level of £3,200. The proposal was judged as "unfair" to students but also as the only feasible option for managing public funds in an environment of fiscal tightening and enrollment expansion. This issue continued in 2011 to threaten the current coalition government's viability. Similar student protests are also taking place in 2011 in California.

7. Consider the following representation: $V = (W - R - A) + (R + A - C) = W - C$, where V is total value, W is willingness to pay, R is tuition revenue, A is public appropriation, and C is opportunity cost of education. There are a many ways of distributing a given value between consumers and producers, and there are many ways of distributing the burden of paying for education. The economics literature has long been concerned with how markets can be organized (monopoly, oligopoly, monopolistic competition, and perfect competition) to both create and distribute value. Much research by engineers and applied statisticians has focused on the techniques for improving elimination of waste processes.

8. Opportunity costs include a rate of return sufficient to retain resources in their current activity; thus, human and physical resources must earn at least what they can obtain in their next best opportunity. The break-even constraint rules out the earning of economic profit, which is a return in excess of opportunity cost.

9. University of Wisconsin, Office of the Chancellor, (2010b).

10. University of Iowa, Office of the Provost (2010).

11. For the strategic plan of UW-Madison, see University of Wisconsin, Office of the Chancellor (2010a); for Penn State, see Pennsylvania State University (2009); and for UC, Irvine, see University of California, Irvine (2007).

12. The distinction between "search" goods, where the quality of a product can be ascertained by the consumer prior to purchase, and "experience" goods, where the quality is learned after purchase, is developed by Nelson (1970).

13. Large lectures given by truly distinguished faculty can provide a unique educational experience. For decades, the eminent space physics professor, James Van Allen, taught basic astronomy to Iowa's undergraduates; this was an unmatchable experience for generations of students. Regardless of class size, to be able to learn from economists Martin Feldstein and Greg Mankiw at Harvard University or John Taylor at Stanford University is both special and distinctive. Experiences such as these unite research and instruction in a unique and effective manner that is difficult for others to copy.

14. In corporate finance, there is much discussion of the so-called "conglomerate discount," where the combined businesses are given a lower value by the market than if they were valued independently. Public universities have conglomerate-like characteristics, and the question is whether their "corporate" administration increases or destroys value.

15. See Delta Cost Project (2008), which compares spending by category for 2,300 public and private nonprofit colleges and universities.

Chapter 4

1. The accounting relation links changes in the university budget to changes in contributing revenues and can be used as a descriptive model for explaining tuition setting.

2. The privatization issue is discussed by Ehrenberg (2006), who endorses the argument made by John Wiley, then chancellor of the University of Wisconsin, that most public universities will be unable to generate the endowment and annual giving levels required to compensate for reductions in state support. The additional permanent endowment required to offset the annual state subsidy to the University of Iowa, using a 5 percent payout, is approximately $6 billion. The actual total endowment of the university in 2011 is approximately $1 billion. Moreover, as private, especially corporate, donations increase, opposition arises to corporations' "buying" the university, creating difficult dialogues about balancing the benefits of corporate financial support against the university's independence.

3. According to Kane (2006, 2007), the consensus estimates indicate that for every $1,000 increase in tuition, enrollment will decline by approximately 5 percent. We adopt a tuition elasticity of −0.50 as being a reasonable approximation in subsequent discussions.

4. There are three competing theories of cost determination in public higher education. The first is the standard notion in an economic model, in which the university selects an array of inputs to minimize total cost. The second, espoused by Howard Bowen (1980), is the "revenue theory of cost," in which, Bowen claims, universities spend whatever revenue they acquire, so the only discipline on costs is the available revenue. The third formulation is that developed by W.J. Baumol and W.G. Bowen (1966), who argue that in higher education, and in many other service industries, labor services *are* the outputs— think of a string quartet "producing" Mozart. With chronic low productivity and the need to provide competitive real wages to attract talent, there develops a "cost disease" in public higher education. Effectively, input costs increase with the general market wage, with no increase in either the quality or the quantity of produced services. Archibald and Feldman (2006) attempt to empirically distinguish between the revenue theory of cost and the "cost disease" notion as each applies to higher education.

5. For a detailed presentation of the process, see Powers (2010).

6. Ibid.

7. In this case, the subsidy is a direct offset against fixed costs. The alternative would be a per enrollment subsidy that affects the marginal cost of enrollment, with a higher subsidy rate decreasing marginal cost at every possible enrollment. The qualitative implications of these two ways of subsidizing public universities are quite similar.

8. Shortages and surpluses occur when markets fail to clear. The predications indicate that the compensation increments between college graduates and high-school graduates will continue to widen.

9. For a revealing report on the expected lifetime earnings of college majors, see Carnevale, Strohl, and Melton (2011). Long (2010) argues that universities need to better align their programs with labor-market requirements and to inform students about market conditions and prospective opportunities in various fields of study.

10. This enrollment expression can be extended to

$$\frac{E}{N} = AT^e \left(\frac{Y}{N} \right)^d$$

It is necessary to track population growth rates to carry out the accounting exercise. The elasticity assumptions we use are $e = -0.50$ and $d = 1$.

Chapter 5

1. The University of California Commission on the Future reports that "indirect cost recovery (ICR) from federal grants does not cover the true overhead costs of research at any university in the nation. The federal government is the largest sponsor of research, providing a total of about \$2.5 billion per year for research at UC. Of this, about \$600 million per year is designated for indirect costs. Yet these ICR funds fall far short of UC's actual overhead costs on federal grants, which are estimated to be as high as \$900 million." (University of California, Commission on the Future [2005, 114]).

2. The University of Iowa employs nearly 18,000 individuals, about 1,500 of whom are tenure-track faculty. The ratio of tenure-track to non-tenure-track faculty at Iowa is relatively low because of the presence of a major hospital. Within the academic core programs, the ratio is higher.

3. The amount of administrative service performed by faculty varies. In business schools and in health care fields, there has been a concerted effort to replace faculty administrative service with professional staff.

4. Case studies indicate that only about half of the return to basic research is captured by private providers; this is used as an argument to justify federal funding of research support on a national level.

5. In the recent report by Lord John Browne (2010), research is not discussed. The otherwise excellent discussion of the critical research challenges facing public higher education by McPherson, Gobstein, and Shulenburger (2010) argues that instruction

does not subsidize research and ignores the complementarity between instruction and research in seeking research support. If instruction is subsidized and there exists a complementary relationship between research and instruction, then an increase in a subsidy to instruction raises the marginal benefit to increasing the amount of research.

6. Under technical conditions of fixed proportions, there is no way to separate the cost function of instruction from that of research. Suppose that the fixed ratio of instruction to research is given by a constant k. If p_1 is the price of instruction and p_2 is the price of research, then the price of the compound output is $kp_1 + p_2$. The standard approach to describing the pricing of a single product can be applied to the compound output.

7. An efficient output mix occurs when the value of additional instruction equals the value of additional research, with both incremental values equaling the incremental revenue associated with faculty input. If the goal is to maximize the revenue an institution can earn from a given faculty input, then it is optimal to allocate more faculty input to instruction when research revenue support falls (see Winston and Zimmerman [2000]).

8. This argument is based on the claim that only specialists in a discipline can judge the research potential of new faculty (see Carmichael [(1988]). Indeed, only casual interest in the teaching ability of adjunct faculty is expressed by tenure-track faculty, but there is keen interest in hiring research-oriented faculty, likely because of the need for collegial fit and the associated commitment of a multiyear contract. Although open for possible termination after three years, the initial tenure-track contract can often result in a six-year commitment, even if tenure is not awarded. Family leave policies for both men and women can, and often do, extend the initial time commitment.

9. Increases in clinical revenues derive mostly from increases in patient visits. There is relentless downward pressure by third-party payers on reimbursement rates for medical services, especially for the expensive state-of-the-art services provided by academic medical centers.

10. Duderstadt and Womack (2003) make a similar point; see their Chapter 6 for a further discussion of the financing of public universities. Ehrenberg (2006) provides a compelling summary of recent environmental factors, which he describes as "a perfect storm."

11. At four-year public universities, aid comes from internal transfers (30 percent), federal Pell grants (25 percent), state grants (25 percent), and other sources (20 percent) (see Baum, Lapovsky, and Ma [2009]). Internal transfers reflect an allocation from high- to low-income students, and it can be argued that they develop in a revenue-neutral manner. State support for low-income students may well come at the cost of the general appropriation. Pell grants presumably provide additional revenue to the university, as do private grants and scholarships.

12. The effect of Medicaid on public higher education appropriations has been studied by Kane and Gunter (2003) and recently discussed by Orszag (2010) in a *New York Times* editorial. The relative price of Medicaid is reduced by the funding formula

where the federal government pays at least half of its cost. Under this arrangement, the reduction of a dollar in state Medicaid spending costs the state one dollar of federal matching funds, but there is no cost, and even a slight tax benefit, associated with reducing state spending on higher education. Most, if not all, of the reduction in the state public higher education subsidy can be associated with an offsetting increase in Medicaid spending. Certainly, one can claim that the health care needs of the poor might have a higher priority than the educational needs of the middle class, which is a legitimate statement of preferences, but the point here is that the Medicaid funding formula is a contributing factor to the decline in spending on public higher education.

13. A second example of an unfunded mandate facing the University of Iowa's hospitals and clinics is the long-standing mandate to treat all state prisoners with no reimbursement. With an expanding prison population in Iowa, this has had significant expenditure implications.

14. Alan Lafley (2009), retired CEO of Proctor & Gamble, argues this point most effectively. To him, P&G was becoming too insular and inwardly focused rather than focused throughout the organization on the varied needs of customers. He saw redirecting the focus as his primary job as CEO.

Chapter 6

1. One administrator asked us, "Is RCM better budgeting theory, or is it just better for the person waving the flag of RCM?"

2. The University of Florida's "RCM Manual" provides a list of RCM adopters as well as a list of institutions that are considering adoption. See University of Florida (2011).

3. Revealing financial information may be difficult. The example provided by Texas A&M of releasing faculty productivity data shows how controversial it can become when the details of cross-subsidies are publicly exposed. See Simon and Banchero (2010) and the *Wall Street Journal* (2011). One of us requested a central administration to prepare detailed summaries of earned revenue, indirect-cost recovery, and the allocated budget for each department in the university. These data, once gathered, were judged to be sensitive because they revealed the internal reallocations among departments and were never released.

4. Establishing property rights for academic programs is critical to the functioning of a market-based system. This is a proper role of regents and central administration under any type of budgeting process.

5. The University of Florida uses the concept of an "off-book" program to describe entrepreneurial programs that are self-funded and independent of state appropriations. The "on-book" programs include everything else.

6. Start-up expenditures are like any capital investment whose cost is covered by a future stream of revenue; start-up investments with negative net present value should

be avoided. The advantage of RCM is that it assigns responsibility for subsequent funding liability to the originating RC.

7. Recently the University of Iowa established a College of Public Health, and UC Irvine established a College of Law. While both aspire to financial independence, it is unlikely that either will be able to generate sufficient tuition and funded research revenue to cover their full costs.

8. Net consumer surplus, which is each student's total willingness to pay minus tuition, is the area under the inverse demand curves above tuition. While there are conceptual problems with this measure of welfare, it provides advantages in application since it is possible to approximate its magnitude by estimating the demand curve. A discussion of the issues surrounding consumer surplus is provided by Willig (1976).

9. Deans of business colleges raise the issue of how implicit taxes will be implemented. There is concern that the impact of introducing a differential tuition will be an offsetting reduction in the level of public support, as appears to be the case at the University of Minnesota. Fethke (2011a) considers conceptual issues regarding a "low-subsidy problem" in a two-stage game between a legislature and a university governing board.

10. While we do not consider social returns from higher education, claims about a loss in social welfare when public funding falls must be able to assert that social returns exceed the gains to taxpayers associated with a decrease in the subsidy.

11. Indirect costs include student financial aid, facilities management, building renewal, admissions, advising, and graduate college expenditures. Each college receives non-GEF revenues and incurs related expenditures; these are included. Benefits are not included.

12. See: University of Minnesota (2009).

13. See Iowa State University (2007).

14. The cost of the MBA-PM program per SCH is on par with the unit cost reported by the Tippie College of Business in Table 6.2. Indeed, if the college's $34.20 subsidy is subtracted from unit cost, the two are about the same.

15. The costs of the law program can be thought of as the SCH subsidy of $343.90, its "profit," which we impute as the same as the MBA-PM program's $259, and a per-SCH cost of $432.

Chapter 7

1. David Segal (2010), reporting a conversation with Nobel Laureate Robert Solow.

2. See StateNews.com (2011) for comments by Senator Tom George, Vice Chairman of the Michigan Senate Appropriations Subcommittee on Higher Education.

3. The *Grapevine* summarizes state appropriations for FY 2010–11 for public higher education. See *Grapevine* (2009).

4. For an alternative derivation of net tuition, see Winston and Zimmerman (2000). Using IPEDS survey data for the years 1986–87, 1990–91, and 1995–96, they

determine that the average net tuition, the average "production" cost, and the average subsidy for all public universities ($N = 888$) were \$1,107, \$9,366, and \$8,257, respectively; see their Table 1.

5. See College Board Advocacy and Policy Center (2010a).

6. These averages mask considerable variation. In 2010, a resident student received a subsidy of \$26,034 at the University of North Carolina at Chapel Hill, while a resident student at the University of Virginia received \$8,601 (*Richmond Times Dispatch*, 2010). In 2009–10, undergraduate students in the United States received an average of \$11,461 in aid per full-time equivalent (FTE) student, including \$6,041 in grants from all sources and \$4,883 in federal loans. Graduate students received an average of \$22,697 in aid per FTE, including \$6,371 in grants and \$15,744 in federal loans. See College Board Advocacy and Policy Center (2010b).

7. Collegemeasures.org (2010).

8. The linear (inverse) demand curve implied by these calculations is $T = 30,000 - 0.667Q$, where T is net tuition and Q is total enrollment. It is assumed that, to meet the break-even constraint, $T = c - s$, where c is unit cost and s is the subsidy per student. The so-called "dead-weight" loss associated with subsidizing tuition in this example is $(1/3)(Q_2 - Q_1)^2$.

9. There is little doubt that students from high-income families receive the most benefit from educational subsidies. Offsetting this is the fact that high-income families pay higher taxes. The distributional effects of this tax-subsidy process depend on whether the received benefits outweigh the higher taxes. Some economists, including Nobel Laureate Gary Becker (2011), argue that the transfer scheme is regressive; others, including William Johnson (2006), claim the opposite.

10. Moretti (2004) found evidence for modest spillover effects in urban areas on the high-school wages of an increase in college graduates.

11. See the position recently take by Baum and McPherson (2011).

12. In their state cross-section regressions, Goldin and Katz (1999, 53) found that state support to public higher education in 1929 was affected by the level of state income, the stability and homogeneity of the population, and the importance of such key industries as agriculture, mining, and manufacturing.

13. Easterlin (1995, 44) argues that "raising the incomes of all, does not increase the happiness of all, because the positive effect of higher income on subjective well being is offset by the negative effect of higher living level norms brought about by the growth in incomes generally." The main implication is that relative income is more important than absolute income for happiness. If this is true, then perhaps policies should be aimed at income equality rather than overall growth.

14. To put this claim in a broader context, the largest government-spending multiplier recently reported by the Obama administration was about 1.6. The controversy surrounding that particular estimate was considerable indeed, with many arguing for multipliers ranging from zero to unity. Using the estimates of government-spending multipliers for the U.S. economy, it would seem reasonable to claim that an additional dollar of state spending on public higher education would increase state GDP

somewhere from zero to $1.5. Since Iowa balances its annual budget, a reasonable balanced-budget multiplier is $1. This is a far cry indeed from $14.50.

15. University of Iowa and Tripp Umbach, (2010).

16. A simple (and familiar) multiplier formulation that nicely illustrates the point describes regional income as being composed of public and private spending. The sum of these two spending components equals the total income of the region. Public spending is given by an externally determined appropriation (subsidy). Private spending depends in fixed proportion on total income:

$$E = \alpha Y + S$$

where total expenditure (E) equals private (αY) plus public spending (S).

$$E = Y$$

where total expenditure (E) equals total income (Y). Substituting for E in the first expression and solving the resulting expression provides the income solution

$$Y^* = \frac{S}{1-\alpha}$$

or income solution, with the multiplier of

$$\frac{1}{1-\alpha}.$$

When public spending changes, the resulting change in total income is larger than the initial change in public spending because of the indirect effect, via income, that public spending has on private spending. The larger the proportion of total income spent by the private sector, the larger the spending multiplier. The critical assumption in this formulation is that there are no capacity constraints on income.

17. This suggests a contraction greater than Iowa's total state spending for Medicaid from state funds which was $606M FY2010 (see Iowa House Republicans [2010]).

18. OECD Directorate for Education (2010).

19. Ibid., table A-8.1.

20. Ibid., table A-8.4.

21. Ibid., table A-9.

22. Basu and Bhattarai (2010) review the empirical and conceptual literature on this topic and find a negative correlation between educational spending as a share of GDP and return from schooling.

23. See Muraskin, Lee, Wilner and Swail (2004) and *Chronicle of Higher Education*, 2011.

24. Fethke and Policano (2011) discuss the efficiency implications of rationing caused by low resident subsidies in capacity-constrained states like California.

25. The Commonfund (2010) annually created the Higher Education Price Index (HEPI), which is used to adjust the nominal values of the appropriation, tuition

revenue, and the General Fund. Data for the state appropriation, tuition revenue, and the General Fund are available from University of Iowa, Budget Development Office (2010); Iowa's enrollment data are from University of Iowa, Office of the Registrar (2011).

26. This already appears to be happening for low-income applicants. There is no assurance that tuition elasticity will not increase as public universities increase their tuition to cover an ever larger share of the costs of education and as fee-paying students become more price and quality sensitive.

27. The appropriation data represent a budgeted amount from *Grapevine* of Illinois State (2011). The student FTE data are from a national survey submitted to the federal government (IPEDS [2010]). When these data are adjusted to account for the primary health care allocation to the University of Iowa, there are no apparent differences in the appropriations per student across the three institutions.

28. There is acknowledgment of a public return to higher education but, citing OECD Directorate for Education (2010) data, it is argued in the report that the private benefit far exceeds the public benefit: "The argument for a private contribution to higher education has been made—and won—elsewhere as well as in England, in countries with a wide range of political values such as Australia, New Zealand, the United States, Canada, Japan, and Korea."

29. The white paper was released on September 27, 2011, to coincide with the Labour Party Conference. Among the nine principles stated are familiar ones: universities provide public benefits that exceed private benefits, build confidence in public debate, ameliorate social inequality and serve local communities. The document also argues that education is not simply a consumer good; that skill training is not the goal of education; that public universities represent a community worth preserving; that similar programs should be funded equally; and that universities had a contract with older generations.

30. This total benefit is simply the area under the inverse demand curve that lies above the common value of net tuition charged by the university.

31. The response of social welfare to an increase in the subsidy is

$$\frac{dW}{ds} = -(s+g) < 0$$

32. For summaries of the substantial research on the empirical relationship between Pell grants and higher tuition, see Gallegos (2011).

Chapter 8

1. The percentage of nonresident students officially listed in the UC-system is below that listed in comparable Big Ten universities. It is not clear whether the University of California actually attracts few nonresidents or whether its criteria for establishing residency is too easily met.

2. At the University of Iowa for 2010, resident tuition and fees were listed at $6,824; nonresident tuition and fees at $22,198. The composite (lower- and upper-division)

unit cost was estimated to be $11,002, and the total unit cost for all students was $17,053 (see Board of Regents, State of Iowa [2010b]). For 2008, the state subsidy per FTE was $7,455. It is estimated that the incoming class of first-year students for fall 2010 will consist of 53 percent nonresident students.

3. An argument is often made that consumers of higher education are ill-informed. Asymmetrical information diminishes the case for maximizing consumer welfare in favor of some type of informed-producer objective function ("the educator knows best"). Consumers of educational services seem to us to be reasonably informed about the market potential of their degrees and are possibly, at times, better informed about employment opportunities than many educators.

4. See Baumol and Bradford (1970, 269–271) and Varian (1984, 276–278) for clearly presented mathematical derivations for the main proposition. The properties of the tuition-setting formulation that we are proposing are developed in the chapter appendix for the special case of linear demand and constant marginal cost.

5. The logic underlying the proposed formulation is to set the tuition markup over the marginal program cost net of the public subsidy proportionate to the inverse of program price demand elasticity. The factor of proportionality varies directly with fixed cost. The higher the fixed cost relative to total revenue, the larger the common markup factor for each program. The more elastic the demand, the closer is the optimal tuition to marginal program cost.

6. It is interesting to use this implied relationship to "back out" estimates of unit cost. For example, using 2009–10 resident and nonresident tuition and subsidy data from the University of Iowa in the formula just given—$T_2/T_1 = c/(c - s)$—implies a unit cost of $10,764, whereas the university reports undergraduate unit instructional costs at $11,002.

7. Tuition and quality might well be related as complements. That is, an increase in the quality of education, as measured by the program's unit cost, implies that tuition elasticity of demand decreases. Consumers are less tuition sensitive for high-quality programs.

8. If willingness to pay curves are linear, nonresident tuition exceeds resident tuition if the maximum willingness to pay by nonresidents exceeds that of residents. The same logic applies to the comparison of tuition rates for any cohorts, including different majors and attendees of different universities within the same system.

9. As a way of accommodating the high-cost majors that provide high returns, the large National Union of Students in the United Kingdom has supported a proposal by Business Secretary Vince Cable to charge graduates a higher income tax rate over their lifetime to repay education costs (i.e., a graduate tax); see NUS (2011).

10. The two linear demand curves are $q_1 = 15000 - .5T_1$ and $q_2 = 15000 - .5T_2$. Here q_1 and q_2 are enrollments and T_1 and T_2 are the associated tuitions. Marginal cost is $c = \$6,500$ and fixed cost is $F = \$125M$. The welfare of each grouping is measured by net consumer surplus (NCS), which is given for each group by $NSC = q_i^{*2} / 2b_i$.

11. The legislature and the university governing board determine an incremental allocation of state funds to the public university. Resident students pay tuition

that is (substantially) below the unit cost of education. Sometimes, agreements are reached between the legislature and the governing board to link the percentage growth in the public subsidy to the percentage change in tuition, but, while well intended, such agreements are flawed because they are not credible.

12. Fethke and Policano (2010).

13. The insights developed in this section draw on pioneering work in the theory of monopolistic competition by Spence (1976) and Dixit and Stiglitz (1977).

14. In 1989, twenty elite colleges were charged with violating the price-fixing provision of the Sherman Act; see Johnston (1989).

15. Similar challenges are appearing even for the elite private U.S. institutions; see *Economist* (2010).

16. Dixit and Stiglitz (1977, 301) argue that the two approaches will yield the same price and the same number of firms: "Thus we have a rather surprising case where the monopolistic competition equilibrium is identical with the optimum constrained by the lack of lump-sum subsidies."

17. Social welfare maximization, with governing boards setting tuition, and profit maximization, with universities setting tuition, focus attention on two different margins of performance. Dixit and Stiglitz (1977) point out that the nature of demand and cost structures will greatly influence outcomes. In particular, inelastic demands combined with high-fixed-cost delivery modes, which we argue describe the very-high-research public universities, may be viable under social optimality but not visible under market competition. While there is high consumer surplus associated with inelastic demand, intense competition disfavors such offerings because it is not possible to take advantage of lower tuitions to increase profitability and thereby permit the research public university to break even. These are the very conditions that provide the rationale for the public subsidy.

18. Net consumer surplus is total willingness to pay minus tuition revenue. With a linear inverse demand, $T(q) = a/b - (1/b)q$, net consumer surplus is

$$\mathrm{NSC} = \int_0^q T(x)dx - T(q)q = (1/2b)q^2.$$

The advantages and disadvantages of this measure of consumer welfare have been discussed for over a hundred years, but the concept is still widely employed, mainly because of its ease of use and intuitive appeal.

19. Equations (2) through (5) are the necessary and sufficient conditions. Substituting the tuition expressions given by Eq. (2) into the break-even condition yields a quadratic expression for the shadow price of fixed cost, with the feasible (positive) root given by Eq. (4).

20. These conditions are an extension of the widely used (second best pricing) formulation described by Baumol and Bradford (1970) to include the enrollment subsidies.

21. The formulation selected here is chosen because it seems apparent that the university is granted a franchise by the legislature, and ultimately the legislature controls the allocation of the public budget.

22. A common argument is made that, because residents or their parents pay state taxes, their education in the state should be subsidized. This claim makes little sense if residents who study elsewhere are denied similar support. Why, according to this argument, should an Iowa student who attends the University of Illinois not receive support that reflects his family's tax payments in Iowa? Reciprocity agreements among states do address this issue.

Chapter 9

1. Crosby (1979) makes the point that inefficient organizations can produce additional quality without having to make difficult cost trade-offs ("quality is free"). Howard Bowen (1980) argues that the cost of education varies considerably among institutions, and he asserts that it is possible to obtain higher economic value at lower cost by placing greater emphasis on cost control. Porter (1996) distinguishes between the relentless quest for operating-cost reductions and the development of positioning strategies that involve trade-offs. If a university is operating efficiently, it must choose to incur higher costs if it wants to offer higher quality.

2. The distinction between search goods and experience goods is discussed in Chapter 3. Many faculty argue that education is an experience good that must be sampled before students can understand its eventual contribution. Some take the argument further and claim that it is the job of faculty to guide students in the right educational direction. While there is some merit to this claim, it is predicated on students deciding to attend a particular institution in the first place, which is based on their perceptions of what that institution has to offer.

3. The framework for this competitive interaction is described by Hoxby, in the abstract of her NBER report (2011): ". . . students previously attend[ed] a local college regardless of their abilities and its characteristics. Now, their choices are driven far less by distance and far more by a college's resources and student body. . . . The explanation is . . . that the elasticity of a student's preference for a college with respect to its proximity to his home has fallen substantially over time and there has been a corresponding increase in the elasticity of his preference for a college with respect to its resources and peers."

4. Christensen (1997) points out that a disconnect can develop between what consumers are willing to pay for products and the features that firms add to attract purchases of a small segment of buyers.

5. McPherson and Shulenburger (2008) provide a complete presentation of these data and an interesting discussion of the related issues.

6. College Board Advocacy and Policy Center (2010a, figure 13).

7. For this table, see Board of Regents, State of Iowa (2010b).

8. A recent Gallop Poll found that 40.9 percent of respondents perceived quality to be higher at private universities, while only 3.7 percent thought quality to be higher at public universities.

9. A survey of adults by the Pew Research Center (Cohn, 2011) indicates that for those not in school and those without a BA, the main barrier to higher education is financial. Almost half reported that they could not afford to go to college.

10. Hoxby (2009) reports that, for over the past fifty years, about 50 percent of colleges have become less selective in admitting students. To attract additional tuition revenues, these colleges have either elected or been forced to reduce the quality of their admissions.

11. While it appears that the "arms race" attribution applies mostly to elite private colleges and universities, its expounders, including Winston (2000) and Frank (2004), are critical of the quest to maintain a strong relative position. Frank argues that the "winner-take-all" aspect of the positional rankings game leads to a perversion of the standard competitive-market outcome.

12. As pointed out to us by John Kraft in a personal conversation in 2010, the existence of rankings implies that students and parents require assistance in evaluating their choices, which implies the presence of a "lemon's" market. While higher education is not a lemon's market in the standard sense, the rankings do create that image.

13. Graduate Management Admissions Council (2011).

14. Large public universities typically feature large class sizes, but increases in class size may or may not imply a decrease in quality. A move to replace smaller classes taught by teaching assistants with large lectures offered by permanent faculty or even teaching specialists may improve the quality of a class. In some states, regional campuses often provide smaller classes than do large public research universities, but it is not clear that these smaller classes provide higher quality.

Chapter 10

1. Michigan, Michigan State, and Ohio State are exceptions, with each having its own board.

2. See University of California (2010).

3. In some university systems, the title of the system head is president and that of the campus administrator is chancellor.

4. Musselin (2011) reviews literature on the structure of the academic profession and summarizes its main activities.

5. The usual defense of tenure as the guarantor of academic freedom seems to provide only modest justification for such an important institution. Carmichael (1988) provides one of the better discussions of why there is tenure. Milgrom and Roberts (1992, 380–385) review tenure as a key feature of long-term contracting in several

contexts. Another explanation for tenure may be that faculty make relationship-specific investments in an area and can be exposed to risk if that area declines in favor. In this sense, tenure ensures the continued payment of quasi-rent associated with specialized investment, and thereby encourages people to make the investment in the first place.

6. In other organizations that provide effective tenure (accounting, consulting, etc.), there are early retirement incentives and disincentives for remaining. In the United Kingdom, there is mandatory faculty retirement at sixty-five.

7. There would be agreement with the statement of the Faculty Council Executive Committee at the University of Texas at Austin: "The Faculty Council reaffirms the principle that faculty should play a significant role in institutional budget planning and decisions at departmental, school/college, and University levels" (University of Texas at Austin, Faculty Council Executive Committee [2010]).

8. Johnson and Turner (2009, 187) assert, "Willingness of faculty members to devote time to internal politics within the university surely affects outcomes in a political economy model of faculty allocation. Faculty in disciplines with lively labor markets will have less incentive to engage in internal politics (and higher opportunity costs in doing so) and their departments will suffer correspondingly in a rent-seeking political competition." Hirshleifer (1995) describes a situation ("anarchy") where strategic groups decide in a contested environment how to allocate resources between productive activities and fighting to retain control.

9. In 2011, the academic senate at the University of California argued to halt all faculty recruiting as a way to maintain its size and to instead use the funds specifically allocated to the current faculty as wage increases; see the section Example: Restructuring the University of California Pension Plan.

10. For a list of collective bargaining chapters, see AAUP (2011).

11. Teaching assistants and lecturers are represented by unions more frequently than are research faculty. In areas of the humanities where it often takes over a decade to obtain a Ph.D. and there are few job opportunities waiting, the "permanent" employment of graduate students is through their teaching assistantships. These individuals seek collective action and the protection of unions. There is little inclination for MBA, law, medical, and dental students to bargain collectively, often because they receive a subsidized education and reasonable assurance of future employment.

12. Ehrenberg (2011), while not endorsing unionization in public higher education, recognizes that the unwinding of collective bargaining agreements will act to reduce the real incomes of faculty.

13. Arizona State offers over 250 academic undergraduate programs and majors (Arizona State University [2010]); the University of Michigan has more than 200 majors and minors (University of Michigan, Office of Undergraduate Admissions [2010]); the University of Kansas has 190 undergraduate majors (University of Kansas [2010]); the University of Oregon, over 75 (University of, Office of Admissions [2010]); SUNY at Buffalo offers 73 degree-granting programs and 39 non-degree-granting programs (at Buffalo, State University of New York [2011]).

14. A detailed response to these solutions is provided by Diehl (2011).

15. Tuition and acceptance rate data for universities and colleges are those provided by *US News & World Report* in their annual publications, "Best Colleges"; data relating to state appropriations in support of higher education are those provided by *Grapevine* (2011).

16. For fall 2010, the entering undergraduate class at the University of Iowa contained more nonresidents than residents, with the administration claiming that there was no rationing for resident applicants. There is a clear and, at least temporarily, successful effort being made at Iowa and elsewhere to attract high-tuition-paying nonresidents to fill the revenue gap created by declining public support.

17. For additional background on Chancellor Martin's proposal, see Finkelmeyer (2011).

18. Pruit, Spector, and Riley (2011).

19. University of California, Board of Regents (2010).

Chapter 11

1. AACSB (2011).

2. The importance of program directors has increased in recent years, particularly for the off-campus and executive MBA offerings, even to the point where a director can reject a faculty member's participation based on lack of experience with mature students, poor performance, and unacceptable student evaluations.

3. Many companies and organizations are currently focused on the concept of sustainable growth, interpreted as growing in a manner so as to not adversely affect the welfare of future generations. It is becoming more common for private businesses and business schools to describe sustainability as part of their vision, which raises the inevitable issue of imitation.

4. Many public universities have developed independent master's programs that are offered for part-time students in the evenings or on weekends, sometimes at off-campus locations. Examples include engineering management, public policy, information technology, liberal arts, nursing, biotechnology management, and software engineering. In some cases, recognition of a growing dependence on tuition and fees is explicit; in others recognition is slow to develop and is inhibited by cultural inertia.

5. Causality in this situation is open to question. As business schools have become more entrepreneurial and financially robust, the level of central support has declined. Recall the RCM implementation at the University of Minnesota, where incremental increases in tuition revenue are offset one to one by a decline in the internal subsidy. Fethke (2011a) calls this the "low-subsidy" problem.

6. In 2010, the Association to Advance Collegiate Schools of Business, International accredited 620 members in 28 countries (AACSB [2011]).

7. It is easy to find examples where business schools, both public and private, extend their brand reputation to international markets but do not staff the programs with the same on-campus faculty and staff. If the motivation for some of these

programs appears to be financial only, we question both their sustainability and quality.

8. At the University of California, Irvine, the development of a joint master's degree between business and engineering was delayed for months while the School of Engineering decided whether it could identify five faculty out of over a hundred who would be willing to teach one class each year at night.

9. Some years ago, one of us was proudly showing a new provost a classroom facility that was built with private funds to meet the programmatic needs of working professionals. This facility was eighty miles from the main campus. The Provost indicated that it was indeed a great physical facility, but that he personally "sure the hell didn't want to make the drive."

10. For many private universities, including Harvard, Northwestern, and The University of Chicago, economics departments with large undergraduate enrollments are in colleges of arts and sciences. Recently, the University of Illinois and Michigan State University relocated economics from business to liberal arts. A primary motivation for this relocation is the lack of fit between business schools and the teaching and research agendas in economics. A viable research base in economics requires a significantly large faculty of specialists, while a viable instructional base in business economics requires a few faculty with contextual expertise. There are many examples where prominent economists in business schools have worked to develop popular economics-based courses that are both conceptually and contextually rich, but in most of these situations the standard and highly competitive economics courses are provided in arts and sciences. A similar conflict emerges in industrial relations and operations research, which, apart from several prominent exceptions, have all but disappeared from business schools. The point is that it is hard to justify a large faculty of dedicated scholars that offer only a modest contribution to integrated teaching programs.

11. This same issue arises in medical schools where discipline-based research is becoming increasingly reliant on clinical revenues. This issue is addressed in the section on the Iowa River Landing Clinic earlier in this chapter.

12. Since its inception in 1983, the Board of Visitors at UI's Tippie College of Business has had two Nobel laureates as members, Merton Miller and Robert Solow. The mixture of eminent academics and top business leaders can provide a most stimulating environment for discussing teaching and research.

13. Board meetings often follow an agenda similar to the following:

1. Overview by the chair, who is not the dean
2. Committee reports
3. Dean's update
4. Review vision
5. Updates on progress and priorities
6. Financial report
7. Prioritization of new activities
8. Break into specialized groups to obtain feedback on specific high-priority issues

9. Report of groups

10. Dean's summary and subsequent action plans

14. In a small state like Iowa having the CEOs of the largest public companies on an advisory board can help the college promote its agenda, even to skeptical administrations and faculty members.

15. Lawson et al. (2010).

16. NCES (2010, tables 271 and 272)

17. This is not intended as a general indictment of entering providers of higher education. Many for-profit entrants are sharply focused and intent on providing a predictable level of quality, particularly in course development and presentation, using modern Internet-based delivery channels. Ehrenberg (2010) discusses innovative for-profit programs that employ untenured faculty. The proposed experiment in the United Kingdom that holds back 20,000 university slots for competitive bidding by all interested providers, profit and not-for-profit, who can hold program cost under £7,500, will be an interesting experiment to follow (see Morgan and Baker [2011]).

Chapter 12

1. The Wisconsin Idea, associated with an early twentieth-century Wisconsin governor, Robert La Follette, was that efficient government required voters, not special interests, to control institutions. He saw the most effective government as involving specialists in law, economics, and social and natural sciences—many from the University of Wisconsin-Madison. Wisconsin State historical Society (2011).

2. Federal loan programs that elevate demand in areas that have limited job market possibilities will require additional subsidized support because many loans will not be repaid.

References and Selected Bibliography

AACSB (Association to Advance Collegiate Schools of Business). 2011. "Business School Data Trends and 2010 list of Accredited Schools." AACSB International, Tampa. http://www.aacsb.edu/publications/businesseducation/2010-Data-TAACSrends.pdf.

AAU (American Association of Universities). 2010. "Public Research Universities." American Association of Universities, Washington, DC. http://www.aau.edu/about/default.aspx?id=4020.

AAUP (American Association of University Professors). 2006. "The Devaluing of Higher Education: The Annual Report on The Economic Status of the Profession, 2005–06." *Academe Online*, March/April. http://www.aaup.org/AAUP/pubsres/academe/2006/MA/sal/.

———. 2011. "Collective Bargaining Chapters." American Association of University Professors, Washington, DC. http://www.aaup.org/AAUP/cbc/colbargainchap.htm.

ACT. 2009. "ACT National Curriculum Survey, 2009." ACT, Iowa City, IA. http://www.act.org/research/policymakers/pdf/NationalCurriculumSurvey2009.pdf.

Adams, Renee B., Benjamin E. Hermalin, and Michael S. Weisbach. 2010. "The Role of Boards of Directors in Corporate Governance: A Conceptual Framework and Survey." *Journal of Economic Literature* 143 (1): 58–107.

Archibald, Robert B., and David H. Feldman. 2006. "Explaining Increases in Higher Education Costs." Working Paper 42, Department of Economics, College of William and Mary, Williamsburg, VA.

Arizona State University (2010). "Academic Programs." Undergraduate Admissions Office, Arizona State University, Tempe, AZ. http://www.asu.edu/programs/.

Bachman, Rebecca. 2011. "UC Regents Approve 9.6 Percent Tuition Hike." *Santa Barbara Independent*, November 1.

Balona, Denise-Marie. 2011. "Lawmakers Take Aim at University Faculty Unions." *Orlando (FL) Sentinel*, March 30.

Basu, Parantap, and Keshab Bhattarai. 2010. "Cognitive Skills, Openness and Growth." Working paper, Department of Economics, University of Hull, Hull, UK.

Baum, Sandy, and Lucie Lapovsky. 2006. "Tuition Discounting: Not Just a Private College Practice." The College Board, New York.

Baum, Sandy, and Jennifer Ma. 2010. "Tuition Discounting: Institution Aid Patterns at Public and Private Colleges and Universities, 2000–01 to 2008–09." College Board Advocacy and Policy Center, The College Board, New York.

Baum, Sandy, Lucie Lapovsky, and Jennifer Ma. 2009. "Trends in College Pricing 2009." College Board Advocacy and Policy Center, The College Board, New York.

Baum, Sandy, and Michael McPherson. 2011. "Is Education a Public or Private Good?" *Chronicle of Higher Education*, January 18.

Baumol, William J., and William G. Bowen. 1966. *Performing Arts: The Economic Dilemma; a Study of Problems Common to Theater, Opera, Music, and Dance*. New York: The Twentieth Century Fund.

Baumol, William J., and David F. Bradford. 1970. "Optimal Departures from Marginal Cost Pricing." *American Economic Review* 60 (3): 265–283.

Becker, Gary. 2011. "Good and Bad Inequality–Becker." *The Becker-Posner Blog*, January 30. http://www.becker-posner-blog.com/2011/01/index.html.

Bloomberg Businessweek. 2010. Financial Aid: Help Is on the Way. July 8.

Board of Regents, State of Iowa. 2010a. Meeting of the Board of Regents, State of Iowa, Des Moines, June 9, agenda item 6. http://www.regents.iowa.gov/Meetings/DocketMemos/10Memos/June2010/0610_ITEM06.pdf.

———. 2010b. Meeting of the Board of Regents, State of Iowa. Des Moines, April 28–29, agenda item 6f. http://www.regents.iowa.gov/Meetings/DocketMemos/10Memos/April/april2010docket.htm.

Bound, John, and Sarah Turner. 2010. "Collegiate Attainment: Understanding Degree Completion." *NBER Reporter 2010 Number 4: Research Summary*. Cambridge, MA: National Bureau of Economic Research.

Bound, John, Michael Lovenheim, and Sarah Turner. 2009. "Why Have College Completion Rates Declined? An Analysis of Changing Student Preparation and Collegiate Resources." *American Economic Journal: Applied Economics* 2 (3): 129–157.

Bowen, Howard. 1977. *Investment in Learning: The Individual and Social Value of American Higher Education*. San Francisco: Jossey-Bass.

———. 1980. *The Costs of Higher Education: How Much Do Colleges and Universities Spend per Student and How Much Should They Spend?* San Francisco: Jossey-Bass.

———, and Gordon Douglas. 1971. *Efficiency in Liberal Education: A Study of Comparative Instructional Costs for Different Ways of Organizing Teaching-Learning in a Liberal Arts College*. New York: McGraw-Hill.

Brandenburger, Adam M., and Barry J. Nalebuff. 1996. *Co-Opetition.* New York: Doubleday.

Breneman, David W. 2004. "Are the States and Higher Education Striking a New Bargain?" Public Policy Paper Series 04-02. Association of Governing Boards of Universities and Colleges, Washington, DC.

———, and Chester Finn, eds. 1978. *Public Policy and Private Higher Education.* Washington, DC: The Brookings Institution.

Browne, John, and Independent Review Panel. 2010. "Securing a Sustainable Future for Higher Education: An Independent Review of Higher Education and Student Finance." Report prepared for the British Department for Business Innovation and Skills, London. http://www.bis.gov.uk/assets/biscore/corporate/docs/s/10-1208-securing-sustainable-higher-education-browne-report.pdf.

Card, David. 2001. "Estimating the Returns to Schooling: Progress on Some Persistent Econometric Problems." *Econometrica* 69 (5): 1127–1160.

Carmichael, Lorne H. 1988. "Incentives in Academics: Why Is There Tenure?" *Journal of Political Economy* 96 (3): 453–472.

Carnegie Foundation for the Advancement of Teaching. 1973. *Who Pays, Who Benefits, Who Should Pay?* New York: McGraw Hill.

———. 2010. "The Carnegie Classification of Institutions of Higher Education." Carnegie Foundation for the Advancement of Teaching, New York.

Carnevale, Anthony P., Jeff Strohl, and Michelle Melton. 2011. *What's It Worth? The Economic Value of College Majors.* Center on Education and the Workforce, Georgetown University, Washington, DC. http://cew.georgetown.edu/whatsitworth.

Cawelti, Scott, and James Lubker. 2011. "The World Has Changed: Universities Must Change Now." *Des Moines Register,* February 20.

Christensen, Clayton. 1997. *The Innovator's Dilemma: When New Technologies Cause Great Firms to Fail.* Boston: Harvard Business School Press.

Chronicle of Higher Education. 2010. "Corporate Chief to Head Review of University Research Support." June 22.

———. 2011. "The Future of Pell Grants: 6 Views." Commentary, March 20.

College Board Advocacy and Policy Center 2010a. "Trends In College Pricing 2010." College Board, New York.

———. 2010b. "Trends in Student Aid 2010." College Board, New York.

Collegemeasures.org. 2010. "University of Iowa Cost per Student." American Institute for Research, Washington, DC. http://collegemeasures.org/reporting/institution/scorecard/cps/153658.aspx.

Collis, David J. 2001. "When Industries Change: The Future of Higher Education." *Continuing Higher Education Review* 65 (Fall): 7–24.

———. 2004. "The Paradox of Scope: A Challenge to The Governance of Higher Education." In *Competing Conceptions of Academic Governance: Negotiating the Perfect Storm,* edited by William G. Tierney. Baltimore: John Hopkins University Press.

———, and Cynthia Montgomery. 1995. "Competing on Resources: Strategies in the 1990's." *Harvard Business Review* 73 (4): 118–128.

————. 2005. *Corporate Strategy: A Resource-Based Approach*. 2nd ed. Boston: McGraw-Hill/Irwin.

Collis, David J., and Michael Rukstad. 2008. "Can You Say What Your Strategy Is?" *Harvard Business Review* 86 (4): 82–90.

Committee on Prospering in the Global Economy of the 21st Century. 2007. *Rising Above the Gathering Storm: Energizing and Employing America for a Brighter Economic Future*. Washington, D.C: National Academies Press.

Commonfund. 2010. "Higher Education Price Index." Commonfund, Wilton, CT. http://www.commonfund.org/CommonfundInstitute/HEPI/Pages/default.aspx . https://dipot.ulb.ac.be:8443/dspace/bitstream/2013/13580/1/dul-0068.pdf.

Courant, Paul N., James J. Duderstadt, and Edie N. Goldenberg. 2010. "Needed: A National Strategy to Preserve Public Research Universities." *Chronicle of Higher Education*, January 3.

Crosby, Philip B. 1979. *Quality Is Free*. New York: McGraw-Hill.

Cunningham, Alisa, Jane Wellman, Melissa Clinedinst, and Jamie Merisotis. 2001. "Study of College Costs and Prices, 1988–89 to 1997–98." NCES 2002-157, National Center for Educational Statistics, U.S. Department of Education, Washington, DC.

Debande, Olivier, and Jean-Luc Meulemeester. 2008. "Quality and Variety Competition in Higher Education. DULBEA Paper 08-12, Université Libre de Bruxelles, Bruxelles.

Delta Cost Project. 2008. "Trends in College Spending (TCS) Online." Delta Project on Postsecondary Educational Costs, Productivity, and Accountability, Washington, DC. http://www.tcs-online.org.

Desrochers, Donna M, Colleen M. Lenihan, and Jane V. Wellman. 2010. "Trends in College Spending: 1999–2009." Delta Cost Project, Washington, DC.

Díaz-Giménez, Javier, Andy Glover, and José-Víctor Ríos-Rull. 2011. "Facts on the Distributions of Earnings, Income, and Wealth in the United States: 2007 Update." *Federal Reserve Bank of Minneapolis Quarterly Review* 34 (1): 2–31.

Diehl, Randy L. 2011. "Maintaining Excellence and Efficiency at the University of Texas at Austin: A Response to the '7 Breakthrough Solutions' and Other Proposals." College of Liberal Arts, University of Texas at Austin. http://7solutionsresponse .org/maintaining-excellence-and-efficiency.pdf.

Dixit, Avinash K., and Joseph E. Stiglitz. 1977. "Monopolistic Competition and Optimum Product Diversity." *American Economic Review* 67 (3): 297–308.

Dranove, David, and Ginger Z. Jin. 2010. "Quality Disclosure and Certification: Theory and Practice." *Journal of Economic Literature* 48 (4): 935–963.

Duderstadt, James. 2005. "The Crisis in Financing Public Higher Education—And a Possible Solution: A 21st Century Learn Grant Act." Millennium Project, University of Michigan, Ann Arbor. http://milproj.ummu.umich.edu/publications/ financing_pub_univ/.

————, and F. W. Womack. 2003. *Beyond the Cross Roads: The Future of the Public University in America*. Baltimore: Johns Hopkins University Press.

Easterlin, R. 1995. "Will Increasing the Incomes of All Increase the Happiness of All?" *Journal of Economic Behavior and Organization* 27 (1): 35–47.

Economist. 2010. "Declining by Degree: Will America's Universities Go the Way of Its Car Companies?" Schumpeter column, September 2.

Ehrenberg, Ronald G. 1999. "Adam Smith Goes to College: An Economist Becomes an Academic Administrator." *Journal of Economic Perspectives* 13 (1): 99–116.

———. 2006. "The Perfect Storm and the Privatization of Public Higher Education." *Change* 38 (1): 46–53.

———. 2010. "Rethinking the Professoriate." Paper prepared for the American Enterprise Institute Conference on Innovation and Entrepreneurship in Higher Education, Washington, DC, June.

———. 2011. "American Higher Education in Transition." Working draft, Departments of Industrial and Labor Relations and Economics, Cornell University, Ithaca, NY.

Ehrenberg, Ronald G., ed. 2004. *Governing Academia: Who Is in Charge at the Modern University?* Ithaca, NY: Cornell University Press.

Fethke, Gary. 2005. "Strategic Determination of Higher Education Subsidies and Tuitions." *Economics of Education Review* 24 (5): 601–609.

———. 2006. "Subsidy and Tuition Policies in Public Higher Education." *Economic Inquiry* 4 (4): 644–655.

———. 2011a "A Low-Subsidy Problem in Public Higher Education." *Economics of Education Review* 30 (4): 617–626.

———. 2011b. "Welfare Effects of Subsidizing Higher Education When Access and Quality Are Endogenous." *Economic Letters* 112 (1): 45–48.

———, and Andrew Policano. 2011. "Get Rid of the UC Tuition Subsidy. Blowback, *Los Angeles Times*, June 26.

Financial Times. 2010. Editorial, October 26.

Finkelmeyer, Todd. 2011. "Biddy Martin Is Latest UW-Madison Chancellor Hoping to Gain Freedom from State Oversight." *The Cap Times* (Madison), January 12. http://host.madison.com/ct/news/local/education/university/article_552b1a7e-1dc9-11e0-bf70-001cc4c03286.html.

Frank, Robert. 2004. "Are Arms Races in Higher Education a Problem?" EDUCAUSE, Forum for the Future of Higher Education, Boulder, CO. http://net.educause.edu/ir/library/pdf/FFP0412S.pdf.

Freedman, James O. 2004. "Presidents and Trustees." In *Governing Academia: Who Is In Charge at the Modern University?* edited by Ronald G. Ehrenberg, Ithaca, NY: Cornell University Press.

Friedman, Milton. 1968. "The Higher Schooling in America." *The Public Interest* 11 (Spring): 108–112.

Gallegos, Shannon. 2011. *Pell Grants Not Linked To Higher Tuition.* News and Views, Institute for College Access & Success. April 12. http://views.ticas.org/?p=676.

Garland, James C. 2009. *Saving Alma Mater: A Rescue Plan for America's Public Universities.* Chicago: University of Chicago Press.

Guardian. 2011. " In Defense of Public Higher Education." September 27.

Goldin, Claudia, and Lawrence F. Katz. 1999. "The Shaping of Higher Education: The Formative Years in the United States, 1890 to 1940." *Journal of Economic Perspectives* 13 (1): 37–62.

Gordon, Larry. 2010. "Three-Year Bachelor's Degree Gains Popularity." *Los Angeles Times*, April 22.

———. 2011. "University of California Weighs Varying Tuitions at Its 10 Campuses. *Los Angeles Times*, May 9.

Graduate Management Admissions Council. 2011. http://www.gmac.com/gmac.

Grapevine. 2009. "Annual Compilation of Data on State Fiscal Support for Higher Education: State Reports for Fiscal Year 2008–09." Center for the Study of Education Policy, Illinois State University, Normal, IL. http://www.grapevine.ilstu.edu/statereports/FY09/index.htm.

———. 2011. "Annual Compilation of Data on State Fiscal Support for Higher Education: Summary Tables, Fiscal Year (FY) 2010–11." Center for the Study of Education Policy, Illinois State University, Normal, IL. http://grapevine.illinoisstate.edu/tables/index.htm.

Grimston, Jack. 2009. "Plan for Tuition Fees to Hit £7,000 a Year." *Sunday Times* (London), July 26.

Hacker, Andrew, and Claudia Dreifus. 2010. *Higher Education? How Colleges Are Wasting Our Money and Failing Our Kids and What We Can Do About It.* New York: Holt/Times Books.

Hamilton, R., and J. Marcus. 2001. "Universities Are Challenged as Demographics Shift." *Texas Tribune* (Austin), January 1. http://www.nytimes.com/2011/01/02/us/02ttstudents.html?pagewanted=1&_r=3.

Hansen, W. Lee, and Burton A. Weisbrod. 1969. "The Distribution of Costs and Direct Benefits of Public Higher Education: The Case of California." *Journal of Human Resources* 4 (2): 176–191.

HECB (Higher Education Coordinating Board). 2010. "2009–10 Tuition and Fee Rates: A National Comparison." Higher Education Coordinating Board, Olympia, WA. http://www.hecb.wa.gov/research/issues/documents/TuitionandFees2009-10Report-Final.pdf.

Hirshleifer, Jack. 1995. "Anarchy and Its Breakdown." *The Journal of Political Economy* 103 (1): 26–52.

Hoxby, Caroline M. 2009. "The Changing Selectivity of American Colleges." *Journal of Economic Perspectives* 23 (4): 95–118.

———. 2011. "Economics of Education Program Report." *NBER Reporter* 2 (1).

Iowa House Republicans. 2010. State Medicaid Spending Since 2007. Iowa House Republicans, Des Moines. http://www.iowahouserepublicans.com/state-medicaid-spending-since-2007.

Iowa State University. 2009. "Resource Management Policy, Procedures and Processes." Iowa State University, Ames. http://www.public.iastate.edu/~budget/buddev/RMMPPP.pdf.

————, Resource Management Model Implementation Operations Team. 2007. "Recommendation #1: Indirect Cost Recovery Revenue Distribution Methodology." Iowa State University, Ames. http://www.public.iastate.edu/~budget/approved/IDCRev.pdf.

IPEDS (Integrated Postsecondary Educational Data System). 2010. "Trends in College Spending 1998–2008: Where Does the Money Come From? Where Does It Go? What Does It Buy?" Institute of Educational Sciences, U.S. Department of Education, Washington, DC.

Jacobs, Andrews. 2010. "China's Army of Graduates Struggles for Jobs." *Asia Pacific New York Times*, December 11.

Johnson, Mark, Clayton Christensen, and Henning Kagermann. 2008. "Reinventing Your Business Model." *Harvard Business Review* 86 (12): 51–59.

Johnson, William R. 2006. "Are Public Subsidies to Higher Education Regressive?" *Education Finance and Policy* 1(3): 288–315.

————, and Sarah Turner. 2009. "Faculty Without Students: Resource Allocation in Higher Education." *Journal of Economic Perspectives* 23 (2): 169–189.

Johnston, David (1989). "Price Fixing Inquiry at Twenty Elite Colleges." *New York Times*, August 10.

Kane, Thomas J. 2006. "Public Intervention in Post-Secondary Education." In vol. 2 of *Handbook of the Economics of Education*, edited by E. Hanushek and F. Welch, 1369–1401. Oxford: Elsevier North Holland.

————. 2007. "Evaluating the Impact of The D.C. Tuition Assistance Grant Program." *Journal of Human Resources* 42 (3): 555–582.

————, and Peter Orszag. 2004. "Funding Restrictions at Public Universities: Effects and Policy Implications." In *Brookings Institution Working Papers*. Brookings Institution, Washington, DC.

————, and David L. Gunter. 2003. "State Fiscal Constraints and Higher Education Spending: The Role of Medicaid and the Business Cycle." Discussion Paper No. 11, Urban-Brookings Tax Policy Center, Brookings Institution, Washington, DC.

Kennan, John. 2010. "Higher Education Subsidies and Human Capital Mobility." Preliminary working paper, University of Wisconsin-Madison and NBER, July. http://www.stanford.edu/group/SITE/SITE_2010/segment_3/segment_3_papers/kennan.pdf.

Kerr, Clark. 1996. "Howard Bowen—Guarded Optimist About Higher Education." Howard Bowen Lecture Series, College of Business Administration, University of Iowa, Iowa City.

Keynes, John M. 1936. *The General Theory of Employment, Interest and Money*. Cambridge, UK: Macmillan University Press.

Kinkade, Tyler. 2011. "Iowa Republicans: Education Cuts Are Not Causing Tuition Increases." *Iowa Independent*, February 21.

Lafley, Alan G. 2009. "What Only the CEO Can Do." *Harvard Business Review* 85 (5): 54–62.

Lawson, Neal, Brendan Barber, Aaron Porter, Sally Hunt, et al. 2010. "We Must Get off the Earn-To-Learn Treadmill." *Guardian*, U.S. edition, December 10.

Leonhardt, David. 2011. "Is College Tuition Too Low?" Business News, *New York Times*, June 30.

Long, Bridget Terry. 2010. "Grading Higher Education: Giving Consumers the Information They Need." Center for American Progress and the Hamilton Project, Brookings Institution, Washington, DC.

Manyika, James, Susan Lund, Byron Auguste, Lenny Mendonca, Tim Welsh, and Sreenivas Ramaswamy. 2011. "An Economy That Works: Job Creation and America's Future." McKinsey Global Institute. http://www.mckinsey.com/mgi/publications/us_jobs/pdfs/MGI_us_jobs_full_report.pdf.

Marcucci, Pamela N., and D. Bruce Johnstone. 2007. "Tuition Policies in a Comparative Perspective: Theoretical and Political Rationales. *Journal of Higher Education Policy and Management* 29 (1): 25–40.

Marklein, Mary Beth. 2011. "College Major Analysis: Engineers Get Highest Salaries." *USA Today*, May 23.

McDuff, DeForest. 2007. "Quality, Tuition, and Applications to In-State Public Colleges." *Economics of Education Review* 26 (4): 433–449.

McPherson, Peter, and David Shulenburger. 2008. "University Tuition, Consumer Choice, and College Affordability: Strategies for Addressing Higher Education Affordability Challenges." Discussion paper, National Association of State Universities and Land-Grant Colleges, Washington, DC.

———. 2010. "Understanding the Costs of Higher Education." *Planning for Higher Education* 38 (3): 15–24.

McPherson, Peter, Howard, J. Gobstein, and David E. Shulenburger. 2010. "Keeping Public Research Universities Strong." Discussion paper prepared for the Regional Meeting on the Research University, Association of Public Land-Grant Universities, Washington, DC, April.

Miles, David, and Jack Evans. 2011. "Stop Cutting Universities' State Funding." *Cedar Rapids (IA) Gazette*, February 25.

Milgrom, Paul, and John Roberts. 1992. "Internal Labor Markets, Job Assignments, and Promotions." *Economics, Organization and Management*. Englewood Cliffs, NJ: Prentice-Hall.

Moretti, Enrico. 2004. "Estimating the Social Return to Higher Education: Evidence from Longitudinal and Repeated Cross-Sectional Data." *Journal of Econometrics* 121 (1–2): 175–212.

Morgan, John, and Simon Baker. 2011. "White Paper: One in Four Undergraduate Places Will Be Up for Grabs." *Times Higher Education*, June 28. http://www.timeshighereducation.co.uk/story.asp?storycode=416653.

Mumper, Michael. 2001. "The Paradox of College Prices: Five Stories with No Clear Lesson." In *The States and Public Higher Education Policy: Affordability, Access, and Accountability*, edited by D. E. Heller, 39–62. Baltimore: John Hopkins University Press.

Muraskin, Lana, John Lee, Abigail Wilner, and Watson Scott Swail. 2004. "Raising the Graduation Rates of Low-Income College Students." Pell Institute for Opportunity in Higher Education, Washington, DC.

Musselin, Christine. 2011. "The Academic Workplace: What We Already Know, What We Still Do Not Know, And What We Would Like to Know. In *Knowledge Matters: The Public Mission of the Research University*, edited by Diana Rhoten and Craig Calhoun, 423–457. New York: Columbia University Press.

NCES (National Center for Education Statistics). 2010. "Digest of Education Statistics: 2009." U.S. Department of Education and the Institute of Education Sciences, Washington, DC.

Nelson, Philip. 1970. "Information and Consumer Behavior." *Journal of Political Economy* 78 (2): 311–329.

NUS (National Union of Students), 2011. "NUS Welcomes 'Fair and Sustainable' Graduate Tax Proposals as Genuine Alternative to Fees." October 21. http://www.nus.org.uk/en/News/News/NUS-welcomes-fair-and-sustainable-graduate-tax-proposals-as-genuine-alternative-to-fees/.

OECD Directorate for Education. 2010. *Education at a Glance 2010: OECD Indicators.* Paris: OECD Publishing.

Okun, Arthur M. 1975. *Equality and Efficiency: The Big Tradeoff.* Washington, DC: Brookings Institution Press.

Orszag, Peter. 2010. "A Health Care Plan for Colleges." *New York Times*, September 18.

———, and Thomas J. Kane. 2004. "Financing Public Higher Education: Short-Term and Long-Term Challenges. In *Ford Policy Forum: The Forum for the Future of Higher Education*, working paper, 33–39. Brookings Institution, Washington, DC.

Pennsylvania State University. 2009. "Priorities for Excellence: The Penn State Strategic Plan 2009–10 Through 2013–14." Pennsylvania State University, University Park. http://strategicplan.psu.edu/enhancesuccess.

Podolny, Joel M. 2009. "The Buck Stops (and Starts) at Business School." *Harvard Business Review.* June, 62–67.

Policano, Andrew J. 2005. "What Price Rankings?" *BizEd*, September/October, 26–32.

———. 2007. "The Rankings Game: And the Winner Is . . ." *Journal of Management Development* 26 (1): 43–48.

Porter, Michael E. 1980. *Competitive Strategy: Techniques for Analyzing Industries and Competitors.* New York: Free Press.

———. 1985. *Competitive Advantage: Creating and Sustaining Superior Performance.* New York: Free Press.

———. 1996. "What Is Strategy?" *Harvard Business Review* 74 (6): 61–78.

———, and Mark Kramer. 2011a. "How to Reinvent Capitalism—And Unleash a Wave of Innovation and Growth." *Harvard Business Review* (January/February): 62–77.

———. 2011b. "Creating Shared Value." Abstract. *Harvard Business Review* 89 (1–2).

Posner, Richard. 2011. "Raising Public College Tuition–Posner." *The Becker-Posner Blog*, January 17. http://www.becker-posner-blog.com/2011/01/raising-public-college-tuitionposner-.html.

Powers, William. 2010. Letter to Dr. David B. Prior, Executive Vice Chancellor for Academic Affairs, University of Texas System. January 29. http://www.utexas .edu/tuition/attach/2010_President_Tuition_Regents.pdf.

Pruit, Charles, Michael Spector, and Kevin P. Reilly. 2011. Letter to Campus Community, February 15. http://budget.wisc.edu/new-badger-partnership/letter-from-kevin-reilly-regents/.

Richards, Alex, and Ron Coddington. 2010. "30 Ways to Rate a College." *Chronicle of Higher Education*, September 2.

Richmond Times Dispatch. 2010. "Virginia Students Facing More Tuition Increases." Business News, June 2.

Roberts, John. 2004. *The Modern Firm: Organizational Design for Performance and Growth.* Oxford: Oxford University Press.

Ronnen, Uri. 1991. "Minimum Quality Standards, Fixed Costs, and Competition." *Rand Journal of Economics* 22 (4): 490–504.

Rosovsky, Henry. 1990. *The University: An Owner's Manual.* New York: W. W. Norton.

Schmidt, Peter. 2010. "Missouri State U. Faculty Members Can Now Be Reassigned Without Their Consent." *Chronicle of Higher Education*, April 12.

———. 2011. "Anti-Faculty-Union Proposals in Ohio Came from Public University Association." *Chronicle of Higher Education*, March 8.

Schneider, Mark. 2011. *Finishing the First Lap: The Cost of First-Year Student Attrition in America's Four-Year Colleges and Universities.* American Institutes for Research, Washington, DC.

Scott, Alister, Steryn Grové, Aldo Guena, Stefano Brusoni, and Ed Steinmuder, "The Economic Returns to Basic Research and the Benefit of University-Industry Relationships: A Literature Review and Update Of Findings." Report prepared for the Office of Science and Technology by Science and Technology Policy Research (SPRU), University of Sussex, Sussex, UK.

Segal, David. 2010. "The X Factor of Economics." *New York Times*, October 17.

Shaw, Jane. 2011. "Is College a Bad Public Good?" Commentaries. The John William Pope Center for Higher Education Policy, Raleigh, NC, February 1. http://www .popecenter.org/commentaries/article.html?id=2471.

SHEEO (State Higher Education Executive Officers). 2010a. "State Higher Education Finance, FY 2010." State Higher Education Executive Officers, Boulder, CO, and the College Board. http://www.sheeo.org/finance/shef/SHEF_FY10.pdf.

———. 2010b. "Supplemental SHEF Data and Tables and Figures, Public Postsecondary Enrollment, Net Tuition Revenue and Educational Appropriation Per FTE, 1984–2009." State Higher Education Executive Officers, Boulder, CO, and the College Board. http://www.sheeo.org/finance/shef/shef_data09.htm.

Simon, Stephanie, and Stephanie Banchero. 2010. "Putting a Price on Professors." *Wall Street Journal*, October 22.

Spence, Michael. 1976. "Product Selection, Fixed Costs, and Monopolistic Competition." *Review of Economic Studies* 43 (2): 217–235.

StateNews.com. 2009. "MSU Second in Michigan for Appropriations." July 19. http://www.statenews.com/index.php/article/2009/07/msu_2nd_in_mich_for_ appropriations.

———. 2011. "House Votes to Maintain Higher Education Funding for 2010–11." June 8. http://www.statenews.com/index.php/article/2010/06/house_votes_to_ maintain _higher_education_funding_for_2010-11.

State of Iowa. 2010. "FY 2009: Year-End Report on General Fund Revenues and Appropriations." "FY2011 Comparison of All Appropriated Funds." State of Iowa, Fiscal Services Division, Legislative Services Agency. Des Moines. http://www .legis.iowa.gov/DOCS/lsaReports/GeneralFundBudget/2009Summary.pdf.

———. 2011. "FY2011 Comparison of All Appropriated Funds." State of Iowa, Fiscal Services Division, Legislative Services Agency. Des Moines. http://staffweb.legis .state.ia.us/lfb/Docs/end-of-session/2010/All%20Funds%20Comparison.pdf.

Stephens, Philip. 2010. Editorial. *Financial Times*, December 7, 12.

Texas Public Policy Foundation. 2008. "Strengthening Higher Education for Texas' Future: 7 Solutions." http://texashighered.com/7-solutions.

Taylor, Paul, Kim Parker, Richard Fry, and D'Vera Cohn. 2011. "Is College Worth It? College Presidents, Public Access Value, Quality and Mission of Higher Education." Pew Social and Demographic Trends, Research Center. Washington, DC.

Tirole, Jean. 1988. "Product Selection, Quality, and Advertising." In *The Theory of Industrial Organization*, chap. 2, Cambridge, MA: MIT Press.

Turner, Sarah E. 2006. "Higher Tuition, Higher Aid and the Quest to Improve Opportunities for Low Income Students in Selective, Public Higher Education." In *What's Happening to Public Higher Education*, edited by Ronald Ehrenberg, 251–274. Westport, CT: Greenwood Press for the American Council on Education.

University at Buffalo, State University of New York (2011). "Undergraduate Admissions: Academic Areas of Study." University at Buffalo. http://admissions.buffalo .edu/academics/areasofstudy.php.

University of California. 2010. "Shared Governance." Regents of the University of California, Oakland. http://www.universityofcalifornia.edu/aboutuc/governance .html.

University of California, Board of Regents, 2010. "The Future of UC Retirement Benefits: 2010 Task Force Report." Regents of the University of California. Oakland. http://ucrpfuture.universityofcalifornia.edu/task-force-inf/.

———, Commission on the Future, Working Groups. 2005. "Commission for the Future: First Round of Recommendations." Regents of the University of California, Oakland. http://ucfuture.universityofcalifornia.edu/.

University of California, Irvine. 2007. Executive Summary to "Strategic Plan.": University of California, Irvine. http://www.strategicplan.uci.edu/?p=19.

University of Florida, 2011. "RCM Manual." Budget Office, University of Florida, Gainesville. http://www.cfo.ufl.edu/rcm/doc/RCMManual3182011.pdf.

University of Illinois. 2010. "Administrative Review and Restructuring (ARR)." ARR Working Group, University of Illinois, Urbana. http://www.uillinois.edu/arr/Reports/.

University of Iowa, Budget Development Office. 2010. "Budget Development." Division of Finance and Operations, University of Iowa, Iowa City. http://www.uiowa.edu/~fusbudg/.

———, Office of the Provost. 2010. "A Strategic Plan for the University of Iowa, 2005–2010: Mission, Aspirations and Values." University of Iowa, Iowa City. http://www.uiowa.edu/homepage/news/strategic-plans/strat-plan-05-10/mission/.

———, Office of the Registrar. 2011. "Past Reports: Total Enrollments from 1963 to Present." University of Iowa, Iowa City. http://www.registrar.uiowa.edu/ReportsStatistics/Census/tabid/132/Default.aspx.

———, and Tripp Umbach. 2010. "University of Iowa Economic Impact Study." Office of the President, University of Iowa, Iowa City. http://www.uiowa.edu/impact/pdf/UI%20Economic%20Impact%20Study%209-29-2010.pdf.

———, University News Service. 2011. "UI Fall Enrollment on Par with Last Year; Diversity Increases." September 7. http://news-releases.uiowa.edu/2011/september/090711enrollment.html.

University of Kansas. 2010. "Academics." University of Kansas, Lawrence. http://www.ku.edu/academics/.

University of Michigan, Office of Undergraduate Admissions (2010). "Areas of Study." University of Michigan, Ann Arbor. http://www.admissions.umich.edu/about/academic/areasofstudy.php.

University of Minnesota. 2009. "Budget Model Overview, November 2009." Office of Budget and Finance, University of Minnesota, Minneapolis. http://www.washington.edu/admin/pb/home/pdf/abb/Univ-of-Minnesota-Budget-Model-Overview_Nov-2009.pdf.

University of Oregon, Office of Admissions. 2010. "Explore Majors and Minors." University of Oregon, Eugene. http://admissions.uoregon.edu/explore/majors.

University of Texas at Austin. 2010. "Class of First-Time Freshmen Not a White Majority This Fall Semester at The University of Texas At Austin." News release. University of Texas, Austin, September 14.

———, Faculty Council Executive Committee. 2010. Resolutions on the Faculty Role in the Budget Process D8631–D8632. University of Texas, Austin. http://www.utexas.edu/faculty/council/2010-2011/minutes/min050911/appendix_A.pdf.

University of Wisconsin, Office of the Chancellor. 2010a. "Connecting Ideas: Strategies for the University of Wisconsin at Madison." University of Wisconsin, Madison. http://www.chancellor.wisc.edu/strategicplan.old/Exec_Sum.pdf.

———, Office of the Chancellor. 2010b. "Mission Statements of UW System Campuses and Institutions." University of Wisconsin, Madison. http://www.wisc.edu/about/leadership/mission.php.

U.S. Census Bureau. "S1401 School Enrollment." *American FactFinder*. U.S. Census Bureau, Washington, DC. http://factfinder.census.gov/servlet/

STTable?_bm=y&-geo_id=01000US&-qr_name=ACS_2008_3YR_G00_S1401&-ds_name=ACS_2008_3YR_G00.

U.S. News &World Report. "Best Colleges" (ranking lists for years 2008, 2009, 2010, 2011). http://colleges.usnews.rankingsandreviews.com/usnews/edu/college/rankings/brief/t1natudoc_brief.php.

Varian, Hal R. 1984. *Microeconomic Analysis,* 2nd ed. New York: W. W. Norton.

Vossensteyn, Hans. 2009. *Cost Sharing and Accountability—Current: European Developments.* Paper presented at the Fifth World Bank ECA Education conference, Montenegro, October.

Wall Street Journal. 2011. "Grading the Ivory Towers." January 10, A16.

Wellman, Jane V. 2001. "Looking Back, Going Forward: The Carnegie Commission Tuition Policy." Paper prepared for The New Millennium Project on Higher Education Costs, Pricing, and Productivity. Institute for Higher Education Policy, Washington, DC, January.

———. 2006. "Costs, Prices and Affordability." Background paper prepared for the Secretary of Education's Commission on the Future of Higher Education, Washington, DC.

———, Donna M. Desrochers, and Colleen M. Lenihan. 2008. "The Growing Imbalance: Recent Trends in U.S. Postsecondary Education." Report prepared for the Delta Project on Postsecondary Education Costs, Productivity and Accountability. Washington, DC. http://www.deltacostproject.org/resources/pdf/imbalance20080423.pdf.

Willig, Robert. 1976. "Consumers Surplus Without Apology." *American Economic Review* 66 (4): 589–597.

Winston, Gordon C. 1999. "Subsidies, Hierarchy and Peers: The Awkward Economics of Higher Education." *Journal of Economic Perspectives* 13 (1): 13–36.

———. 2000. "The Positional Arms Race in Higher Education." Discussion Paper No. 54, Williams Project on the Economics of Higher Education, Department of Economics, Williams College, Williamstown, MA.

———, and D. J. Zimmerman. 2000. "Where Is Aggressive Price Competition Taking Higher Education?" Discussion Paper No. 56, Williams Project on the Economics of Higher Education, Department of Economics, Williams College, Williamstown, MA.

Wisconsin State Historical Society. 2011. "Progressivism and the Wisconsin Idea." Wisconsin State Historical Society, Madison, WI.

Zhang, Liang. 2005. "Do Measures of College Quality Matter? The Effect of College Quality on Graduates' Earnings." *Review of Higher Education* 28 (4): 571–596.

Index

Italic page numbers indicate material in tables or figures.